A MOTHER'S LOVE

I was a real tomboy as a child; not only was I far more likely to play with Matchbox cars than Barbies, but my ambitions knew no gender boundaries: I sincerely believed that I would grow up and become an NFL quarterback.

Mom's reaction: *You can do it, honey.*

And she was sincere: I believe she still has the Matchbox cars and the football to prove it.

Over the years my ambitions changed, but my mother's support hasn't wavered. She's still my biggest cheerleader, the one person in the world who's convinced I can accomplish something before I even set my sights on it. Her support isn't just verbal—my mother was present for both of our children's births, and though she lives on the West Coast, always seems to find a way to get to Texas when I need her.

I called her that awful night Chris died. I don't remember how much I even told her before she declared she was on her way. Just like that, she was with me in Texas: consoling, organizing, and just in general being my mom.

I loved Mother's Day when I was little, because it was the one day of the year when my sister and I could turn the tables on her—we got to do something for her instead of the other way around. Mom was always putting herself out to make others comfortable; she was a great hostess, the sort who

Taya Kyle (right) *with her mother, Kim, and sister, Ashley. The stickers on the girls' foreheads are a bit of a mystery now, but were undoubtedly part of some family fun.*

leaves no stone unturned when you come into her house. She may not have spoiled her daughters—there were careful limits, which we learned to appreciate—but she certainly spoiled her guests.

Mother's Day was her turn. We made her breakfast in bed, of course, and gave her handmade cards and crafty gifts. Those small presents were the sort of thing she loved—gifts of the heart.

Treasuring those gifts was one of the great things I learned from my mother. There was, of course, a whole range of lessons—from grammar to the secrets of a happy marriage. I learned a lot sitting quietly and listening to her and her friends discuss their lives—how to weather the ups and downs, how to cope with the disappointments, how to survive the great tragedies that visit us all.

I'm reminded of those early lessons now when I see my daughter doing what I used to do: quietly sitting nearby while I talk with my girlfriends, listening carefully as we hash out our problems or share our triumphs.

My mom and I are different in many ways—she forgives more quickly, she tends to be formal where I'm come-as-you-are. But in the ways that truly count—as a friend, as a wife, as a mother—we are very similar. We love our families unconditionally, with a love so solid and pure and unbending that it can last through any storm, reverse any disappointment, encourage any dream. It's a mother's love, and there really isn't anything else like it.

Taya and Chris Kyle with Taya's parents in January, 2013.

AMERICAN WIFE

AMERICAN

WILLIAM MORROW
An Imprint of HarperCollins Publishers

WIFE

Love, War, Faith, and Renewal

TAYA KYLE

WITH JIM DeFELICE

AMERICAN WIFE. Copyright © 2015 by 300 Spartans, LLC. All rights
reserved. Printed in the United States of America. No part of this book may
be used or reproduced in any manner whatsoever without written permission
except in the case of brief quotations embodied in critical articles and
reviews. For information address HarperCollins Publishers, 195 Broadway,
New York, NY 10007.

HarperCollins books may be purchased for educational, business, or
sales promotional use. For information please e-mail the Special Markets
Department at SPsales@harpercollins.com.

FIRST EDITION

Designed by Lorie Pagnozzi

Library of Congress Cataloging-in-Publication Data has been applied for.

ISBN 978-0-06-239808-6

15 16 17 18 19   ID6/RRD   10 9 8 7 6 5 4 3 2 1

FOR CHRIS—MY LOVE, MY LIFE

CONTENTS

IF I COULD SUM MY LIFE UP IN FOUR WORDS, THEY WOULD
BE THESE:

Love

War

Faith

Renewal

TAKEN TOGETHER, THESE HAVE BROUGHT ME GREAT JOY,
THOUGH WITH THAT JOY I HAVE ALSO FOUND THE DEEPEST
SORROW.

PREFACE: THE LONGEST DAY

*When life brings you to your knees, you are in the
perfect position to pray.*

FEBRUARY 2, 2013

Saturday, and like a lot of Saturdays, we were going in a dozen different directions. But as always, we began the day together.

First up was a rec basketball game at the local church gym. Both of our children, Bubba and Angel, were on the team. My husband Chris and I made it a point of attending the games together. Not only were we were a vital part of the team's cheering section, but the hour or two in the gym let us reconnect with our friends, maintaining the neighborly ties that are so important in a small town. It was always a fun time.

We took different vehicles—Chris his truck, me the family SUV—because we had to split up after the game. I was taking the kids to friends' and then later the mall; Chris was going shooting at a range he'd helped design.

He was bringing a friend, and another man he knew only as a veteran in need.

A few days before, a woman had approached my husband while he was dropping the kids off at school. He didn't know her, but like nearly everyone in the community, she knew who he was: Chris Kyle, *American Sniper*, former SEAL, war hero, and freshly minted celebrity. The story of his life had been a bestseller for over a year; Hollywood planned a major motion picture starring Bradley Cooper, the hottest actor in America. Since the book's publication in January 2012, Chris had been on TV numerous times, starred in a reality series, and spoken at events across the country. His easygoing smile and matter-of-fact personality attracted admirers near and far.

He also had a warm heart and a genuine reputation for helping people, especially veterans and others in need in our community. And it was that reputation that brought the woman to Chris. She told him her son was just back from Iraq and having a little trouble getting the help he needed from the VA and fitting into civilian life. She asked if he might be able to talk to him.

Chris didn't know the young man, nor was he told the vast depth of his problems: fitting in was the least of them. But as he nearly always did, Chris told her he'd see what he could do. Chris and I talked about where they might go. He settled on Rough Creek Lodge, a serene and peaceful place where they wouldn't be bothered. He recruited our dear friend and neighbor, Chad Littlefield, to come with them.

That was today. It was a long drive, perhaps an hour and a half each way. Chris believed the time in the truck would give them a chance to get to know each other. Once the young man was comfortable, Chris would recommend people who might help him, assuming he thought that necessary. For many veterans coming home from a war zone, just being able to share the displacement they felt was enough to set them onto a normal course.

The young man's name was Eddie Routh. He had been a Marine, and he had been deployed, though apparently he hadn't seen combat. But his troubles started before that. Routh had held his girlfriend and a friend of hers at knifepoint and had a history of problems including drug abuse. Whether he was suffering from PTSD or not, his problems went far beyond that, in a different and far more lethal direction. He had threatened to kill his family and himself, been in and out of mental institutions, and generally acted antisocial—important facts that neither Chris nor I knew that morning.

The game went well. I don't remember the score, but I know we both cheered a lot. Chris's hearty laugh filled the auditorium; it was a day of great if simple joy.

Chris and I had been married now over a decade, and while it may sound like a cliché, our love had grown deeper over time. The attraction we'd both felt at our very first meeting had deepened into something truly beautiful. Like all marriages, we'd had our share of ups and downs, heartache and triumph, but lately we'd hit a kind of glorious plateau. We were spending more time together and had found a rhythm that gave us both comfort and shelter, even as our world had expanded and changed.

Chris left when the game ended, so he could get ready for the rest of the day. I gathered the kids and a friend, then drove Bubba to a buddy's house, where the two boys planned to spend most of the day. I was taking Angel and one of her friends to the mall, but the girls needed the bathroom, so we stopped back at the house before continuing.

Chris was packing his rifles and gear in his truck, a tricked-out black Ford 350 pickup. It was his pride and joy.

We passed in the hall.

"Does this guy know it's okay to talk in front of Chad, even though he wasn't military?" I asked.

While he wasn't a veteran, our friend Chad Littlefield was the sort of man who was great at listening. He was as easygoing as Chris, and if anything even more laid-back.

"Yeah," said Chris. He'd already talked to Routh on the phone, mentioning that Chad was coming.

Running a little late and preoccupied, Chris continued packing the truck. Typically at the range, they'd shoot a few different rifles and pistols at different distances. For people who grew up hunting, especially war veterans, shooting often settled the mind. It was something that required full concentration, and therefore took you away from your troubles, at least for a short time.

"Is he coming here?" I asked Chris.

"Hell no," he said. "I wouldn't give anybody our address. I have to go pick him up."

I went to look after the kids. Then suddenly we were ready to leave. I looked around for Chris to say good-bye but couldn't find him; finally I went back into the house and literally ran into him.

"Hey!" I said. "I was looking for you!"

"I was looking for you!" he said.

"I just wanted to say good-bye." I hugged him.

"Me, too."

"I love you."

"I love you, too," he said.

I gave him a quick kiss and a hug—something we tried to always do when we left the house—and went out to the SUV to take the girls to the mall.

That was the last time I saw my husband, my best friend, my hero, alive.

ONE

LOVE

A little more than a decade before, Chris Kyle was the answer to my prayers.

Literally. I'd been feeling depressed after a series of bad relationships and was unsure of my future. I prayed to God that He would send me someone I could raise a family with. Someone who would value and cherish me—and someone I could value and cherish in return. I didn't care about age, career, looks, or anything; all I wanted was a man with a good heart. I told that to God and admitted that although I wanted to be independent of a man, perhaps I wasn't meant to go it alone.

Within weeks, He sent me Chris, in the most unlikely place to have a prayer answered. But maybe it will make more sense if I start at the beginning—my beginning, at least.

FAMILY BEGINNINGS

I was born in Portland, Oregon, in 1974, to Kent and Kim Studebaker. I spent my childhood in small-town suburbs. Trained as a lawyer, my father gave that up to run a small business; my mom was a teacher by trade, but worked as a bookkeeper for my father.

I had one older sister, Ashley. We lived a pretty typical middle-class life. Family was very important, and some of my fondest memories are of days spent visiting my grandparents, who lived on a lake about twenty minutes from us. Visiting them, whether during the summer or on a weekend or even just for a meal, was like going on vacation. We'd boat and swim, or just sit out on their patio and gaze at the ripples on the water. My grandfather was wicked smart, with a sense of humor to match. One of his favorite things was fashioning limericks on the spur of the moment to keep us amused. He had a huge stock of the witty poems, and could deploy them at will, making crazy connections with things that were going on. I blame my offbeat sense of humor on him.

At the same time, he had an old-fashioned sense of decorum and style, always wearing nice slacks and a button-down shirt, often topped off with a Mr. Rogers–style cardigan sweater. He managed to carry them off with a casual rather than stiff air. He was a calm man, so even-tempered that the very few times he got angry were the stuff of family legend.

That's one trait that doesn't seem to have been passed on in my genes.

There is one unusual wrinkle in my family tree—my mom's mom was married to my dad's dad. They were actually stepbrother and -sister, though they never met until college.

Marion—my father's father—and his wife had four children together, including my dad. (He hated that name, by the way; most people called him "Studie," short for Studebaker, his last name.) When my father was fifteen, his mom died after a long illness. Studie married again soon afterward, then divorced. Following that, and maybe thinking he was done with marriage for good, he moved into an apartment complex on the lake.

Meanwhile, my mother's mother, Emily—gorgeous and very artistic—had married her high school sweetheart in Pasadena. He became a very successful dentist, gave up his practice to join the Navy during World War II, then came out and resumed dentistry after the war. Unfortunately, he seems to have cheated on her; the marriage ended in divorce despite the fact that they had three kids, including my mom.

Emily then married a man from Oregon, moving there to be with him. That marriage also ended in divorce. She moved to an apartment complex—the same one where Studie happened to live.

Two bad experiences were enough to turn her off to marriage forever. Now in her fifties, she was adamant that she would remain single for the rest of her life.

Then she met my grandfather. He set out to woo her practically the moment he saw her.

We have some of the notes they wrote to each other, and based on the evidence, Studie was a master Romeo, even well into his fifties. "Together you and I are meant to be," went one note. "You're going to marry me one day you see." He was the sort of man any woman would find hard to resist—big blue eyes, a gentle heart, brilliant, and a great sense of humor. It took him a while, but gradually he wore Emily down and they were married.

While they'd had a few bad marriages between them, this one was the sort people refer to as made in heaven. They'd have weekly races to see who could do the *New York Times* crossword puzzle the fastest, cooked gourmet meals together, and danced in the kitchen whenever the mood struck them—which was often. They laughed all the time and just seemed to have the most wonderful days together. Visiting their house was like going to a resort where only happy people were allowed.

My sister Ashley once asked my grandmother what the secret of their marriage was.

"Oh, I don't know, honey," she told her. "We just laughed a lot, danced a lot, and loved a lot."

If you could package that somehow, you'd make a fortune.

They were married for twenty-five years before death separated them. I still remember sitting with my grandfather in their living room a few days after she died; we talked about her, remembering good times.

After twenty minutes or so, a single tear rolled down his cheek. It was as emotional as I'd ever seen him.

"She was such a good woman, wasn't she?" he asked.

I could only agree.

He pursed his lips, then smiled and got up. There was deep sadness, great loss, and yet resolve to go on. His energy was happy energy; sadness might weigh him down, but he rarely admitted it to others, and it was even rarer still to see evidence of it.

He'd have my sister and me over for dinner every Thursday night. He'd fuss and cook up a storm, then watch *Jeopardy!* with us in the living room. I'd hold his hand and wonder how in the world he could know so many answers.

Unfortunately, he developed prostate cancer as he aged, and despite aggressive treatments, slowly began to waste away. His body took a beating, yet somehow he managed to smile every time he saw us, whether at home or at a hospital. He was in constant pain, and it must have been hard to keep radiating love and kindness to others. But when I visited him, I always left cheered up, as if I was the one who was ill.

To this day, he's an inspiration.

Where did that strength come from?

I don't know. He'd grown up poor and achieved great success; he'd had a wonderful mother but a terrible father. He'd been through a lot—three wives is a lot of living. But none of those things alone can account for character.

My mom and dad met in college shortly after my grandparents started dating. Actually, my aunt met my father first—and went out on a date with him.

According to family lore, my aunt called up her older sister as soon as she got home.

"I just went out with this guy," she said. "You have to meet him. He was made for you."

That phone call gave my mom "permission" to break the don't-date-the-guy-your-sister-has-dated rule. The next time they were both in town together, they began seeing each other. Both had fiery personalities, yet somehow they hit it off. They ended up getting married about a year after my grandparents.

My grandfather had been an engineer before opening his own business supplying power transmission companies and utilities with equipment. After my father got his law degree, served in the Marine Corps, and worked in corporate law for a decade or so, he decided he wanted more autonomy, and went to work at his father's company. But my grandfather was old school—Dad had to work his way up, learning the business from the warehouse floor to the executive suite before being allowed to buy in. My dad wouldn't have wanted it any other way. It was a small business. Both my grandmother and my mother worked there as bookkeepers, and my sister was also employed there for a while. I was the lone rebel—unless you count the time Dad paid me to pull the dandelions off the office lawn.

My childhood in the seventies and eighties was pretty normal. It was the Reagan era, a time when the Cold War came to an end and women became a fixture in the workforce. Maybe that's why, when I was little, I wanted to be an NFL quarterback.

My next ambition was somewhat more realistic, but not by much: I wanted to be a race car driver.

When most girls my age were asking for Barbies, I was hoping for Matchbox cars. I wasn't a tomboy, exactly, but my interests were definitely all over the gender map.

I grew out of that phase. For college, I followed a boyfriend to Wisconsin—a mistake, but it did lead to more independence. Truth be told, we weren't even getting along at the time, but I wanted to get out of Oregon and spread my wings. It was the best excuse I could think of. I ended up earning a degree in economics with a minor in business, wandering into those fields after dabbling in psychology and philosophy.

I remember my dad laughing when I suggested philosophy as a major: *You're going to major in thinking about thinking?*

There's nothing wrong with thinking about thinking, but ultimately I was too practical for that: if Plato were alive today, odds are he'd be pouring coffee at Starbucks. I wanted a profession where I could get a job and support myself, and economics and business were far better bets.

My first real job out of college was selling advertising for a local newspaper—ironic, since for years I'd sworn I'd never be a salesperson. But I managed to do well, earning a number of promotions over four or five years before Wisconsin's long, gray winters got to me. Looking for something warmer, I started interviewing for jobs in the sunniest place I could imagine—California.

I got a position as a salesperson with an office-supply company. A year of cold-calling convinced me I needed to find something else. A friend recommended pharmaceutical sales, and after a lot of debate—Do I really want to work in sales? Do I want to sell drugs?—I went for an interview and got the job.

My life to that point was a battle between my practical, conservative side and a more free-spirited, dreamer side. The practical side wanted a steady paycheck. The dreamer side wanted the *perfect* job, even though it couldn't define what that job was. I loved sales because it meant I didn't have to stay in an office all day. I got out to meet all different sorts of people; no day was ever exactly the same.

The new position took all that and added the fact that medicine helps people, making pharmaceutical sales a bit more meaningful than hawking pencils. It also paid very well. It may not have been the perfect match, but it was an engaging one. I bought a condo in Long Beach and settled in.

Gradually, the pressures of the job—not only meeting quotas but dealing with the resentment from many doctors and their staffs—started to get to me. I eventually realized that I had a case of mild clinical depression and went on antidepressants. I came to know a lot about the drugs I was recommending.

I went through some difficult emotions. I didn't have a steady boyfriend, and in fact I didn't think I wanted one. Because I was in outside sales, I didn't have even an office full of coworkers to make friends with. Looking back, I feel as if God had to break me, in a way: He had to let me feel the results of my stubbornness so that I could understand the beauty and potential of life. I had to be convinced that I wasn't destined to be a loner, that I needed to walk through this life with a partner.

"It doesn't matter what he looks like," I said. My prayers have always been very personal and specific. "It doesn't matter what he does for a living. Just please, God, send me someone nice."

If I had to have someone in my life, let him be good.

A few weeks later, I met Chris. And he was the nicest person I ever met.

"THAT THING"

Chris and I told the story of how we met in *American Sniper*.

Briefly, I was living in Long Beach at the time. A girlfriend wanted to go down to San Diego—nearly a two-hour drive—to check out some bars and relax. I almost didn't go; it was a long drive and I was tired.

But I went. We ended up in a bar in Coronado, where I found myself drinking Scotch and offering sarcastic comebacks to an admittedly good-looking but obnoxious young man hitting on me.

The man's friend came over and interrupted us, joking that I was abusing his friend.

Now *this* was a handsome man. A bit over six feet, solidly built, he had a warm smile and broad shoulders to go with a sweet Texas accent and an easygoing, aw-shucks manner that instantly melted my cynical heart.

His name was Chris Kyle.

He admitted to being a Navy SEAL, though that wasn't a selling point for me—my sister had had a relationship with a man who wanted to be a SEAL but turned out to be something less than perfect. But before I knew it, I was drunk on Chris's good looks and easy personality.

That and the Scotch I was drinking.

It is unfortunately true that I emptied the contents of my stomach on the way to the car. He sweetly held my hair back to keep it get from getting soaked as I did. When a relationship starts like that, it can only get better.

Our relationship quickly grew. I was living in Long Beach at the time; Chris was in San Diego. Conservatively speaking, that's a two-hour drive. But Chris drove it often. He'd get off work, hop in his pickup, and be at my condo before dark. And not just on the weekends: he often rose before the sun to get to work in Coronado Beach. We'd go out to eat, maybe take in a movie, play miniature golf, bowl, see friends—the usual date stuff. But our most fun was just hanging out together.

I pinned a picture of Chris up near my desk. (It's the profile picture on his Facebook page, if you're interested.) Under it, I taped a quote that went along the lines of: *Life is not about the number of breaths you take; it's the moments that take your breath away.*

Chris was all about those breathtaking moments—riding broncs in the rodeo, jumping out of planes. He worked hard and played hard—but was just as likely to relax completely, sitting comfortably on the couch with a beer or whatever as he took it easy. It was a paradox; I loved both sides.

He could also be terribly romantic and thoughtful. My job was a real challenge. The work was difficult and the boss demanding: he thought nothing of calling or emailing at odd hours, even on the weekend; you ignored him at your peril.

There was a point at which everything got to me. And it was exactly at that moment that Chris stepped in and planned a weekend getaway. He found a little cabin out in the woods where there was no cell phone reception—*yes!*—and without telling anyone, we made our getaway.

Almost. I actually called the boss and told him my cell reception was giving out, and so I wouldn't be able to check messages, something he expected even on the weekends.

As soon as we got to the cabin, I headed to the bedroom. Inside, I opened my suitcase and changed into sexy white Victoria's Secret–style lingerie, complete with corset and thigh-highs. Feeling a little shy and silly, I walked out and leaned against the doorway of the living room where he was sitting.

"Hey!"

"Yeah?" he mumbled from the couch, not bothering to look up from the magazine he was reading.

"Turn around," I said.

He turned around—slowly at first. But as soon as he caught sight of me in that lingerie, he hopped clear over the couch and chased me down the hall to the bedroom. I squealed and giggled the wholeway.

When I met him, Chris had graduated from BUD/S, or basic SEAL training, and was already a SEAL. Chris didn't play the SEAL "card," though; he didn't brag or call attention to what he did or himself. He was just a hot guy with an interesting job that he hardly ever talked about.

There came a point about five or six months after we met that I started to really want to be assured that we had the possibility of a future together. That for me meant the possibility of marriage. I wasn't looking for a wedding date or a ring, but I did want to know that was at least a strong possibility. The question of the future began weighing on me—there was that practical side—so one night on a road trip to Oregon I brought it up.

"I don't expect you to know what the future is going to bring," I told him. "And I'm not asking for a commitment right now. But I do want to know if it's possible for us to be something long term. If it's not a possibility, I'm not interested in doing this."

Chris didn't answer right away, but when he did, his answer was perfect.

"I love you," he said. "And I don't want to spend a day of my life without you."

Whoa!

Whoa?

Instead of feeling happy and confident, I suddenly felt something like fear.

In my mind, what he was saying was that he wanted to marry me.

Was I ready for that?

No.

But I loved that I heard that he wanted to marry me and was so confident and open about it.

I quickly warmed up to the idea. But as the days and then weeks went by, I began to wonder. Did his answer really mean he wanted to get married? We didn't talk about it, and our relationship didn't change in any meaningful way.

So, were we headed toward marriage, or not?

Then came 9/11. The tragic attack, and the implications that going to war would have for Chris, pushed me to think harder about my future—our future.

One day I called him and said, "I just had this crazy idea—let's get married."

I thought he'd say, *Hell, yeah! Let's do it!*

His actual reaction: "What?"

As in, *What the heck are you talking about?*

What!?!

"Oh, it's just an idea," I said, quickly retreating. "I'm kind of kidding. We can talk about it later. I have to go."

I tried to hide my disappointment: not so much at his answer—well, there was that—but at the fact that I had read him so wrongly. I was mortified.

A few days later, we were driving on the 405 Freeway, which is the major north-south connector between Los Angeles and San Diego.

"You want to talk about that thing?" he asked out of the blue.

"What thing?" I said.

"That thing you said on the phone?"

"The thing?" It took a moment before I got which *thing* he meant. "Oh, that thing. Getting married?"

"Um, uh, yeah."

"I don't know. Do you want to?"

"Yeah," said Chris. "If you do."

"I do."

"So?" Chris looked at me. "Are we engaged?"

"Well, yeah," I said. I wasn't about to lose an opportunity like that—if that was the way he was interpreting it. Maybe this was the first of his many records—the record for most awkward marriage proposal ever, courtesy of me.

"I need to get you a ring," he told me. "And I have to ask your dad."

That was pure Chris: old-fashioned enough to actually ask *permission.*

He did NOT want to do it over the phone—he wanted to go all the way to Oregon and ask in person. But I convinced him to use the phone. I was too excited to hold on to the news until we could get up to see them.

I was sitting on the bed when he called my parents a short time later. My father came to the phone.

"Mr. Studebaker," said Chris in his most humble and polite voice. "I want to ask for your daughter's hand."

"Her hand?" asked my father, not losing a beat. "What are you going to do with her hand?"

Chris got a little flustered, but it all worked out. We were getting married.

I didn't want a fancy engagement ring or a gaudy wedding band; for me, a plain wedding ring was a perfect symbol. I like simple, especially in a wedding ring: it reminds you that love is about love, nothing else—not money, not appearances, not showing off. But it seemed almost impossible to convince anyone of that. Including Chris.

He kept asking me what I wanted, and wouldn't take "simple" for an answer. Then my mother got into the act. My grandmother had left her a diamond from a ring that she had had. Mom suggested that I use it as the centerpiece of an engagement ring.

I told her thanks, but no thanks.

"I don't care whether you wear it as an engagement ring or a belly button ring," she insisted after we went around a bit. "But I'm sending it."

She did. It was lovely. Chris and I ended up taking it to a local jewelry store. We found a wonderful setting we both loved and had the jeweler set the diamond in it. We got our wedding rings the same day, adding an engraving on the inside.

"All of me," Chris wrote on mine.

"My love, my life," I said on his.

My dress was another nearly snap decision. I knew the overall look I wanted: sleek and elegant. I found something online I liked, then found a place where similar dresses were sold. When I saw it in person, I knew it was perfect: a strapless, fitted gown with rhinestones across the top and a mermaid bottom. I didn't want a veil, but my mom and the saleswoman talked me into it—and I'm glad they did.

It's funny. I usually think of myself as less than decisive, but when it came to the wedding I was very businesslike and made decisions quickly, without second-guessing. Maybe it was because I just wanted to be married to Chris; the trappings weren't important.

I've modified my view on that over the years, by the way. Trappings—flourishes and celebrations—can help us remember what's important rather than distract us from it.

Another reason I was so decisive may have been the fact that I wasn't planning much of it myself. Weighed down with work— I'd just gotten a promotion that would allow me to move to San Diego—I was far too busy to take care of all the details that go with planning a wedding. Luckily for me, my sister volunteered to step in as unpaid wedding director. She did all the heavy lifting.

The new job as well as the upcoming wedding convinced Chris and me that we should get a house in the San Diego area, where he was based. Buying my condo in Long Beach two years earlier had been a statement of independence, a sign that I was a grown-up. I'd wanted something practical, and an investment; it didn't take long to find. This was different. First of all, there were two of us: buying wasn't a statement of independence but rather interdependence—a new and very different phase.

And, prices were brutal. We were shocked when we saw what we could afford near the city: houses covered with graffiti, places that smelled like cat urine, structures more suitable for demolition than raising a family. We went farther and farther out, until finally we saw something in the suburbs in a decent neighborhood.

By that point, the decision was easy: grab it before someone else does. And so we did.

There was a lot of stress on both of us, and one night we had a fight over some detail about the house. The cause is lost to me, but I know I got really mad—mad enough to knock papers off the kitchen table, and then take a bowl of macaroni and cheese and fling it against the wall.

That's *very* mad, especially for me.

I also remember the solution. Sitting alone after Chris went to bed, I called a girlfriend and poured out my heart. I knew that I had gone too far, but I didn't know how to fix it.

"You love him, right?" she asked finally.

"Yes."

"Then go in there, wake him up, and give him some hot sex."

So I did. We didn't talk, but we sure did make love.

Chris seemed apprehensive when he left the next morning. I later found out that he couldn't quite figure out why his mad fiancée would come to him for hot sex and no talk. He was afraid he would come home and I would be gone.

He didn't mention it, though, because he didn't want to risk a talk when maybe I was over it. If he was wrong and I was gone, he would find me and fix it. Avoiding a "talk" was worth the risk of damage control later. He was his usual confident self, taking life as it came and handling the consequences IF they came.

On my side, I would have panicked if I thought he was going to leave me.

While we hadn't originally planned on living out so far in the suburbs, the location was good for my work as a traveling drug rep. The city and airport were nearby. There was a homey, even country atmosphere in town—the coffee shop was literally a log cabin, and one of the best places to eat was a country-style café. More wide-open areas lay to the east about a half mile, so it wasn't hard to get away temporarily.

There was one feature of the house that nailed it for us: a balcony off the bedroom.

"We'll sit out in the morning and have coffee together," Chris said when we first looked at it. It was a wonderful, romantic idea.

Regrettably, we never found the time, not once, to sit out there together in the morning, with or without coffee.

Chris had a real knack for giving a woman a compliment. He was just so genuine about it.

"Damn, babe," he'd say. "You look so beautiful." Simple words, but the sincere tone and the look on his face made them mean so much.

You're so beautiful.

The words would catch me off guard. He didn't say them in that way often, but that made them more powerful. And he'd do it at the most unexpected times. I might be in the bathroom taking off my makeup and catch him looking at me from the bed.

You're so beautiful.

When the compliment came during a moment when I wasn't feeling particularly pretty, it meant so much.

He tried to hide his intellectual intelligence—he never bragged about being smart, and while he did okay in school, he didn't go out of his way to get good grades. But he couldn't hide his "EQ," or emotional intelligence. It was always obvious in his eyes, and in his voice when he spoke to me, or really to anyone he loved.

Part of the reason I wanted Chris in my life was that he had such a *zest* for things. He was exuberant about even the simplest things: lingerie, a bag of Laffy Taffy, a good meal. And while he was a hard-core warrior, a tough-guy SEAL, he had a romantic side: the idea of spending every morning sharing a cup of coffee with his wife was his idea of bliss. Hearing his laugh, or seeing him saunter into a room—everything he did brought me energy and cheer. I knew I could make him laugh, no matter what was going on—and that laugh infected my soul. The more he laughed, the more I wanted to make him laugh.

Maybe I shouldn't take too much credit: he used to watch *America's Funniest Home Videos* and just guffaw and guffaw. Silly stuff tickled him.

I loved it. As a SEAL, he certainly knew dark times. But he could go from darkness to light with a hearty laugh in zero flat.

THE WEDDING

As a young girl, I had a vision of my perfect wedding: it would be at a lodge somewhere in the Oregon mountains, at night, with the snow falling and a huge fire warming the hearth.

What we ended up having was a wedding on a boat, in southern California, during the day—180 degrees different in nearly every possible way. We had to have it during the day because that was the only time they had available; it had to be in southern California because Chris couldn't get a lot of time off from work . . . you get the idea.

Knowing Chris was getting married, his fellow Team members decided that they had to send him off with a proper SEAL bachelor party. That meant getting him drunk, of course. It also meant writing all over him with permanent markers—an indelible celebration, to be sure.

Fortunately, they liked him, so his face wasn't marked up—not by them, at least; he'd torn his eyebrow and scratched his lip during training. Under his clothes, he looked quite the sight. And the words wouldn't come off no matter how he, or I, scrubbed.

I pretended to be horrified, but honestly, that didn't bother me much. I was just happy to have him with me, and very excited to be spending the rest of my life with the man I loved.

It's funny, the things you get obsessed about. Days before the wedding, I spent forty-five minutes picking out *exactly* the right shade of lipstick, splurging on expensive cosmetics—then forgot to take it with me the morning of the wedding. My poor sister and mom had to run to Walgreens for a substitute; they came back with five different shades, not one of which matched the one I'd picked out.

Did it matter? Not at all, although I still remember the vivid marks the lipstick made when I kissed him on the cheek—marking my man.

Lipstick, location, time of day—none of that mattered in the end. What did matter were our families and friends, who came in for the ceremony. Chris liked my parents, and vice versa. I truly loved his mom and dad.

I have a photo from that day taped near my work area. My aunt took it. It's become my favorite picture, an accidental shot that captured us perfectly. We stand together, beaming, with an American flag in the background. Chris is handsome and beaming; I'm beaming at him, practically glowing in my white gown.

We look so young, happy, and unworried about what was to

come. It's that courage about facing the unknown, the unshakable confidence that we'd do it together, that makes the picture so precious to me.

It's a quality many wedding photos possess. Most couples struggle to make those visions realities. We would have our struggles as well.

We wrote our own vows; I take them to heart even today:

> I give you my heart, soul, and everlasting love.
>
> I promise to be there during both laughter and tears and to protect you in the days to come.
>
> I will be faithful and truthful, whether near or far, and will never give you cause for doubt.
>
> I will embrace your happiness and hold you when you are sad.
>
> I will be your biggest supporter and your constant friend.
>
> I will remind you of who you are when you forget.
>
> I will consider your happiness with every action.
>
> I will celebrate your soul and work to enrich your life as you enrich mine.
>
> Most of all, I will love you and show my love all the days of my life.

Instead of traditional wedding music, we chose Enya's version of "How Can I Keep from Singing." The words of the song talk of a hymn that can always be heard, no matter how dark the night or how difficult the day. The song speaks of faith and endurance, and through it all, music. It seemed to perfectly capture our love and commitment to each other. The words and tune—hypnotic and soaring—would come to me at various parts of my life. I gave birth to it. I hear it in my head today.

He had only three days off, which meant our honeymoon was only two days. We went to Lake Tahoe, and one of the highlights was a snowmobile tour in the mountains. In theory, we had to ride our separate vehicles very placidly, with no horsing around. But Chris—or maybe it was me—discovered that by maneuvering carefully, it was possible to splash up a lot of snow, and as we went up to the top we managed to cover each other with snow. It was the sort of simple joy you vow to repeat as often as you can, even as you realize the moment will be impossible to duplicate.

They were a great two days, though I wished there were more.

I happened to be reading a book around that time that theorized that humans live through many lives. I asked Chris what he thought about the concept. Did he think he had many past lives?

"Oh, I don't know," he said. "That's not in the Bible."

"No, it's not."

"I guess anything's possible," he told me after a little thought. "I don't think we have all the answers. But I do know this: if we get more than one life, I can't wait to spend the rest of them with you."

Chris took his vows very seriously. But even as he said them, he wondered whether the marriage would last.

In retrospect, that's not surprising. He was surrounded by Team guys who'd had their own relationships fail. A common, and tragic, statistic at the time was that the divorce rate among SEALs was over 95 percent—a stunning statistic. Actual statistics are difficult to find, but most experts estimate that the divorce rate in America in general is below 50 percent.

Chris kept his pessimism well hidden, even from me. It wasn't until years later that I found out about it.

He asked why I'd stayed with him through some difficult times.

"I told you I meant what I promised," I answered.

"I know, but I didn't count on it," he confessed. "So few women stick it out."

Maybe. But he was worth it.

TWO

WAR

SEALs train all the time. All . . . the . . . time. That's why they're an elite force.

But with the war in Afghanistan continuing and an invasion of Iraq seeming inevitable, Chris's training schedule picked up considerably right around the time we were married. Within months, he was packing to go to the Middle East.

Technically, I didn't know where he was going or what he would be doing, but wives pick up hints. Besides the "normal" things that SEALs practice—like raiding enemy strongholds to "extract" terrorists or others—they were working a lot on desert warfare and ship takeovers. And his SEAL team was ordinarily tasked to work in the Middle East, which of course included Iraq and the Persian Gulf. There were constant stories in the media about troops being sent to the region in preparation for an invasion. It wasn't hard to figure where he was heading before his deployment orders came that summer.

When it came time for Chris to leave, we drove his Yukon down to the base. Chris was excited to go to war—he'd spent years training for it, after all. He was somber and serious, but also looking forward to it.

Me?

I felt as if a part of myself was leaving, and there was nothing I could do about it. I longed to be with him, but knew that our separation would be deep, and perhaps permanent. I felt trapped by fate, a prisoner of whatever inevitability the future was bringing.

We sat together in the back of the SUV, waiting until it was time for him to board the bus waiting to take him to the plane. Finally, it was time to go. Chris was wearing sunglasses, but I could see his eyes leaking tears under them.

I thought he was nervous because he was going to war and was afraid that he would die. It wasn't until years later that he straightened me out: "I was afraid you wouldn't be there when I came back."

TIPTOEING TO WAR

I might have imagined that Chris and the others would jump right into the fighting, but in fact what happened was more a slow tiptoe to war. President Bush delivered an ultimatum to Saddam Hussein, demanding that he comply with the U.N. resolution that had ended the First Gulf War, which Saddam had agreed to. The Iraqi dictator stalled and stalled; in the meantime, President Bush went to Congress for support to enforce the resolutions and get rid of Saddam. The process took months—the congressional vote was in October 2002; Secretary of State Colin Powell presented the arguments for using force to the U.N. in February 2003. (In the end, though a number of allies joined the U.S. in the war, the U.N. did not vote to sanction an invasion.)

One of the more—*interesting?*—things I did for Chris during that first deployment was send him some sexy photos of me in lingerie.

I knew he wanted something to remember me, and I knew that other wives were doing the same thing. But getting the pictures was difficult.

I finally got my courage up and asked my sister to help. Even then, I was so embarrassed that I needed to have a couple of beers to get through the session.

This was back in the days before camera phones and digital photographs were everywhere, and so the photos were taken on a Polaroid camera. They came home a little worse for wear, so obviously he enjoyed them.

Chris talks about some of what he did in those long months before the war in *American Sniper*. Most of it, including the ship searches, was routine. Even the scouting missions near the Iraqi border were, to a SEAL at least, somewhat boring. But then, these guys hardly get excited even when someone's shooting at them.

A lot of the time, at least from what Chris told me, was spent training. Late one evening Chris called to say hello. It was a very short conversation—he had to leave for a helicopter training mission and had just grabbed a few minutes to chat and say he loved me.

It was a conversation we'd had dozens, maybe even hundreds, of times. He'd steal a moment or two to say hello. My heart would jump answering the phone; for just a few moments, I'd feel the strong love between us. Then it would be back to work or chores or whatever else I had been doing.

This one turned out to be different.

The next morning I flipped on the news and saw a report that a helicopter had crashed during training.

"Special Forces were involved," intoned the newscaster.

My heart stopped.

In the military, the term *Special Forces* specifically applies to the U.S. Army unit known colloquially as the Green Berets. Like SEALs, they're specially trained commandos who routinely go behind enemy lines and carry out dangerous missions. Like SEALs, they are part of the Special Operations Command. But while their missions occasionally overlap, they are separate and distinct from SEALs.

At the time, however, the distinction was lost on most of the news media. They were calling any Special Operations troops, including SEALs, "Special Forces."

So what I heard was that a helicopter with SEALs had crashed.

Maybe with SEALs, the logical part of my brain said.

Probably not SEALs! it screamed.

Definitely not your husband, it insisted.

That was the logical part of my brain. The emotional half was having a frenzy fit of freakin' worry.

I tamped down the emotions, forcing myself to get to work. I went into my office and buried myself in paperwork. As the day continued, I did whatever I could to distract my mind from the possibility.

But dread continued to grow. The emotions were winning out.

Maddeningly, the media didn't carry any more details about the crash. Worse, Chris didn't call. By early evening, when he still hadn't phoned or emailed, I was a wreck.

I phoned my sister in Australia. "I'm trying not to freak out, but I'm kind of losing it here."

She tried talking me through it. I was a little calmer when we got off the phone, but fear has a way of clawing its way back, and in short order I was feeling a panic attack coming on.

I told myself he was fine. I told myself he was busy.

I'm sure it's fine. I'm sure it's fine. Do not freak out. Do not do it.

Finally, the phone rang. It was Chris.

Chris!

"Hey, sexy!" he said. It was his usual greeting.

I started sobbing so hard I literally could not get a word out.

"Babe . . . babe, what's wrong?!" he asked.

I still couldn't get words out. After what seemed like forever I managed to grunt, "I'm just . . . you're okay."

He'd just come in from the training mission. He knew nothing about the crash.

After I managed to explain, he suggested I shouldn't watch the news.

As time went on, I felt I had to pretend that I was never worried or concerned. Because if I didn't—if I let on that I was truly, deeply worried for his safety—that would surely unsettle him. He needed to concentrate on his job. It was an ironic catch-22—if he knew how much I was worried about him, I thought he would turn around and start worrying about me. Taking his mind off what he was doing could be fatal; combat requires intense concentration and constant attention. A worried wife is a distraction no fighter needs.

So not for the last time I pretended that I *knew* he was safe. I might pray like crazy when I hung up, but on the phone I was as blasé as I could possibly be. My tone was the same as if he were down the street—at least that was my aim.

Like all of his regular rotations into Iraq, Chris's deployment was originally scheduled to last six months, but it was extended as the war neared. He took part in the initial assault on Iraq, securing oil fields and a piping area so that Saddam couldn't repeat the environmental destruction he'd perpetrated during the First Gulf War. It was an important mission, but not one that got a lot of press back home.

After that, he went north along the border with Iran, then joined the land war and took part in a rescue operation that remains classified. Our conversations were rare once the war started. If I got to talk to him two days in a row, I was excited.

I was paranoid about missing a call and took great pains to keep my cell phone charged and with me at all times. I was always worried there'd be some glitch in the reception that would rob me of a conversation with him—and my greatest fear was that the call would have been my last chance to talk to him, ever.

Even in war, life consists of inane juxtapositions—life-and-death missions to rid a small section of a city of terrorists, and thoughts of home and "regular" life. One moment, Chris had dozens of lives in his hands; he focused completely on his mission. The next moment—or more likely, an hour later, back at camp—his thoughts were more familiar, at least to me: How were the kids, could he afford a new computer, what sort of truck should he get when he got home?

Talking to me, whether on the phone or in emails, he segregated his world into parts: I heard the concerns about home, the house, our extended family. War rarely entered the conversation. The things I heard were mostly random and trivial—a funny story about how he traveled from one place to another, progress on the hut they were building to live in. The occasional glimpses of battle were brief and without detail: "we rescued hostages," he wrote in one email, and that was all I ever found out until he was working on *American Sniper*.

THE WHOLE STORY

At some point in the first month or so of the war, Chris and his unit began scouting ahead for advancing regular troops in southeast Iraq. During this time, they found themselves surrounded by an unexpectedly large Iraqi force. They fought until they were down to their last rounds of ammunition, then called in air support.

That firefight is detailed in *American Sniper*. It's a dramatic encounter there, with the SEALs outnumbered and ready to go hand to hand with the enemy at any moment.

In the middle of that battle, with the enemy about to charge, Chris called me on the unit's sat phone. Sure he was going to die, he wanted to say one last good-bye.

I wish I could say that I remember that call. But the truth is, it was so normal, he was so completely calm, that I don't. I had no reason to think it was anything but a routine hello in the middle of a hectic day.

Hey, babe. Just callin' to tell ya I love ya. Gotta go 'cause a bunch of guys are waitin' to use the phone.

As it turned out, they were rescued at the very last minute—just before they ran out of bullets, and a few minutes before a fighter jet they were calling in to bomb the area would have attacked. But I didn't know the drama until years later. When Chris sprung the story on me, I was shocked, and not just because he'd been so close to death. He told me he would have preferred to die from an American bomb than from the enemy.

"Why?" I asked. "What sense does that make?"

"Because we didn't want to be captured. We knew what would happen to us."

After he explained it, I realized it made perfect sense from his point of view. It was simply an extension of the SEAL mentality: they would have preferred to die than be taken prisoner. They believed that if they were captured, they would be used for propaganda and completely disgraced, then killed anyway. Why put your family through that? Why torture your own people and suffer besides? Better to go out in a blaze, whether it was glorious or not.

I'm amazed not so much at that attitude, but at the fact that Chris could be so calm when he talked to me minutes before he thought he was going to die.

Then again, that was true of every moment he was deployed. A stray mortar shell or a Scud, later on a suicide bomber or a roadside bomb, could have taken him out at any moment. But he was always calm, always matter-of-fact. Talking to him, he really could be anywhere—safe in a bunker or out in a hide waiting for his target to appear a thousand feet away.

On my side of the phone, I engaged in a certain amount of denial. I would hear gunfire in the background while we were talking, but dismiss it as irrelevant. On the rare occasions that I asked about it, he said it was taking place outside the base and then move on to another topic—without of course mentioning that *he* was outside the base, and the firefight was a few yards away.

I learned early on that the U.S. public was not getting a full view of the war—call it dumbed down by sound bites. A lot of the protests against the war were simply naïve, but even those that were more sophisticated tended to lack a lot of information. It got worse as the war went on. As reported by other soldiers and some news media, the atrocities that were being committed in Iraq, especially by al-Qaeda-affiliated mujahedeen, were outrageous. Civilians were tortured and killed. But this was rarely if ever reported.

I think it is one thing to protest the war and quite another to criticize the soldiers who are sent to fight it. The soldiers are simply doing a job we've assigned to them. They've given their country a blank check on their lives and the lives of their loved ones; we should at least show our sympathy. Protest Congress or the president, the people who are actually making the decision to go to war; support the troops, no matter what.

Some people do do that. Unfortunately, not enough.

COMING HOME

My father had told me that war changes people, and while I knew intellectually that it had to be true, I didn't really understand it emotionally until Chris came back from his first deployment.

It wasn't like he was a completely different person. Casual acquaintances might not even have picked up on the differences. But I certainly could see them.

His temper was shorter, and it seemed to flare at certain things that before would have seemed insignificant. Someone not thanking him for holding the door would make him cross. He'd been in a place where there was no such thing as common decency, let alone courtesy; small failures of courtesy here, in a place where things were supposed to be far different, unsettled him.

Not that he got violent with me, or with anyone, but anger was closer to the surface than it had been.

That's common, I think, among war veterans and others subjected to stress, especially when they've just come home. He was less accessible, too—it was never easy to get him to talk about his feelings, and now it was even more difficult.

We developed a little ritual that we'd follow whenever he came home from war. Chris would spend the first few days at home, without anyone bothering him. Even though neighbors and family members all wanted to see him and celebrate his return, I ran interference, explaining that he needed a little time to decompress. Little by little, he would come out of the protective shell, getting back to his outgoing self.

He never lost his sense of humor, and that may have helped him come back. His belly laugh was a sure sign that he was getting better.

He did drink more. It wasn't a cure, and it wasn't something that made him obnoxious—if anything, it quieted him down a bit. But it always had the potential for becoming something more—a crutch or a problem, or both.

When he started making coffee for me in the mornings again, I knew he was back all the way.

Chris didn't share most of what had happened on the deployments when he got home. Talking too much would probably have detoured him from getting back to normal life. But he was also afraid what my reaction would be to certain things—maybe I might be so worried about him in the future that I would find it impossible to go on.

Eventually, the stories would come out. A few times he'd talk about things in front of other people. I think he planned some of those: he was afraid, maybe, that I'd say *What!* and freak out.

Other times he would tell me at a quiet moment. Alcohol sometimes loosened his lips, though even with me he maintained his silence about classified ops.

What kind of things did he talk about? The things that make war so ugly.

Over the years, he told me about some serious and crazy situations—like the time he was face-to-face with a terrorist but was out of bullets. He got out of that one alive; his antagonist didn't. He talked about laughing as he watched enemy mujahedeen drown. He talked about the way blood smells when it's fresh and still pouring from a dead body.

Gruesome, but the reality of war.

He repeated stories about how guys would laugh at certain things we wouldn't find funny stateside, the way an ER surgeon jokes about an intense surgery with fellow surgeons—you can either laugh or cry, but the emotion has to come out.

I think sometimes he'd throw things out there to see if people thought he was a monster. If they were bothered by the fact that he was proud of his job—which, after all, involved killing people. I don't think that he judged people by their reactions; I think he was more like a scientist, testing to see how abnormal the situation of war truly was.

I wasn't freaked out by what he did, or the strange things that happened. I know the circumstances, and I know the goal. And I know Chris.

War forced him to wall part of himself off. He had to harden himself against the brutality that he was part of. He had to be brutal himself, not only to do his job but to simply survive.

That didn't make him a monster.

People have no idea how horrendous war is until they've lived it. I think that was as true for Chris as anyone. And it's difficult to have an appreciation for the kinds of emotions that the men and women who are in war feel.

It seems especially hard for civilians to understand violent emotions against the enemy. Chris called the enemy "savages"—and with good reason because of the things they did to Iraqis as well as American soldiers, many of which he witnessed. But even without those barbarities, he could only have hated the enemy.

Imagine if you are out somewhere with your family, and one of them gets shot and killed. The next day, another gets shot. Then another. Sooner or later, no matter who you are, you will hate the person who is killing your family. And that hatred extends to the others who are supporting him. It runs deep.

Anger swells.

The guys you train with are your family, especially when you are a SEAL. They call each other "brothers," and if anything, that understates the closeness of the relationship. They depend on each other for a multitude of things, and not just in combat.

In war, you change: you have to in order to survive and to keep the people around you alive. You adapt. You become harder. If you don't, you make mistakes that cost lives.

I remember hearing a story about a soldier relieving himself on a dead enemy's body.

Was that horrible?

No more horrible than war itself.

I'm not endorsing desecration of the enemy or any other bad behaviors, let alone criminal acts. But we need to keep a perspective. War is horrible, and it pushes people to their limits. We need to understand that. It is, after all, one of the reasons we want to avoid war whenever possible.

PREGNANT

One of the greatest blessings a spouse can receive is total, unquestioning support from his or her significant other when it comes to a career. I was so lucky to have that with Chris. He put no pressure on me to work, and no pressure on me not to work. And he took the consequences in stride.

During the early years of our marriage, I was very ambitious and wanted to continue moving up the ladder in my profession. So when I heard there was a manager's slot open, I decided to apply for it—even though it meant leapfrogging an entire level in the company hierarchy.

Chris supported me, even though it would mean more work and stress—and consequently, less time for him. My supervisor didn't. He told me flat out he wouldn't recommend me; I was too young and needed more experience to take that job.

If you want to get me psyched to do something, tell me I can't. I researched managerial styles and prepared a long report on how I would do the job and why I was right for it. Then I gave it to my boss's boss. Yes, I was young; yes, I didn't have great experience; but I was ambitious, I was enthusiastic, and I had already shown that I could work hard.

To everyone's surprise, even mine, I got the job.

It was stressful, but it was also invigorating. I got a chance to work closely with my team members, riding with them and doing my best to help them do their jobs. It was a new challenge that played not only to different strengths but also deeper priorities—my love of helping people was now an important part of the job.

My team's accounts were usually at least an hour away, so visiting them, which I had to do often, meant long car trips and extra-long days. Audiobooks were my saving grace. Tom Clancy, Vince Flynn, even J. K. Rowling, all kept me company on my drives. (I fell in love with Rowling's Harry Potter series, by the way. To this day, I refuse to watch the movies—I just know the wizards and Muggles won't be as good on film as they are in the books.)

Around Christmas 2003, we visited Chris's parents in Texas. I found myself exceptionally hungry, though I couldn't figure out why. When we came back to California, I just felt something was off.

Could I be . . . *pregnant?*

Nah.

I bought a pregnancy test just in case. Chris and I had always planned to have children, but we weren't in a rush about it. In fact, we had only recently decided to be "a little less careful." It was a compromise between our spontaneous impulses and our careful planning instincts, which we both shared. We figured, if it happens somewhere in the next year . . .

I was upstairs in the house working when I decided to take a break and check things out.

Wow.

WOW!!!

Chris happened to be home fiddling with something in the garage. I ran downstairs, holding the stick in my hand. When I got there, I held it up, waving.

"Hey, babe," he said, looking at me as if I were waving a sword.

"Come here," I said. "I have to show you something."

He came over. I showed him the stick.

"Okay?"

"Look!"

"What is it?"

"Look at this!"

Obviously, he wasn't familiar with home pregnancy tests. Maybe that's a guy thing—given that the tests reveal either your worst nightmare or one of the most exciting events of your life. I'd wager every woman in America knows what they are and how they work.

Slowly it dawned on him.

"Oh my God," he said, stunned. "Are you . . . ?"

"*Yes!*"

We confirmed it at the doctor's soon after. I know you're supposed to wait something like twelve weeks before telling anyone—there's so much that can go wrong—but we couldn't keep that kind of secret to ourselves for more than a few days. We ended up sending packages with an ultrasound and baby booties—one pink, one blue—to our parents, telling them we had a late Christmas surprise and to call us so we could be on the phone when they opened them.

Chris accompanied me to most of the exams as we got ready to have the baby. At one critical point, the doctor offered to do a test that would screen for developmental problems. People sometimes use the result of that test to decide whether to go ahead with the birth.

We looked at each other as she said that.

"Do you want to know?" I asked Chris. "I mean, what difference would it make if something was wrong with the baby?"

"It won't change anything. I'm going to love the baby, one way or another."

"Me, too. That's our baby, no matter how it comes out."

We decided not to do the test, leaving the outcome to God.

But we weren't willing to leave everything unknown, or at least Chris didn't: he wanted to know whether it was a boy or girl. A few checkups later, the sonogram proclaimed loudly, "It's a boy!"

I can still see myself lying on my back, belly covered with jelly, and Chris beaming next to me. He'd been sure the baby would be a girl—so many other Team guys were having girls that it seemed to be some sort of military requirement.

I was very excited—and a little nervous. I hadn't had a brother growing up. (Ten male cousins don't count in this equation. Even if I love them all.) Talking to his mother, I mentioned that I had no idea what to expect with a boy. She, after all, was an expert—she'd had two, both of whom turned into fine young men.

"I don't know what to do with a boy," I confessed.

"You just chase them," she replied.

Boy, is that true.

BIRTH

We found out that Chris would be deploying very soon after Bubba was due. I was so thrilled about being a mother that doing it on my own for six months or so didn't scare me. The fact that Chris wouldn't be there to share his early days weighed on my heart, but otherwise I was confident and ready.

Right? You may suspect where this is going.

I planned to stay out on maternity leave as long as possible, then get some help once I had to go back to work.

I remained on the job until a couple of weeks before my due date. I was as big as a house and twice as hungry. Bubba—Chris's nick-name for our son—would move around every so often. Like most moms-to-be, I wanted to share the sensation with my husband. And like many fathers-to-be, Chris was just a little nervous about that.

"He's moving," I'd tell Chris. "Want to feel?"

"No, no, I'm good."

Here's a guy who is totally calm under fire, who can deal with all sorts of difficult physical situations, to say nothing of severe wounds—but put a pregnant belly in front of him and he turns to timid mush.

Men.

"I don't know what that thing is," he said, trying to explain his squeamishness. "When the baby's born, that's my baby."

There's a reason women are the ones who have the babies. Though I will admit that seeing my stomach move and poke out on its own did remind me of the movie *Alien*.

We waited. The due date arrived . . . and passed.

We waited some more. And a little more.

And a tiny bit more.

The doctors decided it was time to induce. I made an appointment, packed everything, and got ready. Chris and I rose early that morning and made our way to the hospital. I was very calm and maybe even a little blasé.

Or just naïve.

I hadn't taken Lamaze or any of those fancy birth classes. "There are girls in third-world countries giving birth without anesthesia all the time," I told friends. "I can handle this."

It also helped to know I was getting an epidural, which would mean much less pain.

I won't feel much, I'll get the shot, I'll push. Done.

Piece of cake.

They prepped me, then started me on an IV with Pitocin, which is a common drug used to speed nature along. And things did move. Within what seemed like seconds, my water broke and the contractions started. Bubba was pushing to get out.

I said to myself, *This is going to be quick.*

I also thought: I'll take that epidural now! Because the contractions were starting to demonstrate what the pain of birth is all about.

The obstetrician came in. I smiled, ready for my shot.

"I don't know how to tell you this," she said. "Your platelets are really, really low."

"Okay," I said. I knew what platelets were—blood cells whose job it is to stop bleeding—but I had no idea why that was significant. "So, my epidural?"

"You can't have any medications."

"Come again?"

"No drugs, no medications," she said. "No epidural. I've called around to different anesthesiologists, and no one will touch you."

"No epidural?"

"Nothing."

There are girls from third-world countries who do it with no drugs, I reminded myself. My mother elected for natural childbirth. How bad can it be?

I got this.

It started to hurt. I thought to myself, I am not going to cuss.

Hell no! I am about to be a mother. I am bringing our baby into a positive environment and must be a good role model.

Wow!

The contractions built up quickly. My pristine vision of perfect, calm, quiet childbirth disappeared. A banshee snuck into the room and took over my body.

Arrrgggh!!!

No cursing!

There was a rocking chair in the birth room. I went over and sat in it and began moving back and forth. Chris put on a CD by Enya that we'd brought to listen to: peaceful, pleasant music. I took a deep breath.

Jeez, Louise! That one was a monster!

Then, a breather.

I'm doing goooooood! Breathe. Breathe . . .

Wow!

Then I said some other things. The banshee had a mind of her own.

"I'm sorry, I'm sorry, I'm sorry!" I apologized to the nurses as I recovered from the surge of the contraction.

"It's okay," said Chris.

The pain surged again.

Dang!

Jiminy!

And other things.

Chris would watch the monitor. Suddenly he'd turn to look at me.

"What?" I asked.

"That was a strong one."

"Uh-huh."

The funny thing is, the stronger the contractions were on the monitor, the less they seemed to hurt. Maybe when things are really bad you focus more on being tough. Or perhaps my brain's pain mechanism simply went on strike when the agony got too much.

Labor had started quickly, but now it went into slow motion. And I mean s . . . l . . . o . . . w. Hours passed. My nurse reached the end of her shift but received permission to stay with me the whole time; to this day I'm grateful.

At some point I tried willing things along, mentally focusing on a rapid delivery. That didn't work. I got up to walk around—

walking is supposed to help you progress—then quickly got back in the chair.

"Argh!!!!!" I groaned. And other stuff.

The way I saw it, my baby should have been out by now, shaking hands with his dad and passing around cigars to the nurses. But he apparently had other plans. Labor continued very slowly.

Very slowly.

We were in that room for eighteen hours. That was a lot of contractions. And a lot of PG versions of curse words, along with the X-rated kind. I may have invented a whole new language.

Somewhere around the twelve-hour mark, Chris asked if I'd mind if he changed the music, since our songs had been playing on repeat for what surely seemed like a millennium.

"Sure," I said.

He switched to the radio and found a country station. That lasted a song or two.

"I'm so sorry," I told him. "I need Enya. I'm tuned in to it, and it calms me . . . ohhhhh!"

"Okay. No problem," he said calmly, though not quite cheerfully. I'm sure it was torture.

Chris would take short breaks, walking out into the waiting room where both sides of our family were waiting to welcome their first grandchild and nephew. He'd look at his dad and give a little nod.

"She's okay," he told everyone. Then he'd wipe a little tear away from his eye and walk back to me.

Chris said later that watching me give birth was probably the most powerless feeling he'd ever had. He knew I was in pain and yet couldn't do a whit about it. "It's like watching your wife get stabbed and not being able to do anything to help."

But when he came into the room with me, his eyes were clear

and he seemed confident and even upbeat. It was the thing he did when talking to me from the combat zone, all over again: he wasn't about to do anything that would make me worry.

I, on the other hand, made no secret of what I was feeling. An alien watermelon was ripping my insides out. And it hurt.

Whoooh!

Suddenly one of the contractions peaked way beyond where the others had been. Bubba had finally decided it was time to say hello to the world.

I grabbed the side rail on the bed and struggled to remain conscious, if not exactly calm.

Part of me was thinking, You should remember this, Taya. This is natural childbirth. This is beautiful. This is what God intended. You should enjoy this precious moment and remember it always.

Another part me was telling that part to shut the bleep up.

I begged for mercy—and painkillers.

The obstetrician had been researching my situation, calling other doctors for advice and trying to find some way of easing my pain. Finally she came in and said she might be able to give me nitrous oxide—laughing gas.

"Will it affect the baby?" I asked.

Now, the answer I heard was: *No. The baby will be fine.*

Chris heard something different. He thought he heard: *There's a chance it will.*

Probably the obstetrician included the standard disclaimer to the effect that there is always a minuscule chance something bizarre will happen. But I'm sure she never would have offered it if a real danger existed. And having worked in the pharmaceutical industry, I knew that low-percentage side effects weren't likely to be an issue, even though doctors were required to state them.

"What do you think, Chris?" I asked.

"Whatever you need, babe," he said, hoping against hope that our baby wouldn't be damaged.

They wheeled me into another room and placed a mask over my face.

"Breathe," someone said.

I did, and instantly I felt a little less . . . everything. The pain retreated far enough across the room that I no longer felt like my pelvis was going to rip into a million pieces . . . only three or four hundred.

"Push!" the nurses told me. "Push."

I did. In my memory, I pushed three or four times, Bubba popped out, and we all lived happily ever after again.

What really happened, apparently, was a little different. I spent forty-five minutes pushing. I would push, then pass out. They'd wake me and I would push again. Again and again.

Allegedly, I soon reached a breaking point. "Pull him the @#$#$ out!" I am supposed to have said.

Now you know that has to be apocryphal, because I do not use unladylike language like that. But the First Amendment does entitle people to render their own memories, I suppose.

Whatever I said, the obstetrician decided to use a device that helps the baby come out. In layman's terms, they put a big suction cup on its head and pull.

Also in layman's terms, the device can cause a temporary side effect—the baby's head gets a little misshapen.

They duly explained this to Chris, who nonetheless approved of the procedure.

Oh my God, he was thinking. I'm going to have a disabled cone-headed laughing-gas-addicted baby.

I'm sure if that had been the case, Chris would have loved him just as dearly. But in truth Bubba was born in perfect health. He was a big kid—eight pounds, six ounces. And no ill effects from the laughing gas.

His head was a little compressed, but it wasn't a cone head and it did get better.

They laid him on my chest.

This is what it's all about, I thought. This is so perfect.

I memorized everything I could about my little boy, to make sure that I knew who he was—no one was going to accidentally switch my kid on me. In fact, I demanded that they keep him in my room with me throughout the entire stay.

Our families came in and took turns holding him. He was an instant celebrity. A little later, the nurse came in with a diaper. Chris took Bubba and laid him on the table nearby.

"What are you doing?" I asked.

"Changing his diaper."

"Really? How do you know how to do that?"

"I just do."

He did. It was Chris—taking care of things without a fuss, even if it meant dealing with poop.

MOTHERHOOD

The first thing Bubba's feet touched when we took him home from the hospital was Texas soil, which his folks had brought west at our request. No child of Chris Kyle's was going to be anything *but* a Texan. He smiled contentedly before nodding off back to sleep; clearly Texas was in his genes.

When I look back, the first months at home with Bubba were as close to bliss as I ever experienced. The first week, though— that was a little rough. I was afraid I wasn't getting him enough milk and was sure he was going to starve. I slept downstairs in a recliner with Bubba on my bare chest so he wouldn't suffocate from any stray clothing and so Chris wouldn't be bothered by the crying when he would wake up to feed. I watched every season of *Alias* on DVD as I fed my son.

(*Alias*—there's a connection there. We'll catch up on that one later.)

Bubba and I bonded despite the fact that I gave up breast-feeding after only a few weeks. He had a voracious appetite, and my breasts and nipples were so tender I couldn't keep up. He'd latch on like— well, no metaphor here is going to do it justice, let alone be proper. Let's just say my son had *no* issues when it came to feeding.

I remember telling the breast-feeding consultant that I wanted to alternate with formula. She gave me a look that said, *Wimp!*

It worked for us. I breast-fed, pumped, and supplemented with formula. A few weeks later I stopped breast-feeding all together. There was a certain amount of guilt—it's hard to escape it when you're a new mom, since you so desperately want to do the best for your baby. But the logical side of my brain argued that Chris had been raised on formula, and he turned out just fine; practicality and comfort won out.

Bubba was such a happy baby that it was impossible not to be energized just watching him. I'd put him on the changing table and he'd start punching the air with his little arms. Then his legs would get going. He was a ball of adrenaline. He'd laugh and I'd laugh, and together we'd face the day.

I had him in my arms pretty much from morning until night. My arms would ache, but I'd never put him down. Slowly starting to get back into a work routine from home, I'd sit at the computer, typing with my right hand while holding him with my left, stopping only to switch him from one side to the other. He was so easy and so happy, it would have been impossible not to love him, or not love being a mom.

I remember saying to a friend, "I don't see why people say being a parent is so hard."

Ha!

I certainly had a lot to learn.

I was determined to do my best. My pediatrician recalls that not only did I ask her more questions than any other patient she has ever had, but I documented every development carefully—not just growth spurts but every bodily function possible. I was amazed that she wasn't interested in my son's poop schedule. And on the rare occasions I had someone else mind him, the sitter would receive a list the size of a telephone book on what to expect, not to expect, possibly expect, and never expect. I had all the bases covered.

At that point, being a mom was the bomb. My son looked so much like his dad, and I was so in love with both of them, that I just didn't think life could be any better.

Well, it certainly could have been better—Chris was away at war. He'd gone back to Iraq within a few days of Bubba's birth.

This was the first deployment Chris spent as a SEAL sniper. As such, it was the beginning of his "legend." In November 2004, while Bubba and I were negotiating nutrition and breast-feeding, Chris was heading to Fallujah to help Marines retake the city.

Fallujah at the time was a stronghold for mujahedeen and other Sunni terrorists and insurgent groups who wanted to topple the Iraqi government and get rid of the Americans. Things had changed dramatically for the worse in Iraq in the year and a half since Chris first deployed there.

People forget that in 2003, most Iraqis actually welcomed the Americans—they hated Saddam. There were terrorists, as well as an underground resistance composed of his loyalists, but they were a distinct minority and relatively disorganized. Even troops coming into a place like Mosul—a stronghold of Saddam's former political party and tribe—were welcomed with cheers from the majority of the populace.

Now the population was disillusioned. Most didn't hate Americans, but they weren't willing to show any sort of enthusiasm for fear of being killed. At the same time, the new Iraq government hadn't delivered on its promises. Corruption was rampant throughout the government, though incompetence was even worse.

Saddam's former backers had joined forces with al-Qaeda-backed terrorists and others dedicated to killing Americans. In the east and around Baghdad, Shia militias—mostly supported by Iran—were also pressing to get rid of Americans and force the new government to do their bidding. The civilian population was caught in the middle. Americans like Chris were tasked to protect them by hunting down the worst of the terrorists, but it was an immense task.

Fallujah had become a terrorist stronghold. It was most notorious as the place where American contract workers were hung from a bridge in March 2004. There were many other atrocities, mostly against fellow Iraqis. By the time the Marines began an assault to retake the city that November, it was an armed camp of terrorists and their families; the neutral civilians had fled.

Chris and other snipers provided what was known as overwatch, striking the enemy from a distance as they came to attack the Americans or Iraqis. The snipers would take up a position and then scan the distance in front of the Marines as the American troops advanced street by street. Spotting terrorists running to attack, weapons in hand, they would shoot them down.

Chris excelled at the job. He was a very good shot, very calm, and keenly observant: "good on the gun," the SEALs called it. Word of his prowess spread through the troops on the ground; he quickly earned a reputation, which would eventually earn him the nickname "Legend." Originally coined as a joke by fellow SEALs, the name stuck among the men Chris was protecting, and even the SEALs quickly came to use it with reverence.

While Chris obviously had great skills, he took pains to tell others that he wasn't the best sniper in the Teams, let alone the U.S. military. Instead, he said his high kill count came mostly from the situations he was in. There were simply a lot of enemy combatants coming at him. It was, as the military would term it, a "target-rich environment."

To put that another way, a heck of a lot of people wanted to kill him and the other Americans in Fallujah.

As Chris details in *American Sniper,* the terrorists eventually caught on to the overwatch strategy and stopped coming out on the street. At that point, Chris decided to go down to be with the Marines. Even though it wasn't his job—and he probably would have gotten in trouble at the time had his superiors known—he thought it was the best way to protect them.

That was also pure Chris. Part of the reason was that he wanted to be where the action was. And another part was that he was a natural-born protector. Just as he'd stood up for kids in the high school cafeteria, he was sticking up for Marines and Iraqis now— though with higher stakes. He felt he could do more to protect them if he was going into the houses with them.

I didn't know that much about what was going on in Fallujah or the rest of Iraq. While I had a general fear that Chris might be hurt or worse, that fear was largely theoretical. I tried to focus on the blessings and not allow fear to take over, even though it was constantly bubbling under the surface. Being a new mother helped. I had plenty of other things to think about.

In fact, I didn't know how much Chris had done in Fallujah until he came home. We were at a car wash place one day when someone overheard his name called and went up to him.

"Are you Chris Kyle?" asked the man. His haircut and build made it clear he was military.

"Yes."

"I was in Fallujah," said the young man, who turned out to be a Marine. "You saved my life."

"Ya'll saved my ass plenty of times, too," said Chris, referring to Marines.

Others came over, including the father of one of the Marines. He had tears in his eyes when he shook Chris's hand.

"Your husband saved my son's life," he said to me. "Thank you."

What an incredibly small world it is, I thought. For all of these people to have been together so far away, and now just meet by chance in the oddest place.

Or was it part of a cosmic plan? A way of showing Chris that he was appreciated?

I felt proud of him, but I also felt sadness—I imagined being the parent of one of these young men, worried about their welfare and yet unable to do anything to protect them. It was an impotence with few parallels.

Chris just took it all in stride, smiling and waving as he left to get the car.

AN EMAIL MARRIAGE

Being a mother and wife was only part of who I was. I was a sales manager for a pharmaceutical company as well. Eventually, maternity leave would end, and I'd have to go back to work. As the date approached, I began to rethink those plans. I wanted to stay home with my son.

"It's up to you," said Chris. We'd been able to put money away while I was working, and while we would have to cut back on many things, we calculated that we could get by on just Chris's salary, thanks to his recent promotions and specialty pay. Granted, it would take careful budgeting, but it was doable.

After a lot of thought, I decided I couldn't leave Bubba. I called my boss. She was a lot more understanding than I'd hoped.

"We're trying to be more family friendly," she said. "You can be a prototype for a part-time salesperson. We'll prorate your salary. You'll work part-time while your kids are young, then go back to full-time."

It sounded like a great compromise. I agreed to try. In fact, I was excited to give it a shot.

I hired a really good friend to watch Bubba on the days when I had to work.

Chris was able to email and call more regularly as his deployment went on. We talked about family things; the war rarely intruded.

I happen to have some of his emails from later in that deployment, so you can see for yourself:

February 17, 2005 7:12 a.m.

Hey baby, I just wanted to let you know that I am okay, and safe. I've been working a lot lately. Right now we happen to be on a base with internet so I wanted to give you a note. I am so sorry I wasn't able to call, at least for Valentine's Day. I love you so very much, and miss the hell out of you. I think I might be able to call later tonight for me, this afternoon for you. I hope all is going well with you, and you're not too worried. I've been thinking about you non-stop. I want to ask how you and Bubba are doing but I probably won't be able to check my email again for a while. Just take care of yourself, and know that I am thinking of you always, and sending my love. You mean the world to me. I love you, sexy woman, with my heart and soul!

—XOXOXOXOXOXXXXXXXOXOXOXXOX

February 22, 2005

I am so happy that you feel so comfortable with the fact that H— is watching Bubba. I do love to hear all the things that go on with him, even if it's just his shit. I really miss you. It's been even worse because of the fact that I haven't been able to talk to you. I've been working a lot. Now I am back with the platoon for a little bit out west. We will probably stay out here now. The phone situation is gonna suck. The only phones are pay phones, and they are always full. The only other option is the sat phone, but I have to be with the platoon to use it. I should be able to call you tonight. I miss you so much, and can't wait for you to wrap your arms, legs, and lips around me. I think I will probably do the same in return. Maybe. Just kidding. You will be begging for some time away from me. I will smother you with all my attention. I can't wait to see you. I love you so much. I really am madly, head over heels, in love with you. I don't know what I would do without you.

Right now the rumor on leaving is the latest the 22nd, but I am still supposed to leave on the first. Hopefully. I want to get home to see my baby and my son. I miss both of y'a'll something awful. Time is going a little faster now because of working again. I had a long enough break and it's about time I got back out. I'm still making a name for myself by adding to my numbers. I know I never say it, but it does feel good to have all the people talking about me in a good way. Anyway, I love you and miss you. You mean the world to me. Please take care of yourself and I will call you soon. Smoooooooooch!!!!! I can't wait to give you a

real one. Carefully go over every inch of your body. I am soooo horny! I
love you, baby!

—XOXOXOXOXXXXX

Chris was hoping to come home that March; in fact, he wouldn't
leave until well into April.

By now he'd gained quite a bit of fame within the military community. He was mentioned as a possible recipient of the Grateful
Nation Award given by the Jewish Institute for National Security
Affairs (JINSA) in recognition of his efforts in the War on Terror.
He didn't get the award that year—he would later on—but he didn't
seem overly disappointed. That was the way he was about all his
commendations: he really didn't care whether he was recognized
by the "head shed" (or higher-ups). He didn't fight for medals; he
fought for his brothers-in-arms.

March 26, 2005

Hey baby. What's up? Same ol' shit here. I found out I didn't get
that Jewish award. They gave it to an officer. They thought that would
look better. Oh well, they needed to spread it out like I told you. You'll
be happy to hear our missions are slowing down. Probably because
it's getting close to going home, and the CO doesn't want any more
casualties. So we are bored. I miss you so bad, gorgeous. When we fly
in we get the first three days off to stay at home free of charge, and
then come in to download the pallets. Once that's done, we can take
leave for a month. Yeahhhhhhhhh! I need to go, just wanted to give you
a hi and I love you (the mostest)!

March 28, 2005

I am so ready to be home I have already gone into autopilot mode.
Just counting the days, waiting for that big bird to take me home. I am
sorry to hear that you are not feeling good. Hopefully getting off the pill
will help. Hopefully when I get home I can help with your emotions.
Whatever you need, just tell me. I want to make things easy for you
when I am home. At least as easy as possible. I love you so much

gorgeous. Glad to hear your dad has busted his ass to help us out so much. We are so lucky with our family, I couldn't have married into a better one. Not to mention couldn't have married a better woman, cause there is none better. I also got an email from your niece. It was a PowerPoint slide that was real cute. It had a green background with a frog, and said she missed me. Sweet, huh. If she didn't forward a copy to you, I can. Oh, about the birth control: You said you wanted ten kids anyway. Change your mind yet? What is Bubba doing that has changed? Is he being a fart or is he just full of energy? I'm sure when I get home you will be ready for a break. How about after I get to see you for a little while, you go to a spa for a weekend to be pampered? I REALLY think you deserve it. You've been going and going, kinda like the Energizer Bunny. Just like when I get home for sex, we keep going and going and going and going and, you get the point. Hopefully you at least smiled over that. I always want you to be happy, and want to do whatever it takes to make it happen. Even if it means buying a Holstein cow. Yuk! That's big time love. Wow. I hope you have a good day, and can find time in the day to rest. I love you more than you will ever know.

Smooooooch!

—XOXOOXOXOXOXOXOX

Even part-time, work ate at my nerves. Frustrated, needing and wanting him home both for selfish and unselfish reasons, I occasionally unloaded on Chris. Communicating by email and sometimes phone was no substitute for having him there.

Yet he tried. One of my cousins was having trouble with her new horse. My cowboy husband counseled her on how to treat it. Mostly, it was a matter of patience and wearing the horse down. "It will take time no matter what you do," he told her. "Some of our horses wouldn't let us touch their feet until we actually rode them. When you ride them you can get them really tired and trusting you."

Some of that advice applies to people, too.

April 13, 2005

It was so nice to be able to talk to you tonight. I miss you something terrible. I can't wait to be with you again, especially the truck ride home while I am teasing the hell out of you. Yea! I love you so much baby. About the computer, how much is too much for a new computer? I got an email through eBay that a guy is willing to sell me that computer I wanted because the winning bidder didn't pay up, but he wants 2500 for it. I know when I get something in my head that I want, I usually don't care too much about the price, so I want a sanity check. The computer is an Alienware computer with 2 gigs of ram and 120 gigs of hard drive. It's top of the line, but is it too much? I know you can bring me back to earth if I am over-anxious. Anyway, I love you so much, baby. I will call you again tomorrow night for me, day for you. Take care of yourself and think about the ride home!!!!!!!!!!!!!!

Chris did end up buying that computer, which was a fairly hot gaming rig at the time. He played mostly sports games on the PC and consoles, and while he tried the original Call of Duty series, it was never among his favorites.

After roughly four months of work, I couldn't stand leaving Bubba anymore. It was an effort to get into the car. I felt as if I was abandoning my son, especially since his dad was still away. Finally, after a few months, I just had to give up and became a full-time mom.

It's not the right thing for every woman, and certainly I was lucky to have the option. But it was also one of the best decisions I've ever made.

It was around this time that a routine medical screening warned that Chris might have tuberculosis.

We talked about it on the phone. I remember the discussion vividly, not because of the disease—I thought further testing would say he was fine, which it did—but because of his attitude.

Namely, that he was replaceable.

"If I die, you could just get a new husband and Bubba can get a new dad," he told me.

It made me furious. Heartbroken. It was as if he didn't understand how irreplaceable he was to me, to our son, and to the rest of the family.

It was as if he didn't know how much I loved him.

I realized later that, in his mind, he was only being realistic. He wanted what was best for me. He had seen death up close and watched the mission go on, lives go on, whether people wanted it to or not. If he couldn't be there, he still wanted me to be happy.

Even so, it was a devastating statement at the time. In some ways, I never got over it.

A GIRL!

Having children changes things in a marriage. There are good changes and bad changes. One of the worst is that it tends to shorten tempers. That made things a little testy around our house after Chris came home.

I saw it as the natural state of things—and only temporary. Chris was surprised, I think, that things weren't as smooth between us as they had been.

"Oh, we'll get through it," I'd tell him.

"I don't know."

"Other people go through this all the time, especially with a new baby. Didn't your parents ever argue?"

Actually, they don't seem to have argued at all, at least not in front of the kids. Maybe there's a lesson for us in that—it's okay to argue in front of our children; it prepares them for later in life.

And those of you with idyllic marriages where you never fight at all—fake it a few times for the rest of us, okay?

Just joking.

Chris's enlistment was nearing its completion, and we began talking about whether he would stay in the Navy or not. Having lived through two deployments already, I was more than ready for him to come out.

I thought he was, too. In his letters home he said he couldn't wait to be home and spend more time with us; he said he hated being away. We had started our family, and both of us wanted a more stable life with him home and involved with the kids.

This was all true, but it turned out that I wanted that more than he did. He loved being a SEAL more than he loved being home, or at least he loved them equally and thought he could continue doing both. I didn't.

It took only a few conversations before I realized that he was leaning heavily toward reenlisting. If he did, he knew he would redeploy back to Iraq within a year. To look at it from his point of view, he thought he still had work to do there. And truthfully, few people could protect as many people as Chris could; even though I told him he had already done his bit, he felt it was his duty to continue fighting for his country.

"If you tell me not to reenlist, I won't," Chris told me.

"I don't want that on my shoulders," I answered. "Telling you not to live your dream. You love your job. But I also want to be honest. If you do reenlist, it will change the way I think about things. It will be different. I don't want it to be, but I know deep in my gut it will be. You keep saying romantic things, things about wanting to stay and build your home here. If you go and reenlist, then I don't know that I'll think they're true."

In retrospect, I think those romantic dreams were true for Chris. It's just that he thought he could have his career in the Navy and his family life. Many people do. And I think he realized that while I might discount what he said about wanting to be home, I wouldn't give up loving him.

I prayed that God would help him make the best long-term decision for our family. I was disappointed when that answer turned out to be reenlisting.

No, I didn't stop loving him. Things did change between us, but it was more than just his enlistment: soon after he re-upped, we discovered we were expecting again.

We got pregnant with Angel almost by accident. I was thinking it was just about time to go on birth control and wham—it happened. We wanted two children, but were thinking of spacing them out a little more. God and Angel had other plans.

I'm so glad. Bubba and Angel are so close in age and such good friends that I can't imagine it any other way. But at the time, I was more than a little apprehensive about it. Once again, it worked out that Chris was preparing to leave just when I was due.

They say God only gives you what you can handle. Chris didn't cope with crying babies very well. So either he paid the military to deploy him with each baby, or God was looking out for him with well-timed, newborn-avoiding deployments.

This time, the Team guy karma worked: the sonogram technician confirmed it was a girl several months into the pregnancy. She was going to be the first female born into the Kyle side of the family in eighty years. Which made her unique, and her grandparents particularly tickled.

Chris couldn't resist the opportunity to tease them with the news.

"We're having a boy," he said when he called them back in Texas with the news.

"Oh, how nice," they said.

"No, we're having a girl."

"Whoo-hoo!" they shouted.

"No, we're having a boy."

"Chris! Which is it!?"

"A girl!"

If they could have gotten away to visit us that night, I doubt they would have needed an airplane to fly.

One of the things I loved about Chris was his sense of humor, which seemed perfectly matched with mine, even at its most offbeat. April Fools' Day was always a major highlight. A month before our daughter was due, I woke him up in the middle of the night.

"Don't panic," I told him, "but I think I'm going into labor."

"Do we have a bag?" he asked, jumping up immediately.

"No, no, don't worry." I slipped out of bed and went to take a shower.

Chris immediately got dressed and, calmly but very quickly, gathered my clothes and packed a suitcase.

"I'm ready!" he announced, barging into the bathroom.

"Babe, do you know what day it is?" I asked sweetly. It was two A.M., April 1.

"Are you kidding me?" he said, disbelieving.

I laughed and plunged back into the shower.

He quickly got revenge by flushing the toilet, sending a burst of cold water across my body.

In retrospect, maybe I'd been a little cruel, but we did love teasing each other. At our wedding, we'd smooshed cake into each other's faces. That began a tradition that continued at each birthday—whether it was ours or not. The routine never seemed to get old. We'd giggle and laugh, chasing each other as if we were crazy people. Our friends and neighbors got used to it—and learned to stay out of the line of fire.

I had a routine appointment with the obstetrician roughly a month before Angel was due. Ordinarily Chris went with me to the appointments, and this one was no different; we planned to meet at the office. But when I got to the building, he wasn't there.

One thing you have to know about Chris: if you set a watch by him, it would have been ten minutes early. He was *never* late for anything he considered important. And he considered his babies very important.

So when I was called in and he still wasn't there, I was concerned. I knew something must be up.

There was nothing to worry about, I told myself. He was still in the States, far from danger. Something must have come up and he couldn't use his phone for some reason.

Your loved ones don't have to be in a war zone for you to worry about them. In fact, there are all sorts of statistics on how dangerous life can be outside of a war zone. It's just that ordinarily we don't think about that. We don't focus on our anxieties.

I put all those possibilities out of my mind as I went into the exam room. I was relaxed. I'd been through one birth, and I knew what to expect. Even better, my platelets were under control this time.

Except . . .

They hooked me up to the ultrasound machine. The operator's brows knitted. Before I could ask what was up, she'd gone to get the doctor.

The ultrasound showed that Angel was in a breech position. It meant that she was backward in the womb; rather than her head, her feet were positioned to come out first at birth.

That is much more difficult for the baby than a "normal" birth, but it's hardly an emergency. More critically, the image showed Angel's amniotic fluid was low and the umbilical cord was wrapped around her neck.

The technical term for the latter is *nuchal cord,* and in a small number of cases, it can lead to a constriction of the umbilical vessels and hypoxia. (*Hypoxia* is a fancy term for "not enough oxygen," and in the case of a developing baby, this lack can cause developmental problems or even, potentially, death.) The bad stuff happens only in a very small number of cases; in fact, many times the baby untangles itself before birth and there isn't even a hint of a problem. Low amniotic fluid, or *oligohydramnios,* can cause developmental problems for the baby. The exact danger depends on a number of factors.

In my case, the doctors were confident that neither situation would be critical, as long as I gave birth soon. After laying out the specifics, they recommended I have a C-section as soon as feasible—no later than the next morning.

I have to confess that having the cord wrapped around my baby's neck was always one of my worst fears. It's the one thing you really can't feel or sense as a mother; you know the kicks and the movements intimately, but the cord's placement is as much a mystery to you as it is to everyone else.

So okay. C-section in the morning? Why not?

Chris still hadn't shown up when I left the examining room. Nor had he answered my call asking him what was up.

I got in my car to drive to the hospital, then did what a lot of women do in that situation: I called my mom.

"Hey, honey, are you okay?" she asked.

"Yes." I burst into tears. Until that moment, I hadn't realized how close to panicking I really was.

"What's wrong?" she asked.

"I . . . don't know where Chris is. I have to go to the hospital to have the baby—"

"It'll be OK," she said quickly. "I'm going to the airport. I'll be there."

I didn't even get to explain the full situation.

Then Chris called. "Where are you?" I asked. I was somewhere between relieved and angry—or maybe I was both angry *and* relieved.

"I just had some stuff happen," he said. "I'm okay. I'll tell you when I see you."

"I need you now," I said, telling him about the baby.

If you've read *American Sniper,* you know what had happened to him: he passed out during what should have been a very routine procedure to remove a cyst in his neck. It was a freak thing that led to what we think was a temporary seizure.

Some "thing." But being a SEAL and being Chris, he completely minimized it. In fact, I didn't know what had happened until later. All I knew was that he met me at the hospital and was by my side when I needed him.

There is a bit of a funny story attached to the incident. A friend of Chris's happened to be with him when he passed out.

"Stand back," his friend told the corpsman.

"What? Why?" the corpsman asked.

"Because when he comes to, he's going to come up swinging."

"No."

The corpsman leaned down. Just then, Chris came to and, as his friend had warned, started swinging. Fortunately, the corpsman jerked out of the way just in time.

Chris said in his book that the incident was nothing. From his point of view, he was right: there were no ill effects, and he never had a seizure again. He was cleared for the deployment, which was scheduled to begin in a few days.

But from my perspective, he shouldn't have deployed at all. He should have let the doctors fully investigate the situation. Someone should have figured out why exactly he passed out—even if it was just that he didn't like the sight of spooky long needles.

But you can't tell a SEAL that. SEALs may not think they're indestructible—most if not all are too smart for that—but they are all absolutely 100 percent convinced that they will let their brothers down if they are not in the fight, no matter what. And something like this was, not only to Chris but I'm sure to any SEAL, truly insignificant.

But anyway . . .

ANGEL IS BORN

I hated getting the C-section. The idea of it was bad enough—getting cut open rather than giving birth naturally, as painful as that had been. But even getting ready was difficult. They strapped my arms out like I was being crucified. They gave me a shot for pain, but apparently an air bubble interfered with the injection, because I felt tremendous pain in my neck right after the needle went in.

Then I got pretty numb. Chris held my hand, watching calmly. "It's all good, babe," he said calmly.

That was as much as he said—wisely. It wasn't a good time for talking, even if I was under sedation.

They put a big blue sheet over me, blocking off my view of what was happening. Nurses and doctors and lord knows who else were gathering at my feet, getting ready to go in and get my baby out. Meanwhile, the talk in the room was incredibly banal:

So, what are you doing this weekend?

Going on a hike. What about you?

All of a sudden, the chitchat stopped. The conversation became sharp and terse, precise and very medical.

Scalpel.

Scalpel.

Sponge.

Sponge.

You can fill in the rest from your favorite medical drama. I was cruising along—figuratively, not literally—grooving on the medication, assured by Chris's rock-steady calm, until a splash of blood went *pooof* on the blue sheet in front of me.

Hmmmmph.

I looked at Chris. He squeezed my hand gently, smiling at the same time. We could have been strolling in the park on a summer's day, not a care in the world.

The doctors had hit an artery, which is not standard procedure.

They worked quickly to deal with it—to this day I have no idea what actually happened, but whatever they did worked, because our beautiful Angel was born soon after.

Chris was the first person to hold her. The word *beaming* was invented to describe the proud expression on his face.

I went into the recovery room and slept for a while. When I woke up, Chris was holding Angel. He looked so natural with her—a big six-footer holding a six-pound bundle in the crook of his arm, already bonded to her.

"Do you want to hold her?" he asked.

I was exhausted, and I knew she was safe with him, so I told him no.

He forced himself to smile. He explained later that he thought my response meant I was rejecting the baby—having worked on a ranch, I guess he had seen animals do that, with dire results for their new offspring. But of course I wasn't; they just looked perfect together, and I was barely conscious.

I asked for her a few minutes later, when I felt stronger. He passed her on gently, and I held her for the first time. There is no way really to describe how that feels.

In many ways, the birth was a miracle, not a disaster. Because of Angel's dilemma, her father was able to be there at her birth—something that wouldn't have happened had that ultrasound been routine, since I would have waited another four or five weeks for her. A potential tragedy had been turned into something beautiful. It was quite a miracle, I thought, that he had been present for both births, despite the long odds against it.

Sometimes God's plan for us is difficult to decipher, but the end result can be far more wonderful than we thought.

I knew that. I felt that.

And yet, I had a terrible feeling, lying in the bed that night, one I couldn't shake and one I didn't dare put into words:

Maybe God gave Chris this chance to be with his daughter because he's going to die in Iraq.

Angel was born with jaundice, a not uncommon condition for babies born prematurely. She was also on the small side because of having been born so early. In the grand scheme of things, neither was very important. But they did add to my concern. And I was really scared about Chris going on that deployment, partly because of his having passed out before he left, and partly because of reports about the uptick in violence in Iraq at the time.

Adding to my angst was a difficult recovery from the C-section. I'd heard women say they were up mopping the floor within a day of the operation. I couldn't mop the sweat off my brow. Maybe it's a mind-over-matter thing, but if so, matter won.

I hurt!

And I hurt for a long time—eight weeks at least.

Add an active toddler to the mix and anyone would be a little stressed. The postpartum hormonal changes hit me hard. I was probably a little depressed, though not to the debilitating degree that sometimes hits new mothers. I would breast-feed with one hand while running to grab Bubba with the other. I was exhausted, worried, and ultimately angry with Chris for leaving me alone.

I certainly didn't want to worry Chris by sharing my feelings. Yet I found it impossible not to, largely because he knew me so well.

One night he called while the kids were sleeping. I was sitting on the bed, exhausted but unable to sleep myself. He must have heard something in my voice. "What's wrong?" he asked.

"I don't want to tell you this, but I'm angry with you," I burst out, starting to cry. "I don't want to be angry with you. We didn't know we were going to have another baby when you reenlisted—but we did, and it's hard. I miss you."

My emotions flooded out. Everything was contradictory. I wanted to support Chris—I wanted to be okay with his being gone, and yet I wanted him there with me.

I was angry with myself, too. I had had such a perfect time with Bubba, and now I was having great difficulty. Some of it had to be my fault, I thought. I wasn't happy—but I *should* be happy. I was a new mom again. I should feel overwhelming love and joy at having another child. A girl.

I couldn't be the kind of mom I wanted to be, and that made me feel even worse.

I don't remember how the conversation with Chris ended. Possibly Angel woke up, and I had to go comfort her. She would always cry in the middle of the night and wake me up.

Some nights I thought, Stop crying! Just stop!

A wave of guilt would come over me.

She's an infant, of course she's crying! What's wrong with you? How are you mad at this little baby?

It was a vicious cycle. I hated myself for not loving her perfectly, then grew angry that she had needs, then loved her immensely for who she was—all at the same time.

It was a brutal few months. Eventually, things started to settle and I felt better. I was fortunate not to need medication or serious intervention.

Not having Chris around made everything several times worse. We hadn't known I was pregnant when he reenlisted, but here we were. I was really sad, and I didn't want to be a bitch, but I was at times. It wasn't until I started getting myself back into shape that I began feeling better. Or maybe it was the other way around. I got a double stroller and I started wheeling both kids out. It was still tough, but the physical exercise helped.

RAMADI

Many people not familiar with current military tactics criticized Chris and all snipers for somehow fighting unfairly in Iraq, as if they were hiding far from danger when they went into combat.

I wish those critics could have spent five minutes in the hell that was Ramadi to see how wrong they were. Far from being "safe," snipers and the others with them were constantly targeted by large groups of terrorists and insurgents, who used every weapon they had to try and kill them.

Chris went to Ramadi in 2006, during his third deployment to Iraq. Like Fallujah, Ramadi was in Anbar Province, an area rife with al-Qaeda and former Saddam loyalists. Sunni extremists had taken hold of the city and the SEALs were part of a push to pacify it long enough for the local Iraqi tribes to retake control. In the media, the efforts were hailed as "the Great Awakening," supposedly because the Iraqis had finally decided on their own that they wanted peace and were going to kick the bad guys out.

The reality was a lot messier. The Americans had been criticized for operations in Fallujah and elsewhere that did a lot of damage to the buildings and local infrastructure. And unlike in Fallujah, there were still many civilians in Ramadi, as well as tribal leaders whom the Americans felt could be won over. For all of these reasons and more, the strategy in Ramadi was very different than Fallujah. Rather than moving through the city block by block, securing each area before moving on, the SEALs and others established small outposts in the worst parts, providing overwatch for operations on the streets nearby and helping arrest known terrorists. As soon as their positions were known, they became the targets. Insurgents, often using civilians as cover, would concentrate their attacks on the areas where snipers were posted. A group of three or six Americans would be attacked by dozens of enemy combatants.

By now, Chris had a reputation as one of the best snipers in the military—he got his hundredth kill soon after he arrived. And things continued to intensify. It was during this deployment that posters began to appear naming him as the "Devil of Ramadi" and offering a reward to anyone who could kill him. Those rewards eventually reached sixty thousand dollars.

But his emails back home barely hinted at the carnage.

April 22, 2006

Hey baby, sorry I wasn't able to call you, but our phone line is down. I will try to call you one more time before I leave. I'm sure you haven't even checked your email yet, so by the time you do I will be gone. I love you very much. You are an extremely strong woman. I don't know anyone else who could put up with all you do, and still hang in there. Tell Bubba and Angel I love them. I will call or write as often as I can. I love you so very much.

May 5, 2006

Hey baby, I'm back for the day and then I leave again tonight. Things are going well, just extremely busy. It's gotten to where people call up, they don't ask for SEAL snipers anymore; they are asking for me by name. The bad thing is there are too many for me to do, so I have to pass a few on to some of the other guys. My platoon is very supportive of me (probably because I always take a few of them), but my sister platoon has a lot of resentment towards me. It's pretty funny. They are just a bunch of whiny bitches anyway.

How are you doing? Are you healing up, and able to get around? I hope you can do all the things you used to real soon. I know that has to be a real bummer to be limited physically. I also hope you are being able to keep yourself a little bit happier. If you need to resent me to be able to make it through, I understand. I know you love me, and support me in whatever I do. I don't have to hear it all the time, or call home to hear just good things. If you need to unload on me when I call, then do it. Whatever it takes to make you feel better.

Is Bubba feeling any better? I hope his cold has gone away or goes away real soon. Maybe he will also be a little happier, and not so emotional. I miss that little guy so much. I carry around a picture of the three of us. The picture is of you and me in Oregon, one of Bubba is the one he pulled out from the computer cabinet with me and him sitting on the couch, and I have a picture of Angel and you in your bed at the hospital. I have such a beautiful family. I could not have asked for more. I am extremely happy.

Sorry babe, but I have to go now. I thought I had the day off until tonight, but I guess there is a mooj [enemy = mujahedeen] sniper I have to try to get before I leave tonight. I will try to call you before I leave tonight. I love you so very much, baby, and miss the hell out of you. You truly are a dream come true. I love you, Taya!

June 6, 2006
Hey sexy

Hey baby, it was very nice to talk to you last night. I am gonna try to call you again tonight. I can tell you a little more than I can on email. We did a big hostage rescue the other night, and did it very well. I can't tell you who or any other specifics, but it was a big deal. Everything is really going well out here. I am staying safe and not taking any stupid chances. I have too much to come home to. I miss y'a'll so bad. I would love to be able to hold you, and kiss you right now. I am not going anywhere tonight. I was, but it got canceled. I will be gone later though. On one of my ops, a guy asked me to carry an American flag in my gear and bring it back to him. He wanted to give it to his dad, and say it was carried on an op in Iraq. This guy is a reservist, and doesn't go on any of the ops. I told him I would. When I got back I gave it to him and told him what had happened on the op, and how many people I killed. Later he came up to me to show me a certificate. It was very well done, and looked sharp. He said with the way I am going he is gonna save the flag to give to the SEAL and UDT museum. He is on the board of directors. He thinks I am gonna be in the SEAL hall of fame. All the other guys keep saying someone is gonna write a book about me, whether I allow it or not. All the army guys have already been spreading the stories all over base. I go to the chow hall and overhear people talking about me not knowing who I am or even that I am sitting there. It's funny. When I reenlisted they held the flag I carried up behind me for the pictures. I think it maybe is getting a little out of hand with the "legend" status. But in a way it's also kinda nice. Anyway, I hope you are having a good day. It is always nice to hear Bubba's voice when I call home. He is such a little grown-up already. I can't wait to be with y'a'll again. We will finally have some time to be a real family. Can you imagine what that would be like? Wow.

Well, tell everyone hi, tell the kids I love them, and give them a hug and kiss from me. I love you so very much. I miss you even more. Take good care of yourself. I love you, sexy!

June 23, 2006

Sorry, I didn't get a chance to write you after we got off the phone last time. It was a short turnaround. I should be able to call you tonight. I just wanted to let you know how important you are to me. I love you so much. You really do mean the world to me. I appreciate you taking a back seat so I can do what I want. You are extremely selfless. Soon I will be able to make it up to you. You have always been there for me, and supportive no matter what. Even when you hate what I am doing. I do realize this, and could never tell you enough how much I thank you for it. Hopefully someday I can do the same for you. i owe you the world.

I hope you are having a safe and quick trip back from Texas. I know mom and dad loved having y'a'll out there. I'm sure it'll be an emotional goodbye for them. Especially if dad has been feeling a little depressed. I could imagine with Bubba being there it has to take him back in time to simpler times. I will try to call later to give you enough time to get home and situated.

When are you going to Oregon? I hope things go as well there with Bubba. I know wherever he goes, people will spoil him rotten. We are so extremely blessed with the families we have. They are always supportive, and loving of everything. . . .

What are you gonna do about Max [our dog] around the kids? I'm sure he would be fine, but you never know. And the fact that Bubba is probably gonna want to play with him. Whatever. I know y'a'll will have a good time.

Anyway baby, I love you more than I could ever express. You are so kind, gentle, loving, and just knockout gorgeous!!! Did I mention sexy? I can't wait to wrap my arms around you. I love you so much, and miss you. Take care of yourself, and give the kids a hug and kiss from me. I love you, sexy.

July 14, 2006

Hey gorgeous, it was so good to be able to talk to you tonight. It really made my day to talk to you and Bubba. He is able to communicate very well. I could understand most of what he was saying. Maybe it's because we're both childlike. Sorry to hurt your feelings with my joke, but that's all it was. I promise. I call you every chance I get. I love being able to talk to you and find out about your day or days.

Things here are about the same. We are constantly working. Most of the time I don't even know what day it is. Which sometimes is good. I'll look at the day and think, wow, the time has flown by. Other times it's like, what, it's only been two hours? The average day is about 115-120 [degrees]. The dust storms are kicking up more. But when the dust storms aren't blowing, sometimes there's a good breeze. I'll sit there in my hide drenched in sweat. I had to make a new hole in my belt. I think it's mostly water weight I'm losing. Sometimes it feels like I'm in a human stew. It's hot enough to boil in your own sweat.

On to more appealing things. I can't wait to get your pictures. You are the sexiest woman ever. I love looking at the pics I already have. I just can't wait to see you in person when I get back. Thank you so much for all the packages and emails you have sent. You are always trying to make me feel loved and comfortable. You have so much to do already, but you still make the time to take care of me. I appreciate it all. You are the best thing that God has ever blessed me with. One day I will make it up to you. I will be there every day and every night. I'll be around so much you may wish I had a trip or deployment to go on. I look forward to those days. I love you and the kids with all my heart. I keep y'all in my thoughts and prayers every day. I love you, sexy!!

Bubba was learning to talk. He could say "flute," "trumpet," and "violins," and knew the difference between each. He was climbing over everything, drawing all the time. Angel, though now more comfortable, was still a fussy infant—maybe, I worried, because I couldn't keep her in my arms all day as I had with Bubba.

At the time, I thought Chris didn't mind missing so much of the kids' early stages. He seemed like the kind of person who didn't get sentimental about first steps or first words, first bites of real food, the baby talk and the silly games. But I realized years later that he actually felt the loss of his kids' early days acutely. We were at the hospital, waiting for my sister-in-law to give birth. Chris's niece had missed her nap and hadn't eaten; inevitably, she got cranky. She ended up throwing a mini-tantrum, which only her grandmother could calm.

Chris turned to me and leaned over, his hand on my knee and a serious look on his face.

"You know, babe," he said, "I wish I'd been here more when our kids were this age."

To say that, in a moment when a child was throwing a fit—I think that's a depth of incredible love. It made me sad, realizing that he had missed those moments, good and bad, that end up being so much a part of our experiences as a parent.

"You were there," I told him. "You were there. We felt you every day, whether we talked to you or just about you, you were always there."

MARC AND RYAN

As the deployment continued, Chris felt more and more confident. He was doing what he loved, and he was doing it well. Just as important, the Americans were succeeding in Ramadi. It wasn't exactly a paradise, but the level of violence declined dramatically while the SEALs and other Americans were there. The aggressive policy was working, or at least so it seemed.

Because of his experience, Chris had more responsibility in the missions. Where once he had acted as a navigator, assisting the driver, now he would help plan and lead during the operation. He was very close to all of the men who worked with him, but especially those who acted as security for him while he was "on the gun," which was the slang term snipers used for working.

Often SEAL snipers would work in pairs during long missions, alternating—while one was manning the rifle, the other might be sleeping. But this was just a general pattern. Many times, both men would be looking for attackers. In some cases only one sniper would be with two or three other men. Typically in Chris's platoon, these men would include a machine gunner. Once the sniper's position became known, he usually became the focus of the enemy attack, and having a gun with extra firepower was welcome.

Among Chris's closest friends in the platoon were Marc Lee and Ryan Job. Both were hardworking SEALs, but they were different from each other in many ways. Marc was an athletic, all-American type, good enough at soccer to be offered a tryout in the professional league. He had a thoughtful, gentle side to him—he was a quiet intellectual, which was not as rare among SEALs as might commonly be believed.

Ryan, on the other hand, was as close to class clown as a SEAL could possibly be. While he wasn't out of shape—no one could get through BUD/S in poor physical condition—he was hardly the most imposing physical specimen, and when he first joined the platoon, all of the other SEALs, including Chris, made fun of him because of his weight.

But Ryan was a SEAL through and through. He pushed himself every bit as hard as the other members of the Team, and was absolutely dependable in a firefight. He also cracked everyone up with jokes constantly. Like Marc but in a different way, he was the kind of guy you just couldn't help but like.

In early August of 2006, the platoon went out on a mission that, though dangerous, by now was almost routine. While men patrolled on the nearby streets, Chris provided overwatch from a rooftop at an intersection. The mission went very smoothly at first; they got on the roof with no trouble. Chris set up and began watching for terrorists attacking his men.

At some point, he and the other two men on the roof came under fire. They ducked quickly. It was a momentary attack, a burst of fire so brief that Chris thought it was nothing. He got up and looked across the roof.

"Hey, Biggles," he said, using Ryan's nickname. "Get up, dude!"

Ryan didn't get up. It took another second or so to realize that it wasn't one of Ryan's classic jokes. Blood was gushing out of his head.

They called for an evacuation. Chris started to carry Ryan down the stairs. Ryan objected—he didn't want to take anyone else out of the fight. He struggled down the steps, but by the time he was packed into a vehicle, Chris was sure he was dead; no one could survive those wounds.

The platoon went back to their base, reeling. Ryan was the first serious casualty they'd had, and one of the first SEALs injured in all of the Iraq deployments.

A short time later, someone came in with intelligence about the mujahedeen who'd targeted the roof. They'd been located in a house a short distance away.

The platoon decided to get some revenge. They suited up, got into their vehicles, and drove to the neighborhood where the house was. Chris assembled a team to do overwatch from a nearby building. They took the house quickly and began running up the stairs.

Marc Lee, one of their best assaulters—those are the men who lead the charge into a building—got about halfway up the stairs when he saw something through an open window. He stopped to warn the others. Before he could say anything, he was shot.

The men immediately began returning fire. As soon as things calmed a little, Chris and another man picked up Marc and began carrying him down the stairs. Once again, the platoon retreated to base.

Chris and the others learned a short time later than Ryan, though severely wounded, would survive; Marc Lee had passed away.

Chris called me shortly after hearing the news. His voice was far different than anything I'd heard before. It was pure pain.

He cried as he spoke. I don't know that I'd ever seen or heard him cry before. Certainly not like that.

I immediately started to cry myself, but I muffled it as best I could. I didn't want him to hear my sobs, because I knew they would add to his distress and despair.

Chris didn't give me many details—he never wanted to worry me—but honestly, how much more did I need to know? One friend was dead, another badly hurt, and he blamed himself, since he'd been in charge in both instances.

Tears rolled down my face as I listened. I said very little until he was done.

Never have I been aware of distance so acutely as when he finished. I wanted to comfort him, to hold him, cradle him, kiss him, cry with him. But that was impossible. The best I could do was simply tell him I loved him.

The words never felt so empty.

He asked if I could call and tell his parents what had happened. He wanted them to know, but was so upset he didn't feel like talking. I told him I would.

When he ended the call, I immediately called Marc's mom, Debbie, telling her I'd heard the awful news and offering to do whatever I could for her. It was hard to get the words out. She was brave, but the pain in her voice was overwhelming.

I called Chris's parents and got his mom.

"Chris is fine," I told her. I took a breath. "But two of his close friends were shot. One is dead and the other may not make it."

The rest of the conversation blurred.

There is such a feeling of impotence in grief. You watch someone else in pain and you think, I have to take that pain away. I have to do something to help that person! I love them. I don't want them to hurt.

And yet nothing you can do, let alone say, can lessen the pain.

CONTINUING ON

The platoon rested for a few days, then went back to work. Somehow, they managed to carry on. Life didn't return to normal, but they did manage to continue their missions.

August 18, 2006

    I know it's about time I got these [pictures of Chris with some of the members of the platoon, and an Army unit he was training] out to you.

Sorry it took me so long. After all you do for me to make me feel good and comfortable, the least I can do is get a few pics to you. And you are right about deserving them. I know you were kind of joking, but you do deserve them and more. For right now, this is what I have, but you will be getting more.

It was so nice to talk to you tonight. I always wind up in a better mood after talking to you. Somehow you always manage to brighten my life even when in a hell hole like this. You are the greatest woman ever, and I will never understand how I got so lucky to have been blessed with you. I appreciate all you do. You are the strongest person I know, and I admire you, and respect you. I am always extremely proud of you. I know with all that has happened with Marc and Biggles, you have gone out of your way to try to make everyone feel better. Even though I know that is your worst nightmare. I don't know many people who could be there, and put themselves through the pain just to make someone you don't even know more comfortable. You are an angel sent by God. Now you have given me two more angels. Remember Satan was once an angel of God, so Bubba is an angel, but just which side is sometimes debatable. Just joking. I know he can be very trying sometimes, and you have kept your cool way better than I ever could have. Our kids are so lucky to have you as their mother. So am I.

I cannot wait to get back into your arms. Talking about it tonight felt so good. Knowing that this whole thing is coming to an end. I dream about the day I step off that plane to see you. Hope you have no plans for the rest of your life, because you're gonna be a little busy. I miss you so much!!!

I loved talking to Bubba tonight. I love hearing him tell me he loves me, but I also don't want to force him to say it. I know inside that he loves me. He just gets a little busy with everything going on around him. I can't wait to play with him and chase him around the house. I was also thinking, all this time I've been wanting to talk to Bubba because he can talk back to me, but I want Angel to hear my voice, too. I want her to be a little familiar with me if at least my voice.

Anyway, I love you with all my heart, and can't wait to see you again. I am gonna smother you like crazy. You'll be begging me to go on another deployment so you can get a little break. Too bad. You're stuck with me now. I love you, sexy!

XOXOXOXOXOXOOX

....

The danger Chris and the others were in had become less theoretical for me after Marc and Ryan went down. Yet I still tried to keep the idea of it at bay. I didn't want to worry. And, I told myself, the last thing Chris needed from me was fear. If he knew I was worrying, he might worry, too. The distraction might be enough to get him killed.

Our conversations circled around the reality of where he was. We talked about things at home because they were safe; no one was in danger of getting shot or blown up.

I knew there were bullets flying all around him. I just became very good at not focusing on that part of the picture when we spoke.

Later—much, much later—Chris told me a story about being confronted by two insurgents while he and a friend were in a back alley relieving themselves.

There was a moment of stunned silence—he guessed the pair might have been about to do the same thing—then everyone grabbed for their guns.

Chris pulled his pistol from his drop holster first; he shot the others dead.

"I'm damn glad you're a quick draw," I told him.

A postscript on Ryan: Ryan did recover, but he was left permanently blind. His girlfriend Kelly stayed by his side through his recovery, and they soon married.

I'm happy to say that we all became good friends. Ryan had an indomitable spirit that infected everyone he met. He used to say that he suspected God had chosen him to be wounded, rather than someone else, because He knew he could bear it. If so, it was an excellent choice, for Ryan inspired many others to deal with their own handicaps as he dealt with his. He went hunting with the help of friends and special devices. His wound inspired the logo Chris would later use for his company; it was a way for Chris to continue honoring him.

Ryan and his wife were expecting their first child in 2009 when Ryan went into the hospital for what seemed like a routine operation, part of follow-up treatment for his wounds. Tragically, he ended up dying.

I remember looking at his wife at the funeral, so brave yet so devastated, and wondering to myself how we could live in such a cruel world.

My enduring vision of Ryan is outside one of the hospitals where he was recovering from an operation. He was in his wheelchair with some of the Team guys. Head bandaged and clearly in pain, he asked to be pointed toward the American flag that flew in the hospital yard; once there, he held his hand up in a long and poignant salute, still a patriot.

BACK WITH US

It may not have been directly related to my fears for Chris when he was gone, but I grew more apprehensive about being alone with the children in the house. We lived in a relatively quiet suburb, and yet—what would I do if there was an intruder?

Before we had kids, the answer was simple: I'd hide or run away. I didn't want to hurt anyone, even a thief. But now that I had children my attitude changed:

Take one step inside my house and I will put a bullet through your skull.

One day after he'd returned home from the Ramadi deployment, Chris and I went down to a gun range. As he showed me some of the basics, I started asking questions.

And more questions.

And more after that.

Why this, and why that.

"Really?" he said finally. "Are you challenging what I said?"

"No, no," I tried to explain. "I just want to know everything about it."

Maybe husbands shouldn't teach wives about certain things, and vice versa. I did eventually get pretty good with a gun—but that was after enlisting a friend of Chris's to help teach me. Somehow those sessions were a little easier.

It was during Chris's time back home after Ramadi that Mike Monsoor was killed in Iraq after courageously saving the lives of his fellow SEALs and Iraqi soldiers by leaping on a live grenade. Chris and I attended the service in San Diego.

We stood toward the back of the cemetery as the coffin was prepared for burial. As is customary, the SEALs pounded their Tridents into the top before it was lowered into the ground. I couldn't help but think of the danger Chris had been in, and how thin the line of fate was that kept him from being the one laid to rest.

When the services were over, I went off to see some friends while Chris went with a few of the others to a bar in Coronado. That was the night that the infamous incident with Jesse Ventura occurred or didn't occur, depending on whose account you believe.

I didn't think much of the incident when I heard about it the next day, and I doubt Chris did, though gossip about it spread quickly around the SEAL community. There was no knowing then that the details would eventually become the subject of a court case.

ONE LAST TIME

Chris's time home passed quickly, and in the spring of 2008, his unit was ready to deploy again. This tour, he found himself assigned to the area near Baghdad; he was in and near the notoriously dangerous Sadr City and some of the villages outside the capital for a good stretch of time.

The kids were bigger and more of a handful. I was having trouble keeping up. More and more I felt overwhelmed. I blamed Chris—surely things would have been easier if he had been there.

I would vent to Chris on the phone when he called, then feel sorry.

"I fall apart and then try to explain it all and tell you I am proud of you even though the whole situation is hard," I wrote in an email after one of those conversations. "I probably don't even need to write all that anymore since you've heard it before and I guess you understand."

This was his response:

May 2, 2008
Sorry I haven't written but the internet was actually down. Just as I told you that it was dependable. About the emails once every deployment, I don't care if you send them once a week. If you are feeling down and need to talk about it or write about it, then do so. I already told you, I am here for you to cry on, or dump your emotions on. I know these deployments are rough on you, especially now that you need some help with two kids, and all the regular chores of the day. So

please feel free to unload your worries and troubles on me. I am glad to hear Bubba is doing so much better. Hopefully he will get over the cold soon. I love to hear that he is saying so much, and climbing in the seat all by himself. Wow. He is shooting up like a weed. Next you're gonna email me saying he was driving my truck. Hope you are feeling better each day. I can imagine how it would feel to have so much to do, and not be able to physically do them. I don't envy you. I do love you so very much. I miss you like crazy. Can't wait to touch you again. Well, I just got back from working, and I am gonna go to bed for a while now. Like three days! I wish, but I do have some down time now. Anyway, take care of yourself and the little ones. Tell them I love them, and give them a hug and a kiss from me. I love you, baby!

Around this time, Chris and his platoon were on a patrol in Baghdad when they came under attack. Chris was shot in the head—fortunately, he was wearing his helmet, and between that and the grace of God, the bullet did nothing more than ring his ears. But for him, I think, it was the start of the end. The impact of the round had slammed his helmet and vision gear down so that he couldn't see; for a moment, he thought he was blind.

While Chris continued to work just as hard as he always had, he was as aware as ever that he was vulnerable—friends had been killed, he'd been hit. At the same time, he had three big reasons to want to come home in one piece: the kids and me.

That didn't change the fact that he loved being a SEAL and was dedicated to saving people. It was just something that clouded his vision of those things.

May 9, 2008

Thank you for all your emails. I loved opening it up and seeing you all over it. You made my week. I love you so much, and miss the hell out of you. I love to hear about the kids and orange poop, too. Hope your gums are feeling better. Do you like your hair the way it is now? Wish I was there to see it for myself. We are really staying busy here. Work is good and the morale is high. The army is in love with us. We have already done so much to save them. They never want us to leave. Good news for me. The quality of life is OK. We all live in open bay, and the food isn't bad, but we aren't here often to enjoy even that. We came in last night and it looked like we just crawled out of the sewer. I had several days' growth on my beard and it caught all the dirt. My face was almost black from all the soot, gunpowder, and everything else. Our uniforms were almost completely brown. By the way, we are wearing army cammies that are more green, so that should tell you how dirty we were. But we are loving what we are doing. I am gonna try to call you tonight. I really miss talking to you. I love to hear your sexy voice and picture being able to see you in front of me. Can't wait to see you again. I gave Mark Spicer your email address and phone number in case he or Diane wanted to talk to you. [Mark Spicer was a British sniper whom Chris had befriended; they would later start Craft together. Diane was his wife.] Hope you don't mind. Tell everyone there I said hi, and tell the kids I love them and miss them. Please give them both a big hug and kiss and tell them it's from daddy. I am sending you tons of them. Just can't wait to deliver them. I love you more than anything in this world, baby. You are everything to me. No more leaving you to fight some war. You are all I need. I honestly feel now I have done my part, and don't mind someone else fighting the next one for me. Take care of yourself, gorgeous. I love you!

While he was in Baghdad, Chris was involved in one other incident that illustrates his character and the lines that he drew.

People have criticized him for his willingness to shoot a woman and her child who had a grenade and were about to blow up American Marines. (The incident is described, though toned down, in the first pages of *American Sniper*.) Though he balked until ordered to shoot, Chris realized that the mother and child were already dead, thanks to the woman's pulling the pin on the grenade. Because of that, his decision to shoot didn't bother him—his action saved a number of Marines.

Contrast that with this incident in Baghdad, also in the book:

A Shia terrorist armed with a grenade launcher attempted to kill American soldiers building a wall around the worst part of the city slums. Chris killed the man, who dropped the grenade launcher. Over the course of several hours, other would-be terrorists attempted to retrieve the launcher. Chris shot them all.

Finally, a young boy was sent to retrieve the launcher.

Under his rules of engagement, Chris was entitled to shoot the boy. In fact, you might replace the word *entitled* with *obligated*—that grenade launcher was clearly going to be used against Americans or Iraqi civilians at some point.

Chris chose not to shoot.

His explanation years later for why he didn't shoot: "I could have, but I couldn't."

Though the incident was included in *American Sniper,* not one person has ever commented on it, let alone asked him about it, in the course of all that's been written about him and his service.

Maybe that says as much about some of the people who criticized him as it does about Chris.

THE TOLL

By the midpoint of his fourth Iraqi deployment, Chris was exhausted. It wasn't so much that stint in particular as it was all the deployments and special missions that came before it; the cumulative effect on his body—his knees were shot, his hearing damaged—would eventually cause him to be classified as 90 percent disabled, if not more. And that was just the physical side. But he didn't admit it, certainly not to himself.

There were hints, though, and warning signs. In June 2008, while giving me instructions on bidding on a truck he wanted to buy, he mentioned that he couldn't sleep.

At the same time, he was in great demand for special missions and training sessions. Journalists started to ask the command about him, interested in doing stories on his prowess.

The Navy promoted him to chief petty officer while he was in Iraq. That's an important rank, one of the highest an enlisted man can attain. It was a tacit recognition of his contribution to the war. It also meant a little more money for the family, since a pay raise came with it.

As always, Chris was pretty laid back about the promotion. For him, neither promotions nor medals were what serving was all about; protecting others and serving our country were what he'd signed up for.

Toward the end of their scheduled six-month deployment, Chris's platoon went out west. Terrorists were not extremely active in the area, and the number of missions decreased. Chris and his fellow SEALs spent more and more time at their base.

To a civilian back home, that might seem like a good thing—no missions meant less fear. But it had an odd effect on Chris. His blood pressure was surging. He couldn't sleep. It was as if now, when he finally had a chance to relax, everything was finally getting to him.

I'll let him describe it:

August 10, 2008
  Well, I guess all the shit has finally caught up to me. Remember the tightness in my chest I was telling you about? I felt like I could

never relax, grinding my teeth, felt like curling up in the corner and crying, and my blood pressure is thru the roof. I finally decided to talk to someone because I wasn't able to sleep, and when I could it was nightmares. I just wanted to take a deep breath and relax, but nothing would work. I talked to a doctor here, and looks like I am gonna be sent to Al Asaad in a week or so to see another one. . . .

Looks like I will probably go to Germany a little early. Don't know if that means I will be home early or if I will come home with the rest. They said I won't go home late. They prefer I see a specialist at home, but want to make sure all is good enough before I am resubmerged into the real world. I will call as soon as I can. I am doing OK. Already on some meds that are helping me relax a little and sleep. Spirits are OK, just feel all fucked up in the head. Not crazy though; don't want you to worry about my sanity. I still know right from wrong, and would never do anything to hurt myself. Just wanted to let you know how things are going. I love you very much.

But in the end it wasn't his health that got him to come home; it was his daughter's.

Angel came down with a fever, and when I went to the doctor, they mentioned the possibility of leukemia.

It was a distant possibility, but when I said that to Chris, what he heard was: My baby has leukemia.

He was scheduled to come home within a few weeks anyway, but his command arranged for him to get an earlier flight.

Just like that, he was home. This time, for good.

THREE

FAME

W e don't talk enough about what happens to servicemen when they leave the military, especially men like Chris who have seen a lot of action. I've come to learn that when these guys get out, they really need a year or two before they're resettled. It's bigger than changing a job or moving to a different state—they've given up a brotherhood. Everything about the civilian world is completely different than the one they've left. For SEALs, especially. We see these men as so strong and capable, and just assume that when they're home, they'd adjust.

It's not that easy.

Unfortunately, I didn't realize that at the time. I thought things would be perfect if he got out.

A NON-ULTIMATUM ULTIMATUM

It turned out Angel was okay. Her dad, though, was a different story.

Back home, Chris struggled to readjust, physically and mentally. He also faced another decision—reenlist, or leave the Navy and start a new life in the civilian world.

This time, he seemed to be leaning toward getting out—he'd been discussing other jobs and had already talked to people about what he might do next.

It was his decision, one way or another. But if I'd been resigned to his reenlistment last go-around, this time I was far more determined to let him know I thought he should get out.

There were two important reasons for him to leave—our children. They really needed to have him around as they grew. And I made that a big part of my argument.

But the most urgent reason was Chris himself. I saw what the war was doing to him physically. His body was breaking down with multiple injuries, big and small. There were rings under his eyes even when he had slept. His blood pressure was through the roof. He had to wall himself off more and more.

I didn't think he could survive another deployment.

"I'll support you whatever you decide," I told him. "I want to be married to you. But the only way I can keep making sense of this is . . . I need to do the best for the kids and me. If you have to keep doing what is best for you and those you serve, at some point I owe it to myself and those *I* serve to do the same. For me, that is moving to Oregon."

For me, that meant moving from San Diego to Oregon, where we could live near my folks. That would give our son a grandfather to be close to and model himself after—very important things, in my mind, for a boy.

I didn't harp on the fact that the military was taking its toll. That argument would never persuade Chris. He lived for others, not himself.

It didn't feel like an ultimatum to me. In fact, when he described it that way later on, I was shocked.

"It was an ultimatum," he said. He felt my attitude toward him would change so dramatically that the marriage would be over. There would also be a physical separation that would make it hard to stay together. Even if he wasn't overseas, he was still likely to be based somewhere other than Oregon. We'd end up having a marriage only in name.

I guess looked at one way, it was an ultimatum—us or the Navy. But it didn't feel like that to me at the time. I asked him if he could stay in and get an assignment overseas where we could all go, but Chris reminded me there was never a guarantee with the military—and noted he wasn't in it to sit behind a desk.

Some men have a heart condition they know will kill them, but they don't want to go to the doctor; it's only when their wives tell them to go that they go.

It's a poor metaphor, but I felt that getting out of the Navy was as important for Chris as it was for us.

In the end, he opted to leave.

Later, when Chris would give advice to guys thinking about leaving the military, he would tell them that it would be a difficult decision. He wouldn't push them one way or the other, but he would be open about his experiences.

"There'll be hard times at first," he'd admit. "But if that is the thing you decide, those times will pass. And you'll be able to enjoy things you never could in the service. And some of them will be a lot better. The joy you get from your family will be twice as great as the pleasure you had in the military."

Ultimatum or not, he'd come to realize retiring from the service was a good choice for all of us.

It was around this time in 2006 that Chris began texting with an old girlfriend—something he also talks about in the book.

There's not much more to add to what he said there. I felt sick to my stomach when I realized what was going on.

Was I jealous?

No. I was just hurt that our marriage had taken such a dive. And for Chris to do something that extreme, I worried he'd lost all faith in us. Another woman was getting more attention than I was, or so it seemed. Certainly it had the potential to break up our marriage.

Fortunately, Chris didn't want that, and neither did I.

When I told him what I thought, he was devastated—in fact, I have never seen him so devastated.

We talked again, later that night.

"I love you and I want you to stay," I told him. "If you want to go though, you are free to. You are not trapped here. If you want to stay, I want you to find a counselor for us, book a weekend away for us and leave a message for her that you will not talk to her anymore. And agree to tell me when she contacts you again."

As we both cried, he told me all day at work he was thinking of "suck starting his pistol." I couldn't imagine it ever being that bad or him feeling so horribly. But that was Chris. Harder on himself than anyone else ever would be.

I don't know if that was the worst threat to our marriage. Chris certainly felt that it was a very serious issue, and so did I. But the problem wasn't really the old girlfriend. The problem was that we had stopped focusing on each other. We had become distracted and harassed, and we weren't taking care of our relationship. We needed to get back to the reasons we had gotten together in the first place— the mutual respect and love, the support, and the genuine interest in the other person.

The big problem was realizing that.

We both learned a lot about each other in counseling. One of the issues that I always struggled with was communication. Chris could be pretty subtle about expressing his emotions. There were things I didn't pick up on. At times he thought he was communicating, but it went past me. He would say "A" and think that I understood B, C, and D.

So what was the solution?

Talking more. Understanding that there were gaps. Knowing that I did have to try and figure out B, C, and D.

Two people communicating, even when they love each other, is not an easy process. I'm sure we still missed things. But working with the counselor helped give both of us a vocabulary. The fact that we were starting from a really strong foundation of love made it possible to use that vocabulary, even if it wasn't always perfect.

BUSINESS

The Navy made a halfhearted attempt to get Chris to reenlist, telling him they would assign him stateside. But they wouldn't put it in writing, and in the end Chris's pledge to me and our family won out. His official discharge papers list his commendations. Among them: two Silver Stars, five Bronze Stars with "V" ("V" for valor, meaning they had been earned in combat), two Navy and Marine Corps Achievement Medals, a Navy and Marine Corps Commendation Medal, five Armed Forces Expeditionary Medals, an Iraq Campaign Medal, and three Good Conduct Medals. He was also awarded the Grateful Nation Award by the Jewish Institute for National Security Affairs.

Chris kept what he considered the most important medals in a small box in a desk drawer, shoved in with other paraphernalia. The rest . . .

Having decided to leave the Navy, the next big question was: What should he do for work?

Chris had struck up a friendship with Mark Spicer, a British sniper and commando who was now providing military-style training in the U.S. Together they formed a plan to open their own training facility. The idea was to teach military and police personnel how to work in realistic settings. Sniping was the most obvious skill—Spicer was also an accomplished shooter—but there were a variety of other combat-related specialties they felt would round out a curriculum. At the time, there were few if any such training facilities in the country, and none could boast the military's most lethal American military sniper as their head instructor. The two found a suitable property in Arizona, and made plans to establish their school there.

But before they put that plan into action, Texas hedge fund owner Kyle Bass approached Chris about doing security work for him. While being a bodyguard wasn't Chris's favorite thing, he felt the job might be a good opportunity: not only would it pay well, it was in Texas.

Emphasis on the latter.

Bass flew Chris to Dallas to talk about the job. The interview went well, though Chris still had misgivings. On the way back to the airport, Bass asked Chris where he saw himself in a few years. Chris mentioned the training facility.

Bass was immediately interested. So much so, in fact, that he asked if Chris had ever thought of putting together a business plan.

"As a matter of fact," said Chris, "I have one."

Chris gave the plan to Bass, who was impressed enough to offer to help establish the business, Craft International. The billionaire lined up some investors and put up a major portion of working capital himself, through his firm. The protection job went by the way-side, except when Bass had a special need. (The company eventually did provide protection services, including to former governor Sarah Palin and to Chris himself when *American Sniper* was published.)

The opportunity to have a facility he loved in Texas was a dream come true for Chris. He got ahold of Spicer, and together they re-worked the plans to establish Craft in Texas.

That meant moving from San Diego.

I was ready. San Diego had been convenient when Chris worked there, but I wanted a place where we could have more space. The cost of living in San Diego was outrageous. And believe it or not, the near-perfect weather had become a bit of a bore. I like changing seasons.

Most of all, I was ecstatic to have Chris home. We were finally going to settle down and have a normal family life, one where he wouldn't be traveling all the time—and one where I would never have to worry about him getting shot at or blown up by an IED.

Life was going to be perfect, and Texas was going to be a piece of heaven.

ROCK-BOTTOM TEXAS BLUES

The Texas part came true. It was the first place I've ever lived where I instantly felt at home.

Texas has a way of getting in your blood. I like the open space, the style of a lot of the houses, and, most of all, the people. New-comers often fear that "native" Texans will look down on them or treat them differently, but that's never been my experience. And traditional family values are as strong here as any place I've been.

Even stronger is patriotism. There are more flags per acre in Texas than any place outside a flag factory. And the communities tend to be God-based in a friendly, nonjudgmental way. Faith is an easy, accepted thing. There are places you live in where you would be cautious talking about God, because you don't know how other people think; here it's just accepted.

We'd always been a religious family. That's "religious" with a small "r." We believed in God and prayer. We'd read the Bible—Chris especially. But I wouldn't say we were regular churchgoers. We went when we felt the need, maybe once or twice a month. Every night we would say a little prayer together with the kids. Many nights I simply said to Chris, "Look how blessed we are. You, me, and the kids."

"Yes," he'd reply. "Blessed." And we'd thank God for something specific, maybe a friend who'd helped us or a prayer that had been answered.

I don't know if those brief sentences count as "real" prayers, but they were true emotions, and an honest testimony of our faith.

Chris had to start quickly. We put our San Diego home on the market; in the meantime, we needed a place to stay near Dallas. Kyle Bass had just moved into a new house, and he offered us his old home temporarily. It was large—far bigger than our San Diego home—and it was furnished. But despite its size, it soon began to feel very cramped.

One of my relatives was having assorted troubles. I invited her to live in our house, which turned out to be a mistake. She began drinking more than I thought she should, couldn't or wouldn't find a job, and ended up sleeping in much of the day. Worse, she brought along a dog that absolutely hated Chris.

Needless to say, none of this improved the family situation. Nor did the constant stream of friends and acquaintances who seemed to stop by every time it looked like Chris and I would have a moment alone together. I'd never been in a situation before where I resented visitors, but I quickly reached that point. The perfect life I'd envisioned was anything but.

Our marriage hit a rock within the first six months of moving. The unfamiliar neighborhood, the revolving door of visitors, the kids—those were just normal stresses. There were others: Spicer lost his wife, which affected his ability to help with the company. Our house back in California wasn't selling; we were asking roughly the same price we'd paid when we'd bought it eight years before, but with the housing bust it wouldn't move. An investment soured. Craft went through typical startup pressures: Chris threw himself into work, but the company struggled.

Not surprisingly, he started having second thoughts about leaving the Navy. He seemed to stop taking care of himself physically. He didn't work out. He started drinking heavily.

I think it didn't help that many people treated him like a show pony. Having heard of his military accomplishments and the fact that he was a SEAL, people would befriend him, then want to show him off to others. It was as if they gained a contact high from being around him and claiming that they were good buds.

They'd say: *This is my friend Chris Kyle. He was a bad-ass SEAL.*

What they were really saying was: *Look at me. I know the top SEAL sniper ever! Aren't I cool?*

It grated on Chris. He'd gone from being surrounded by guys who would die for him to phonies who were using him, even if it was in an innocent way.

Leaving the war zone didn't translate immediately into leaving the war. He had bad dreams, reminders of the brutality he'd seen. His blood pressure remained high.

I have to admit, I didn't really appreciate all he was going through at the time. I was thinking: My husband is finally with us! We're going to have the perfect family life! I was impatient for that to start, and baffled when it didn't.

I was as disappointed and confused as he was. I didn't like the drinking, either by him or by friends. And the more the distance between us grew, the more I resented everything that added to it. Little things that he did or didn't do—like not holding me when I was feeling blue—grated, becoming bigger and bigger things. It worked both ways—I was certainly distracted and often couldn't help commenting negatively on things he'd say, even when I should have held my tongue.

I'm sure he must have blamed me for what he felt, because I was the major reason he'd left the Navy. To his credit, though, he never said that and never tried to make me feel bad because of it. (We only talked about it in depth much later—while he was working on *American Sniper*.)

We started arguing a lot. Some of the things I said were very hurtful, and vice versa.

I can see why your family thinks you don't want to have anything to do with them!

Silly stuff, yes. The worst of what we said doesn't even seem like much of anything except a stupid misunderstanding now.

And yet, it seemed life threatening, or at least marriage threatening, at the time.

Things finally came to a head one night. But the truth is, I didn't see it coming.

"I don't think this is working out," Chris told me.

"What?" I said, stunned.

"It's not working out."

"Please," I said, feeling like a drowning swimmer groping for a rope. "We're just under stress. We—of course it will work out. We have a good marriage."

Chris saw the relationship in much starker, and maybe more realistic, terms.

"I'm going hunting this weekend," he told me. "Let's take this weekend to think about whether we want to stay together."

I wasn't ready to give up. I don't think he was either. We both took our characteristic approaches to problems: he went off and cleared his head; I dug in and researched how to fix our marriage.

Among the things I read that weekend was *The Proper Care and Feeding of Husbands.* Maybe it has a silly title, but the book gave me some good insights on what I could do better. It also reassured me that I was right about the most important issue—we *did* have the basis of a great marriage, and we could make it even better.

It was just a question of getting there.

When Chris came home, we put the kids to bed, then went into the living room to talk alone.

"Did you have time to think?" I asked.

"Yeah. I don't know if we can make it, Taya. I really don't."

"I love you," I said.

"I love you, too," he answered, with his sincere cowboy eyes. "I just don't know if we can be happy."

"I think we can."

I started telling him about the book I'd read. He laughed at the title. But the tactics it suggested were serious, and also fairly achievable.

"I'm going to do these things," I told him. "And I'll keep doing them or whatever it takes. Just give me a chance."

I don't think the conversation lasted more than a half hour. There was no yelling or anything like that. It may sound a little corny in the telling, but to us it was one of the most heartfelt half hours we'd shared in years.

I think Chris was wondering why things weren't okay when we'd finally reached a point where we'd thought they would be. I was wondering the same thing. So as usual, we were working together; we just didn't know it.

Looking back, I can understand exactly why we were having trouble. No privacy, work pressure, major relocation, excessive drinking, little sleep, two little kids, crazy dogs—you name the stressor, we had it.

But a key part of the problem was our—*my*—expectation of perfection without effort. Or even *with* effort.

Gradually we removed stressors. I told my relative the stay was over. The dog went with her. We cut out some of the friends who were contributing to chaos.

But the real thing that got us over that hump was simple: *We focused on each other.*

I don't mean that Chris and I were together 24/7 from that point on. In fact, the increase in our time together may not have amounted to a few minutes a day, if that. But we made a conscious effort to be together mentally as well as physically. We both tried hard to think about the other person, and to take them into account—to hold them dear.

It was the whole reason we'd gotten married in the first place.

Staying in Kyle Bass's house had always been a temporary measure. As part of the effort to change the atmosphere around us, we started looking for a new place to live, outside the city. It came to symbolize a whole new start.

Our initial idea was to rent—we were still trying to sell the San Diego house—and we looked at a number of places in the general Dallas area. One day we drove out to a neighborhood that looked almost ideal. There was a house there that was nearly perfect—all it lacked was a fence for the dog in the back.

"Put in a fence and we'll take it," we told the Realtor.

She got a funny look on her face.

"I want to show you another house," she said. "It's actually for sale, but it's been on the market almost a year. Sometimes when houses sit that long, people are willing to rent instead of sell."

We went along, not expecting much. Then we saw it.

A sprawling ranch-style home, it was fairly new, with a very nice kitchen, nice bedrooms, and a single room upstairs we could use as a playroom for the kids. There was an office for Chris and a nice little den tucked toward the back. The backyard—which was fenced—had to be six times the size of the one in California. The local schools were good and the neighborhood was quiet. It was the perfect place to raise our kids.

Oh my God, I thought when I walked in, I want this house.

Instead of renting, we came up with a plan to buy. Chris decided he would sell one of his guns to pay for the down payment; we'd get a mortgage for the rest. When he heard that Chris was going to sell the gun, Kyle Bass offered instead to loan Chris the down payment in exchange for the gun, and then arranged for his company to hold the mortgage on the house. It was the perfect arrangement, and a generous one.

The night we closed, we slept on a blow-up air mattress. We probably would have floated above the floor anyway.

"Can you believe this is ours?" we said to each other, over and over.

"They'll bury me in the backyard," I told Chris.

Chris loved the house, but he had other ambitions. What he really wanted was a place where he could have horses and shoot. Which meant a lot more acres, a barn, a corral—your typical Texas ranch. We couldn't afford that—yet. For him, the new house was going to be a stepping-stone to someplace bigger. But in the meantime, if the kids and I were happy, he was happy.

DAUGHTERS OF SARAH

The idea behind Craft was a good one, but like any new business, attracting clients and just getting normal working procedures into place was a grind.

To start the company and cover initial expenses, Kyle Bass and a group of other investors loaned Craft a considerable amount of money—it would eventually come close to $2 million in 12 percent convertible preferred notes, according to court documents—to get started. Chris felt obliged to each of the investors and worked hard to make their investments pay off. He owned 85 percent of the company, which to him meant that its weight was on his shoulders. He made cold calls to police agencies and contacted military units, trying to drum up business. Not only did Craft personnel teach classes themselves, but the facility they had obtained in Arizona was used for training sessions.

As the pressures of starting the new business built, I made suggestions to Chris about different things he could do to improve the company. I had a background in sales and management, and while pharmaceuticals are nothing like tactical training, I still thought I could contribute.

I'd suggest management books he could read, only to be met with a shake of the head.

"I'm not going to do that."

All Chris really wanted to do was train people. Management? No way.

Sniping, surveillance, even security—another name for being a bodyguard—were what he loved to do, and teaching these skills was the reason he started the company. The other parts of running a business had relatively little interest for him. Not that he didn't do them, but there wasn't the same level of enthusiasm. He was happy to turn over duties like keeping the books to his employees and partners.

For quite a while, I was frustrated that he wouldn't take my help. I felt hurt and rejected, not allowed to contribute. I surely became a bit of a nag, second-guessing or criticizing his decisions.

That, too, must have worn on our marriage, or at least on Chris. Then one weekend we took the kids to a lodge for a few days away. While Chris, Bubba, and Angel were out, I started to read a book a friend of mine had recommended called *Daughters of Sarah*, written by Genevieve M. White. I was skeptical, but I saw a lot of things that were not only true but that could be easily applied to us, and me specifically. Basically, I had to learn to trust Chris more—one of the ideas in the book—stop second-guessing him, and, more to the point, stop nagging him to do things my way. I had to learn to listen without offering opinions unless asked.

For us, the advice applied to Craft, which was truly his thing. But it applied to our family decisions as well. I had to let him lead, and help when he wanted help. In the end, if I trusted God, then I had to trust Chris as well.

And I did. So why did I have a problem?

I cried my way through the book because I knew I needed to change and didn't know if I could do it. I wondered if I would become invisible or insignificant in the process. My desire for happiness and faithfulness won out. Driving home after our stay, I told Chris a little about the book. I was going to let him lead and make a real effort not to second-guess or nag. I'm sure he doubted that would happen, but it did. It was amazing how things in our relationship worked so much better from that point on.

There's a lot more in that book, of course. Some people will find the religious angle comforting; others won't think it will work for them. But my father gave me a piece of advice that has stuck with me over the years: you don't have to follow the Bible to get to heaven, but it is a recipe for happiness. And it's the same way with that book.

At first it seemed like I was giving up a lot: disagreeing meant a chance to change a decision, and frankly I would have changed several of Chris's decisions. But the reality was that I gained much more than I lost. Once I stopped questioning everything he did, Chris consulted with me more. I changed my attitude to one that was more accepting and supportive, which made both of us happier.

Did he do everything the way I would have? No. But who's to say that his solutions weren't miles ahead of mine?

It may seem ironic now, but Chris and I never really settled on a "home" church, even in Texas. We went to several, trying to find just the right one to fit in. But while we were comfortable in many, including what's known locally as a "cowboy church," we couldn't really pick one as a permanent home. Faith remained an important part of our lives, but for some reason we just never found the right place to worship.

I guess the exterior walls aren't important, as long as you worship in your heart.

AMERICAN SNIPER

Even before he left the Navy, Chris had heard that people were interested in writing about him. He was adamantly opposed. Chris didn't want the attention or even feel that he deserved it. Toward the end of his service, he met a man named Scott McEwen in a local bar. They got to talking, and Chris told him some war stories. At some point, McEwen suggested that they should write a book together. McEwen was an attorney, but he had always wanted to try his hand at writing.

Chris eventually agreed.

"This guy's a lawyer?" I asked. "Not a writer?"

"Yeah."

"Why would you consider him doing it?"

"I don't think anything's going to happen anyway," he said. "But this way I can say someone's working on it and maybe other people won't do it."

I was like, okay.

McEwen eventually presented Chris with a contract that had McEwen owning 30 percent of the story, a similar percentage to what an attorney often gets in a contingency agreement. Publishing agents in New York typically get 10 to 15 percent of the author's money; lawyers doing book contracts are often paid on a per hour basis. (Film agents are a little different; in California, they must be registered and usually are limited to 10 percent; attorneys in the movie business usually review contracts and do other legal work on a percentage basis, generally around 5 percent of the deal.)

They started working, though in my opinion haphazardly. They never got very far, and then we left San Diego for Texas. I suspect Chris wanted to let it go and see if he really *had* to write the book—as if it were one of the high school assignments he used to try to duck, only to finish at the last minute in the cab of his truck before running in for class.

And that was where things were in the summer of 2010, with us fitting into our new home and Chris busy with Craft, when an email came to Chris from Peter Hubbard, an editor at William Morrow. Peter had heard about Chris from another SEAL, and in the email asked if he'd ever considered writing a book about his experiences:

Dear Chief Chris Kyle,

By way of introduction, I am an editor at the William Morrow imprint of HarperCollins Publishers. I'm writing to ask if you've given any thought to writing a book about your personal experiences in the military as a sniper. It's my understanding that you have a superb reputation and an outstanding service record that might be of interest to a wide audience. I hope we can be in touch further if this is an opportunity you'd like to explore at this time.

Many thanks.

Best regards,
Peter

Peter Hubbard
Senior Editor
HarperCollins Publishers

Chris's response:

> I would be very interested in talking with you. I am packing right now for an antelope hunt my company is putting on for several wounded vets. I will be back Wednesday, and I will reach out to you then. Thank you for your email.
>
> Chris Kyle

They talked. Chris told Peter that Peter would have to talk to Scott, who represented him as attorney and agent on the book deal and, later on, the movie. Scott kept the original contract in place, even though he wasn't going to write the book; in addition to taking 30 percent of the proceeds, he got his name on the cover as an author and ended up on the copyright. (Harper looked at a sample he had prepared and made it clear they wanted a professional writer. Scott's material was not used to prepare or shape the book.)

Peter recommended Jim DeFelice as the writer. Jim had collaborated with a number of other men on memoirs, and was a bestselling fiction and nonfiction writer. Among his partners was Richard Marcinko, the "father" of SEAL Team 6. That was actually not a selling point for Chris. Jim prepared a vision for the book talking about finding the deeper themes and insisting on a raw, no-holds-barred story that would be in Chris's voice and tell people what war was really like.

Chris talked to Jim by phone a short time later. Chris explained that he was reluctant to do the book at all but had been persuaded that another book was going to be done, and so he'd decided to go ahead.

"Why do you want to write the book?" Jim asked.

"I want to honor the guys who fought with me."

"Tell me about them," Jim said, not knowing whether to believe what might be a stock answer.

Chris talked about the two men who had been shot while under his command—Marc Lee and Ryan Job—and how he wanted to honor them. He was so sincere and open, that before five minutes had passed they were set. Within a week or two—even before there was a formal contract with HarperCollins—Chris and Jim were working.

Chris and Jim's process was deceptively simple. Basically, the two men talked. And talked and talked and talked. The phone bills must have been outrageous. They also worked together in person on a ranch a friend of ours owned; Jim also stayed with us in Texas, and we stayed with him and his family in New York.

From the start, Jim wanted me to be part of the book. He argued that my contribution would make the book truly unique: to that point, no one had included the family in a military memoir, certainly not one involving a SEAL. But Jim and then Chris argued that the family went through their own kind of war while their loved one was away. Just as Chris felt that his story was every veteran's story, telling my side would illuminate what spouses go through during a deployment.

I was nervous, though. I wasn't sure about it for several reasons. One question was the kids' privacy: Would people—the enemy Chris fought abroad—be out to take revenge against Chris by harming his children?

Chris assured me that wouldn't happen. My other objections were more personal. Frankly, I didn't think people would care about me. In fact, I was still undecided in mid-December 2010, when I drove out to the ranch where Jim and Chris were working.

"We think it's a good idea," Chris told me over the phone when

I called on the way to say I was having second—or by that time, third or fourth—thoughts. "It will give people a better idea of what families go through."

Still unsure, I went in and met the writer. Before I knew it, we were sitting in front of a fireplace and talking. It seemed incredibly natural, even when the topics became heavy.

We were all in. Before I knew it, Chris was needing a drink, and Jim was taking a lot of notes.

The book took the better part of a year to write, even though they were working every day for stretches.

Or at least they claimed to be working—I have a rather incriminating photo showing them playing Xbox. Maybe it was for research.

Chris wanted to come across in the book the way he was in life— humble, not bragging. He didn't want to seem as if he was full of himself, or making too much of what he'd done. That was a tricky proposition, given that the book was in his voice and about things he had done that were, by any measure, heroic.

One of the criticisms that came up later was the fact that, because he was a sniper, Chris was always "safe," since he was shooting from a distance. Of course, if you actually read the book, you know that's not true: he often fought "on the ground," and in fact snipers were primary targets for the enemy—the guys they all wanted to kill.

He also was worried that some of the stories—like the one where he shot the terrorists who were swimming across the river—might make him look like a monster. But the stories were real, and in the end, he decided to tell them without spin and let people make their own judgments.

One thing Chris and Jim—and the publisher—discussed quite a bit was the number of kills to use in the book. The number that is published—over 160—is the "official" number, and is technically correct, but it's short of the actual number by quite a bit. The Navy demanded that he *not* use the actual number, claiming that a large portion had come on missions that were tangentially involved in classified actions, and therefore shouldn't be published.

Jim and Chris debated quite a lot about that. Chris reasoned that the number was so high largely because he happened to be in a lot of battles; many other snipers, Chris claimed, were just as good as he was, but didn't have the opportunities. Nonetheless, some number had to be used; otherwise there would always be questions about Chris's record.

Chris never dwelled on the number of kills, though it was common knowledge in the SEAL community and something that others often mentioned. What was important to him was the lives he was saving—and the two lives that ultimately he couldn't save, the lives of his friends Ryan Job and Marc Lee. If it were up to him, Chris wouldn't have used any number at all. But as the publisher pointed out, there had to be some number in the book, to show what he had accomplished.

Finally, they decided to use the round number the Navy uses, which itself is higher than any other American sniper has been publicly credited with. They explained that the actual number is more, though few people pay attention to that part, let alone Chris's reasoning on why the number itself isn't important.

As far as I know, Chris still has the "record," if you want to call it that. One thing that he always made clear: the number did not mean that he was the best shot ever. On the contrary, he considered himself only a good shot, often pointing out that his brother Jeff was better. His number of kills was due primarily to his "luck" of often being in combat.

Another thing to note: even Chris's unpublished "real" number doesn't represent the number of people he killed in combat. That number was much higher—he shot people before he was a sniper, in actions when he was "on the ground," and even as a sniper a kill was only recorded when a combatant's death was recorded by a witness.

A lot of people died because of my husband's skills.

A lot of people die in war. Machine gunners in World War I, artillerymen in World War II, bomber pilots in both wars, all killed hundreds of enemy soldiers. There are endless examples, and the truth is, compared to some of those tolls, Chris's exploits were modest.

The difference here was that there was a specific record and acknowledgment of each kill. Somehow, that offended some people's sense of propriety.

While Chris was proud of the job he did and certainly knew the exact number, to him, the significance was that he had saved other people. Every one of those kills represented one, two, three, twelve—countless lives that were protected. And given that more Iraqi citizens were killed by terrorists than by American soldiers during the conflict, most of the people who owe him their lives are Iraqi, and Muslim. So when he's called a racist or anti-Islam, I just shake my head.

Chris knew and worked with Iraqis and Muslims in Iraq. Following the war, he happened to meet a man who had acted as an interpreter for SEALs and other American and Iraqi forces in Iraq. Johnny Walker—that's a pseudonym he adopted to protect his family—had been helped to immigrate to the U.S. by SEALs after his life was threatened several times.

Chris publically thanked and praised Johnny at a book event. He then persuaded William Morrow to publish a book about Johnny's experiences. Written with Jim DeFelice's help, *Code Name: Johnny Walker* talks about what it was like to be an Iraqi during the war. Johnny praised Chris—and other Americans—freely in the book, and continues to do so.

Certainly Chris hated the terrorists and insurgents he was fighting. But that hatred didn't translate into blind rage against all Muslims.

A lot of people have asked if writing *American Sniper* helped Chris heal.

No!

If anything, it reopened many old wounds, maybe including some Chris didn't even realize he had. But once he decided to do something, he was committed. If he wanted to quit at any point, he never told anyone, including me.

The beauty of *American Sniper* is that it is raw. Chris was upfront about his flaws. And it reflects his viewpoint on the war, one that wasn't polished or buffed, let alone made "politically correct." I think that was an important reason people were able to relate to it.

Anyone who has served in the military and writes a book about their experience is supposed to submit the manuscript for a legal and security review before it is published. Many, many authors ignore that requirement, but Chris insisted that the book be submitted. And so it was.

The Department of Defense coordinates the formal procedure,

sending the book to other agencies and services, then passing judgment on the legalities and making formal recommendations.

The Navy did its own review and came up with their own "suggestions." Chris thought a few had nothing to do with classified missions—he had been very careful not to mention any, even in cases where reports had already been published. Possibly he didn't have to agree with all of the "suggestions," but he had agreed to go through the process, and so he made the changes, deleting material at their request.

Chris and Jim finished working on the book in the fall of 2011. Except for blocking off some time to do an interview or two for the media the following January, Chris put it out of his mind and concentrated on his business. There was more than enough to keep him busy.

I had had my own dream of writing. The dream stayed with me on and off, and with Chris working on his book, he encouraged me to work on my own.

But my time was tight. I was volunteering at the kids' school, helping Chris, and just being a mom. Finally, Chris pushed me to get going.

"Couldn't you run to Starbucks for a few hours when I get home and work on it?" he asked.

I did that for a while. I'd make dinner before I left, then go out and work. Unfortunately, it was still very hard to be consistent—the kids might get sick, or there were just other interruptions and things that had to be done.

Finally, I got to the point where I thought, God is telling me you'll do it, but not now.

Now that I've gained some distance from it, I've realized that putting it down temporarily was actually a blessing. Not only have I gained a perspective on what I was trying to say, but I've also gotten more insights into people and situations that are similar to those I was trying to write about.

And I wouldn't trade the time I spent with Chris for a dozen novels, all of them bestsellers.

Since coming to Texas, Chris had begun visiting with veterans who were having trouble readjusting from the war. Many were disabled; others just needed to talk to someone who knew what they'd experienced.

Chris's attitude was to treat them all absolutely the same, as if they were regular guys hanging out together—because in his eyes, that's what they were. He went out a few times on organized "retreats"— trips to ranches in the area where vets could spend weekends hunting or shooting or just chilling.

He also spent time talking to people informally. Guys he knew and some he didn't would call him up and just need to talk. I remember him leaving the house one night at eleven thirty after a call when he thought the guy was close to committing suicide.

Chris was never much of a talker, but maybe that's why people felt they could talk to him. He'd been through the war and the transition to civilian life. He knew what it was like. He also wasn't the kind of person who would gossip about you to others—what you said to him would stay with him.

He had a soft heart, but you could trust him, too.

The conversations would start casually: *Have you ever had bad dreams?*

Yes, Chris would answer, then simply listen. There were certain topics that I'm sure hit him very hard—like the guilt one feels after a buddy dies, or the conviction that you might have done something more to save other lives. Mostly Chris would just listen, nod, and add a word or two of encouragement. Sharing with someone who knows what you're going through is sometimes the best medicine you can get.

BACON AND OTHER SILLY STUFF

Among the many veterans Chris helped was Omar Avila, who'd been badly wounded in an ambush and IED attack in Iraq in 2007. Burned over 75 percent of his body, Omar managed to largely recover from his wounds, but even three years after the attack was still suffering psychologically. Chris met him after a friend invited him to hang out with some disabled vets at a ranch for a weekend. It was an informal gathering—the kind Chris liked the best. Most of the guys were going hunting, but Omar didn't feel much like hunting that weekend. He was, he said later, in a dark hole.

Chris saw him hanging back and went over to talk. Omar suddenly opened up about survivor guilt—he'd lost his best friend in the attack. Finding someone to talk with about the war was difficult, Omar said; he just didn't feel right talking about it.

Chris suggested that Omar write his experiences down. Omar not only did that; he soon began putting them into poetry, and today has a fair number of touching and eloquent war poems.

More than that, the two became good friends. Today, Omar mentors other wounded warriors and works as the Texas coordinator of Feherty's Troops First Foundation.

It was amazing how wise Chris could be. Recently, someone who had randomly corresponded with him sent me an email Chris had sent to his son about joining the service and college:

From: "Chris Kyle"

Date: December 25, 2010 at 12:55:57 AM EST

I appreciate your upbringing and your respect. My dad would have kicked my ass if I didn't call everyone sir or Mr. until they notified me otherwise. So I am telling you, my name is Chris. Please no more sir bullshit.

I went to college right out of high school, but did not finish. Sometimes I do regret that. Now that I am out, I could really use the degree. Even if you think you will retire from the service, like I did, there is life after the military. I joined at 24 years old. I had some mental maturity over my teammates due to joining later. I also got to enjoy my youth. One thing about being a SEAL, you age fast. I was only in for eleven years, but I spent over half that time in a combat zone. Unlike other combat units, SEALs in a combat zone are operating. That means getting shot at on a daily basis. I had a baby face when I joined, and within two years, I looked as if I had aged 10 years. I am not in any way talking you out of joining. I loved my time, and if I hadn't gotten married and had two kids, I would still be in. Unforeseen events will come at you in life. Your plans today will not be the same in four years. I am just trying to prep you for what is to come. I sit in an office or train other people on a range all day, every day. I would much rather be in Afghanistan being shot at again. I love the job and still miss it today. There is no better friendship than what the teams will offer. Once you become a SEAL, you will change. Your friends and family may think you are the same, but if they are really honest, they will see the difference. You will no longer have that innocence that you have now. Sometimes I even miss that person I used to be, but do not regret in any way who I have become. You will be much harder emotionally than you have ever imagined. The day to day bullshit that stresses people out now, fades away. You realize, once you have faced death and accepted it, that the meaningless bullshit in day to day life is worthless.

I know this was a long answer to an easy question, but I just wanted to be completely honest. Take your time and enjoy your youth. The SEALs are one of the greatest things that have ever happened to me, but once you are in, you will no longer be the same.

Chris Kyle

One of the things that I admired about Chris's relationship with our kids was his insistence that each be his or her own person.

Even when that meant rooting against his beloved Dallas Cowboys. Though in that case, there were limits.

He and Bubba were watching a football game one Sunday, with Dallas playing the Philadelphia Eagles.

Philadelphia started winning from the get-go. Decisively. And Bubba rooted for them. Loudly.

Finally, Chris could take it no more.

"Bubba, you can root for whoever you want," he said at last. "But today, you're going to do it in your head."

Silly stuff could tickle him no end. Chris loved practical jokes, even when they weren't planned.

One day he brought home a large kudu head to keep for a friend. (Kudus are large African antelopes; this one had been shot and mounted as a trophy.) I was in the kitchen getting something out of the refrigerator. I heard a noise and looked up—there was a beast in my house!

I screamed.

Chris appeared behind the head. For a brief moment his face was tight with concern and worry.

It was a *very* brief moment. When he realized he'd scared me with the silly head, he began laughing so hard the house shook.

"I'm sorry," he said, gasping for air. "I didn't mean to scare you."

He laughed some more.

"Oh, I'm sorry," he said when he managed to stop momentarily. "I'm sorry."

Another five minutes of hysterical laughter. By now it was contagious, and I started laughing, too.

"I didn't mean to do it," he said finally. "But it couldn't have worked out better."

I liked to make stuffed baked potatoes with all the trimmings, in-cluding bacon. But being a health-conscious cook, I cut all the fat parts off, using only the meat. One day I was in the middle of cook-ing and had piled the bacon on a plate. The fat, still hot, was on another plate waiting to go in the garbage.

Chris walked into the kitchen.

"Bacon!" he said, practically licking his lips.

"Don't eat any of this," I told him. "There's not enough for the potatoes.

His eyes twinkled. I left the kitchen for a moment. When I came back, all of the bacon meat was still there.

The plate with the fat, however, was empty.

Oh. My. God.

"Tell me you threw out the fat!" I said.

He just smiled.

I'm sure it tasted really good, at least to him. As for the health consequences, he couldn't have cared less. To his way of thinking, when your time came, it came, and there was nothing you could do about it beforehand. So why not eat all the bacon fat you wanted?

As we settled into our home, we developed some family rituals. There was dinner together every night. Saturday sports with the kids. Watching football on Sunday, of course.

At night before bedtime, we'd gather the kids on our bed and read a bedtime story. Then we'd each take a turn saying what we were grateful for, thank God, and pray. It was always fascinating to hear what the kids were thankful for. They'd come out with things

I had never thought of, sometimes an innocuous thing that had happened during the day.

I never once heard bacon fat mentioned, but I wouldn't have been surprised if it were.

For most people who have kids, "dates" are pretty much a thing of the past. But Chris and I were able to get some breaks thanks to our family and the occasional babysitter.

One of our best dates was actually a weekend when we went to the wedding of a friend from the Teams. The couple married in Wimberley, Texas, a small town maybe forty miles south of Austin and a few hours' drive from where we lived. We were having such a pleasant day, we didn't want it to end.

"It doesn't have to end," suggested Chris as we headed for the car. "The kids are at my parents' for the weekend. Where do you want to go?"

We googled for hotels and found a place in San Antonio, a little farther south. Located around the corner from the Alamo, the hotel seemed tailor-made for Chris. There was history in every floorboard. He loved the authentic Texan and Old West touches, from the lobby to the rooms. He read every framed article on the walls and admired each artifact. We walked through halls where famous lawmen—and maybe an outlaw or two—had trod a hundred years before. In the evening, we relaxed with coffee out on the balcony of our room— something we'd never managed to do when we actually owned one. It was one of those perfect days you dream of, completely unplanned.

I have a great picture of Chris sitting out there in his cowboy boots, feet propped up, a big smile on his face. It's still one of my favorites.

People ask about Chris's love of the Old West. It was something he was born with, really. It had to be in his genes. He grew up watching old westerns with his family, and for a time became a bronco-bustin' cowboy and ranch hand.

More than that, I think the clear sense of right and wrong, of frontier justice and strong values, appealed to him.

We never did find a buyer for the San Diego house. The bank foreclosed that fall. We were officially broke.

HELLO, AMERICA! HELLO, CHRIS KYLE!

A week or so before Christmas 2011, the publisher contacted Chris and told him that *Time* magazine had read the advance copy of *American Sniper* and wanted to interview him. It was the first indication that there was going to be a lot of interest in the book.

Chris flew up into the cold Northeast, did the interview, and met with the publisher. While he was there, he learned that the interview was just the start. Television news shows were lining up to talk to him. The lineup included *The O'Reilly Factor*.

Getting on *O'Reilly* is the book world's equivalent of performing at the Super Bowl; there are no guarantees in life, but being Bill's guest is as close to a guarantee as there is that your book will become a bestseller.

Actually, the advance sales were so strong that *Sniper* was already going to be a bestseller, but we didn't understand that. In fact, while Jim and the publisher had told us *some* of what to expect, even they didn't know just how big it would be. No one wants to be too optimistic in a world where even the best books can beg for an audience.

To me, it was all a little surreal. *O'Reilly?* Really? This could really be . . . big. I think.

The funny thing is, Chris would have been completely happy if only ten people bought the book. If it had been sitting on a shelf in the back of the bookstore somewhere, he would have been fine. In fact, I think that's pretty much what he expected.

Chris came home and we had a wonderful Christmas. On New Year's Day, he flew back to New York. *O'Reilly* was just the start.

It didn't take long before he was exhausted from back-to-back-to-back interviews and other events. Things blurred together as he went from studio to studio before crashing in his hotel room.

Sometime during this week, he went on the *Opie & Anthony* show. Toward the end, a caller came on and asked if he'd been in a fight with Jesse Ventura. He said he had; the hosts laughed and shared a joke, then moved on.

Chris promptly forgot about it; there were many other things to concentrate on.

Later that day, he and Jim went down to the World Trade Center site. After going through the temporary museum nearby, they walked a few blocks in silence, found a bar, and had a drink before continuing the day's interviews.

Back in Texas, I sensed things were going well, but I didn't know how well. I hadn't read military books, so I didn't know how they sold or what they could be compared to. And while I knew Chris's life was heroic, I didn't know whether it would really translate into something that would interest other people. They'd had to leave a lot of things out—books can only be so long—and besides, words rarely if ever can get to the real essence of a man. So I didn't know.

Then came the book signing in Dallas.

Fearing there might be threats from al-Qaeda or some other terrorist group, the publisher arranged for security to cover the signing, which was to be Chris's first. As is common, the security team sent an advance man to the Dallas Barnes & Noble bookstore a few hours ahead of the event to check things out.

He called back with an incredible report: there were people lined up around the store already.

Wow, I thought.

Wow!

Wow didn't begin to cover it. People lined up on two floors of the store to talk to Chris and get their books signed, hours before he was even scheduled to arrive. Chris was overwhelmed when he got there, and so was I. The week before, he'd been just another guy walking down the street. Now, all of a sudden he was famous.

Except he was still the same Chris Kyle, humble and a bit abashed, ready to shake hands and pose for a picture, and always, at heart, a good ol' boy.

"I'm so nervous," confided one of the people on the line as he approached Chris. "I've been waiting for three hours just to see you."

"Oh, I'm sorry," said Chris. "Waitin' all that time and come to find out there's just another redneck up here."

The man laughed, and so did Chris. It was something he'd repeat, in different variations, countless times that night and over the coming weeks.

We stayed for three or four hours that first night, far beyond what had been advertised, with Chris signing each book, shaking each hand, and genuinely grateful for each person who came. For their part, they were anxious not just to meet him but to thank him for his service to our country—and by extension, the service of every military member whom they couldn't personally thank. From the moment the book was published, Chris became the son, the brother, the nephew, the cousin, the kid down the street whom they couldn't personally thank. In a way, his outstanding military record was beside the point—he was a living, breathing patriot who had done his duty and come home safe to his wife and kids. Thanking him was people's way of thanking everyone in uniform.

And, of course, the book was an interesting read. It quickly became a commercial success beyond anyone's wildest dreams, including the publisher's. The hardcover debuted at number two on the *New York Times* bestseller list, then rose to number one and stayed there for more than two months. It's remained a fixture on the bestseller lists ever since, and has been translated into twenty-four languages worldwide.

It was a good read, and it had a profound effect on a lot of people. A lot of the people who bought it weren't big book readers, but they ended up engrossed. A friend of ours told us that he'd started reading the book one night while he was taking a bath with his wife. She left, went to bed, and fell asleep. She woke up at three or four and went into the bathroom. Her husband was still there, in the cold water, reading.

The funny thing is, Chris still could not have cared less about all the sales. He'd done his assignment, turned it in, and got his grade. Done deal.

As the book sales shot up, more media interviews and book signings were added. Chris was a sensation. But that also meant he had to keep working at it, and traveling.

He wanted me to come on the book tour with him, and so I did. There were plenty of times I wondered why I was even there—I tried to stay in the background. But inevitably he would point me out, and people would come over and thank me as well.

To be honest, most of the time I felt as if I didn't really deserve their thanks. I loved Chris, and that's why I was his wife and full-time mother to our kids. Getting through his deployments was just what I did. I wasn't a hero; he was.

And, as I've said here, and as I relate in *American Sniper*, I had reached a point where I needed him home. That was selfish. A lot of these women had stuck it out for years and years longer than I had. A part of me felt embarrassed that I hadn't stuck it out longer.

I finally realized that the thanks wasn't about me. Even the out-pouring of emotion for Chris wasn't just about him. We both came to represent every serviceman and -woman, and every family that supported them. People acknowledged our sacrifices on behalf of all military families.

One thing that was interesting to me: many of the people who thanked me had either had a spouse deployed overseas or been close to someone who had. Maybe it takes going through that experience to really appreciate all it involves.

We traveled through Texas for a couple of weeks, then went to the West Coast. In San Diego, near where we'd lived, a friend came up to me and said she was so glad to see us together.

"We really haven't had much quality time," I confessed. "Chris is always so busy with the media and everything."

"Yes, but I can tell he needs you."

"Really?"

"Whenever you walk away, there's a look on his face. He's looking around, wondering where you are."

Just being present for him turned out to be more important than I realized. Part of it was the toll the attention and the interviews were taking on Chris—he was reliving Iraq yet again, over and over, several times a day. But I came to realize the need was deeper than that. Having come through so much together, we had each reached the point where our love reinforced and nurtured us. Having me physically close gave him a safe base no matter how unusual or crazy the rest of the world got. With the tumult of demands for interviews and face time and all the rest, he knew he could just reach out and touch me to relax, if only for a moment.

He was my strength at home. Now, on the road, in a slightly different way, I was his.

While as a general rule Chris didn't really care what people thought about either him or the book, there was one major exception: the SEAL community. He was worried that other SEALs would think he was bragging or would get angry with him for sharing his opinions.

The book signing in Coronado put his mind at ease. One of the commanders he had respected greatly showed up with his wife and congratulated him. Just as important, his close friends all responded with enthusiasm. They were proud of him for sharing his story with humility—and especially for talking about Ryan and Marc.

We were in West Texas for a signing one evening in late January when, at the very tail end of the night, a peculiar-looking fellow ambled up to the table where Chris was standing.

"You're Chris Kyle?" said the man.

"Uh, yeah?" answered Chris.

The man handed Chris a piece of paper. "You've been served," he intoned in an overly dramatic voice.

Jesse Ventura had decided to sue Chris, claiming he had been defamed by his statements. According to Jesse, the incident never happened.

One of the unique aspects of the lawsuit was that it charged Chris with "unjust enrichment." In layman's terms, as I understood it, this meant that Jesse claimed people bought the book because he talked about decking him.

So all that information about Chris's childhood, his days as a cowboy, his time in Iraq, his medals, the people he saved, the people he couldn't save, his difficulty transitioning home, all the things I said in the book about raising the kids, how hard it was to get on without him . . . all of those things weren't the reason people bought the book? They were interested in the four hundred or so words tucked toward the back about a fight that didn't even name the principal—details that anyone could find for free on the Internet?

Awesome.

Chris wasn't worried about the lawsuit. He believed what he said and had witnesses who remembered the incident as he did.

It was an issue that would smolder for more than two years, and cause a great deal of pain.

POLAND

Jesse aside, most of the people who came to know Chris because of the book were generous when we met them and went out of their way to make Chris and me feel welcome. My uncle arranged for us to have a day together at a simulated shooting range near where he lived on the West Coast. The entire staff turned out to make sure we had fun—and to catch a glimpse of the newly famous hero.

I went through the range with him, and the results were not quite what I expected. I did well, but . . .

To give you some background: The range featured tactical situations where you did more than stand behind a bench and shoot at a paper target and a bale of hay. Videos supplied an immersive experience; it was a little like being part of a video game, except that you moved around and had a full-sized weapon as opposed to a game controller.

The results were recorded, and we reviewed them later on.

Chris's shots were all head and chest.

Mine were all in the crotch.

"Do we need to talk?" asked Chris.

I swear, there was no hostility. I was just aiming low, expecting the recoil to bring the shot up.

Really.

The most exotic place we went on the book tour was Poland. Chris had served with the GROM—Poland's equivalent of SEALs— during the war and they really took a liking to him; The Polish publishers were one of the first foreign companies to pick up the book. They worked closely with Jim on the translation, getting the nuances right, and they wanted to make a really big splash for Chris when the book came out. So they invited him to come over for the publication.

I was excited when he asked if I wanted to come. I was also a little nervous—not only had I never been out of the country before, but I'd never left the kids for so long or been so far away from them.

Not that I was worried—they were with their grandparents—but still . . .

Before we left, Chris and I got out some index cards and wrote little notes for the kids. Each note was specific for the kid:

Bubba:
Your smile makes me smile and your laugh makes
my heart happy.
You make my life happy! I love you!!!
Love, Mama

Bubba:
I love to see you smile even when you are upset.
You are a great kid. I love you so much.
Love, Daddy

Bubba:
I love having fun with you and being with you. I am so
blessed and happy you are my son!!!
I love you!!!
Love, Mama

Bubba:
You are the greatest little man in the whole world. I love
you so much and miss you.
Love, Daddy

Angel:
I love how kind you are. Your smile and laugh make
my days happy. I love you!!!
Love, Mama

Angel:
You have such a tender heart. I love and miss your hugs.
Love, Daddy

Angel:
You are very helpful and loving. I am proud of you and
love you with all my heart!!!
Love, Mama

Angel:
You are a kind-hearted girl, and you make
me proud every day.
Love Daddy

We later framed them and hung them in their rooms.

The Poles treated us like movie stars. We got a tour of the Polish White House, and we got to spend some time on a shooting range together. It wasn't exactly a vacation, but it was close.

It was interesting to watch Chris during interviews. The Poles asked some harder questions than I expected, but he was always comfortable answering.

Not me. I had to walk out of the room during one interview when the questions seemed to be accusing him of being a murderer—but Chris was always Chris: straight to the point and never really bothered by the attitude of the person interviewing him, good or bad.

BRADLEY COOPER

The success of the book generated a lot of interest from Hollywood. Even before Chris started working with Jim on the book, he had spent some time with a screenwriter from Hollywood, Jason Hall. Jason came out to Texas and spent a few days talking to Chris about a possible script, but he hadn't finished it yet. The book put a new impetus on getting that done.

To make a movie based on a book and someone's life, the movie producers have to obtain the rights. Among the people who asked about them was Bradley Cooper, thanks to Jason, who'd championed Chris and the book. Cooper was already a huge star, one who had a reputation for taking big risks and trying a variety of roles (including one in the TV series *Alias*—the connection I promised earlier).

None of that was important to Chris. If there was a movie, he wanted the actor who portrayed him to be a *true* American. He couldn't stand actors who would make unpatriotic statements against the war and then turn around and do war films. He'd told Jim he didn't want a hypocrite playing him. I think he would have chosen not to let a movie be done rather than agree to let people proceed with it whom he didn't consider patriotic.

And so for Chris, the most impressive thing about Bradley Cooper was not his acting ability or the enormous research he put into his roles, but the work he'd done helping veterans. He was a supporter of Got Your 6, an organization that helps veterans reintegrate into family life and their communities. He had also done some USO tours. I couldn't imagine a better match.

Still, Chris didn't just say okay. He talked to Bradley before deciding to let him option the book and his life rights.

I remember Chris coming out of his home office after the final conversation. He was smiling; Bradley had a great sense of humor, which was probably the first thing they bonded over.

"How'd it go?" I asked.

"Went good. I told him, 'My only concern with you, Bradley—I might have to tie you up with a rope and pull you behind my truck to knock some of the pretty off you.'"

Bradley laughed. Still, he did just about everything short of that to prepare for the movie. He grew a beard, studied photos and videos, and worked out like a madman, getting himself into the proper shape to play a SEAL in the movie.

Many, many things had to be done before the movie actually was made. The most important was finding a director.

We had no say in that, but it was fun to fantasize. One night when we were in the kitchen, I looked over at Chris and asked, "Who would you want directing the movie?"

"I don't know." He shrugged.

"Wouldn't Clint Eastwood be fantastic?"

"Hell, yes," he said.

In truth, everything was fantasy: many books are optioned but few become movies, so we couldn't even be sure there would be a movie. Given that we had no control over it, we turned our attention to other things.

TV SHOW

That spring, some television producers approached Chris through his agents and asked if he'd be interested in starring in a show called

Stars Earn Stripes. Produced by Mark Burnett, the show paired celebrities with former military and law enforcement professionals in a range of missions from airborne drops to shootouts. Chris was paired with Dean Cain, aka "Superman."

Before going on set in California, the producers had Chris fill out a form that, among other things, listed some of his special qualifications. His answer: *Shooting, shit talking, and beer drinking.*

Chris thought the show would help advertise some of the different things that military people were trained in. I think the final product veered a little too heavily toward special effects, smoke and mirrors, and the normal show business trappings for his taste—it was fun, certainly, but not very educational. The training that the celebrities had to do generally didn't make it to the actual show; missing that may have left viewers with the wrong idea that what they were doing was a lot easier than it was.

Chris's favorite part of the project may have been the remote location—he didn't have cell reception through most of the training and shooting sessions, so no one could bother him for nearly a month. That was even better than a vacation for him.

The day the show premiered, a friend hosted a little party to celebrate back in Dallas. Someone came up with the idea of making T-shirts; it was very last minute, so we all grabbed some Magic Markers and white T-shirts and scrawled "Team Kyle" on them. Chris loved it, even if he did think it was a bit much.

Dean won four out of the six competitions, though in the finale he lost to WWE Divas Champion Eva Torres.

The TV experience was novel, but Chris was starting to accept the fact that he was a celebrity. If it had happened twelve months before, it might have seemed surreal. Now it was just the way things were.

One of the great things that Chris taught me was not to get crazy about how things looked—specifically about how the house looked when people came over. I'd grown up in a home where nothing was out of place when company came over, and I always obsessed if we were having company. This meant running around like crazy straightening the house, vacuuming, mopping, cleaning.

Chris would look at my frenzy and ask, "These people are our friends, right?"

"Well, sure."

"Then why are we going through all this trouble? They'll love us the way we are."

He was right. Appearances don't matter—though company *was* a good excuse to clean the house.

Gradually, I learned not to obsess. Now, if you come to my house, some days it'll look really good. Other days, it'll look like a tornado hit. I've come to accept that it really doesn't matter.

The success of *American Sniper* encouraged the publisher to ask Chris to do more books. After tentatively agreeing to do a series of fictional novels with Jim based on some of his experiences, Chris decided to put that project on hold and do a nonfiction history book. He'd been interested in history from the time he was young, and after talking with Peter Hubbard, his editor at HarperCollins, came up with an idea that intrigued him—telling the history of America through the story of ten different guns that had helped shape our country.

The book had a very tight deadline—it was due at the end of 2012. Chris simply added it to his list.

Meanwhile, his celebrity brought him a lot of other opportunities. The number of people and companies approaching Chris for product endorsements and speaking engagements made it clear that he could look far beyond Craft to make a living. He commissioned a personal logo and began exploring his options.

PRESSURES

All my life, fame had been for someone else: the movie star, the football hero, the politician. Now I was living with it.

Chris's "role" as a hero had never seemed strange: it had evolved naturally from who he was. He was a strong man, emotionally as well as physically—my rock, to use an old cliché. His personality demanded that he protect other people, and put in the right situation, he would do that again and again. So the fact that he was a hero on the battlefield made absolute sense. Of course he was brave and had done a lot of courageous things in combat: he was Chris.

But becoming famous? That was something in a different direction. Chris was a humble man—that was every bit as critical to his personality as being a protector. He retained that. He still didn't brag; he talked about his experiences in very direct answers, as he always had, but the reluctance remained in the tightness of his grin. The difference now was that people knew what questions to ask because of the book. And of course they knew to ask them because he was *Chris Kyle!*

Exclamation mark intentional.

His humility managed to come through in person, but that only made him more endearing. Being humble and honest made him even more of a hero—and more famous.

Movie stars and football players and all sorts of celebrities now wanted to meet him. He had become famous himself, joining whatever magical circle that is.

Yet so much of our lives didn't change. We still lived in our house, we still struggled to have dinner together and make sure the kids got to school on time. Chris took the garbage out like everyone else.

But he was *famous!*

Was I famous, too?

I didn't think so. I went to the book signings and the events and enjoyed being who I was—wife of an American hero. Chris Kyle's wife. That was my identity; I was wife and mother. I wanted to be the best possible wife and mother, but you don't get famous for that. Which was fine.

I think for Chris, all the notoriety became an extension of his natural friendliness. Even before all of this, people said he could make friends just walking down the street. In a way, this was more of the same—though on steroids.

He wasn't always comfortable with the attention. It put pressure on him in a way that I didn't entirely understand at the time. He didn't feel he needed to live up to people's expectations, but he did feel he owed them something, if only politeness. Meanwhile, he owed himself the knowledge of who he really was—not the person they thought he was.

I was his rock, or maybe his touchstone with reality. I wasn't famous, and in his mind, he wasn't famous either. Because fame wasn't real. But Chris Kyle was.

Fame is a funny thing. In one sense, it brought us a lot of new friends and acquaintances from all different walks of life. On the other hand, it closed our circle down. You can only spend so much time with people.

And you can only spend so much time straightening out misconceptions. I didn't realize this at first; it was a lesson I had to learn as time went on.

Fame for any reason tends to bring out detractors and haters, people who whisper things that aren't true or are distortions of the truth. Online especially, people would simply make things up, projecting their own hang-ups and hatred on Chris in comments on Facebook, in online book reviews, and the like. People said all sorts of BS.

Chris ignored most of it, pretty regularly. I tried to, but occasionally I'd see something and burn.

There were so many things that were so far from the truth that they're not worth mentioning.

It got worse with the lawsuits. But I'm getting ahead of myself.

It's one thing to see criticism and made-up baloney in online comments from anonymous sources, and another to hear echoes of it from people you think are friends. Chris was mostly able to shrug and move on. I found it more difficult.

I want people to like me. And I want to like them. Even casual acquaintances, professionals like lawyers and accountants, or office workers—I feel a need to deal with them as friends. As Chris's fame brought us in contact with more and more people, I struggled to deal with them all as friends. Anything less just didn't feel right.

Eventually, that would have to change.

In late fall, Chris was called to give a deposition in the Ventura case.

Chris took it very calmly, sitting for hours and answering the questions politely.

It had been six years since the incident, and memories had faded. While we knew from working on the book and discovery in the lawsuit that other people who'd been there remembered it roughly the same way, there were some very minor discrepancies in the accounts. But Chris was careful not to speak with people who were going to be called as witnesses. "I'm not supposed to," he told me. "And besides, I know from our intel work that if there *aren't* discrepancies, then it's very likely the story is made up. If everyone remembers it the same way—especially after time has passed—well, something is up."

He was extremely confident that the trial would go his way. He always insisted on taking the high road. When asked about it after the suit was filed, he would smile and not say anything more.

Maybe not smile. Maybe grit his teeth, at least at home.

Chris and I met with a financial adviser to help plan how to give proceeds of the book away. Before we began, Chris told him that, in the event of his death, all of the money was to go to me and the kids.

"You'll be the family of the fallen, then," he said when I tried to object.

Some of the families Chris wanted to help told him that while they appreciated the thought, they didn't want the money. While we did give away a portion, his intentions were soon overtaken by events.

The kids weren't oblivious to the new demands on Chris, but we insulated them as much as possible. Their dad was often away for TV or other appearances. But overall he was home a lot more than he had been when they were younger and he was a SEAL. He brought them a lot of joy, whether by tossing a ball around or tickling them, teaching them how to hunt or just watching TV. Angel loved to climb into his lap and cuddle. His tensions and cares would melt away as he held her.

I know there's a saying about "Daddy's little girl wrapping him around her finger." Chris and Angel didn't have that kind of relationship, exactly. She was definitely *his* girl—he was closer to her than probably any other female on the planet, including me. But he also held her to high standards. She couldn't get away with being bad or taking advantage of him.

She could see in his face that he was absolutely delighted by her. He "got" her humor, and he definitely got her.

One day he had to leave on an overnight trip. We said good-bye and closed the door; Angel and I went into the kitchen.

She had tears in her eyes.

"Okay, honey?" I asked.

"Yeah. I know he's coming back tomorrow," she said. "I guess I just miss him already."

I told Chris what she'd said later on that night when he called to check in. It was something cute she'd done.

"Wow," he said. "I feel like I've just been punched in the stomach."

He slid down the wall to the floor, hand to his face, devastated by his daughter's simple statement of love.

"I wasn't trying to make you feel bad," I told him. "I'm sorry."

"It's okay."

We talked a little more, then he hung up the phone. The man he was traveling with said later that he looked wounded the whole rest of the trip.

The business, the fame, and just the everyday things that a father and husband has to deal with—it must have been a heavy load. I think back about it now and I'm truly sorry that he had to bear all of that.

He didn't complain. That wouldn't have been Chris.

Around Thanksgiving, Chris mentioned to his brother Jeff that he was thinking of getting rid of his truck. I was floored. He'd wanted a tricked-out black pickup for years before he got it, and labored so hard to get it just the way he wanted.

"Babe," I said to him later on, "I'm shocked—why are you going to get rid of your truck?"

"Ah, I don't know," he said.

"What are you going to get in its place?"

"A 250 or something," he said, referring to a good-sized Ford work truck. "Something inconspicuous."

Not too long after that, one of our friends died in an accident. We drove up to the funeral and I was struck by how strange it was—how vastly the family's lives had changed because of the death, while for us everything was still "normal." We would grieve with them, but things would continue as they were.

Chris and I talked about the ceremony on the way home.

"There were a lot of people there," I said. "I would like a small ceremony."

"For a funeral?"

"Well, yeah."

"I want a big funeral," he said. "I'm gone, right? Blow it out."

He wanted bagpipes, music, and a large crowd.

We talked a bit more. "Do you still want to be buried in Arlington National Cemetery?" I asked. We'd discussed the possibility several times; it had been among his dearest wishes.

"I don't know if I feel that way anymore," he confessed.

"Why is that?"

"I just want to be wherever is best for ya'll."

I was so taken aback by that. But it stayed with me.

FRIENDS—CHAD

Leanne Littlefield and I met each other on the local soccer fields where our kids were on teams together. We were friends, close friends, for a while before her husband Chad and Chris met. Once we introduced them, the two men seemed to bond very naturally. Chad's easygoing personality matched well with Chris's. Chad didn't want or need anything out of the friendship; he just genuinely liked Chris, and vice versa. They started hanging out on weekends, watching football or fooling around with the kids. Leanne and I would hang out in the kitchen and we'd all have a relaxing, fun time. Chad even helped Chris clean out the garage one day—if there's a stronger test of suburban male friendship, I can't think of it.

"You know, I think Chad would take a bullet for me," said Chris one night when we were getting ready for bed.

"Really? That's an awfully big thing."

"Yeah, but I really do."

We were on a brief vacation trip with the kids when our tenth wedding anniversary came up.

It was almost an afterthought for both us. *Hey, it's our anniversary! We should do something special.*

We didn't. We both thought that the fact that we were together and happy was enough. There was no need to clink champagne glasses or have some special night out, let alone invite friends or have a party. We knew, and that was what mattered.

In retrospect, I think this was a mistake. You should do anything you can to strengthen your marriage and celebrate it. Milestones help you appreciate what you have. I think it's too easy to forget how much you love someone if you don't celebrate once in a while. If nothing else, those special occasions give you a chance to focus on the other person and spend some meaningful time with them.

Chris and I talked about it later. We decided that we would never let the anniversary pass again without some sort of celebration and formal acknowledgment.

It turned out we never got the chance.

I don't know if it was the pressures or what, but toward the end of 2012, Chris mentioned that he was thinking of giving up "dipping"—chewing smokeless tobacco.

Chew had been part of Chris forever, certainly since I'd known him. It certainly wasn't healthy for him—especially since he generally would swallow the spit, if not the tobacco. *Ewww—yuck!* But he always felt that it was something he wanted to do and didn't worry about the health consequences.

"You're really thinking of quitting?" I asked when he mentioned it.

"Yup."

"Well, anything I can do, let me know."

"I will."

ATTENTION AND TEMPTATION

Chris's activities took him to many places. His new status as a celebrity brought many more invitations to events like charity hunts and fund-raisers.

It also brought a lot of attention from people he didn't know. Mixed in there were a few female admirers, attracted to either his fame, what he represented, or his good looks—can't blame them for that!

There were a lot of temptations, I'm sure. Most of his events had hotel rooms, ranches, alcohol, and women. Granted, they were all somebody else's wife or girlfriend, but my memory of Team infidelities hadn't quite left me. Sometimes opportunity knocks and sometimes people are just plain stupid in the moment. I had to remind myself of the good man I was married to each time he left.

I *did* trust him. I didn't bother checking on his phone or social media accounts—I didn't even write down the passwords, though he made no secret of them to me. Still, as confident as I was that he would remain faithful, there must have been a small sliver of doubt in my mind, given what had happened with the old girlfriend.

It was getting close to Christmas. My parents were visiting. I got up early and saw his iPad happened to be sitting in the kitchen. The screen was lit with a message stream from a young woman who had struck up a conversation. They'd exchanged over two hundred messages over the past month. Most of it was innocuous—at least from Chris's side.

> HER: How old are you?
> CHRIS: I'm an old man.
> HER: Look at this buck I just shot.
> CHRIS: That's a good one.

What bothered me wasn't so much the girl's obvious flirting, but the fact that Chris hadn't cut it off. I mean, two-hundred-plus messages? *Come on!*

But my reaction may have been over the top.

"I don't need this shit!" I yelled, storming into the bedroom where he was still asleep. I threw my coffee—lukewarm, fortunately—all over him.

"What? What?" he mumbled, not yet awake.

"Get the hell out!" I screamed.

There were a lot of expletives. As a Navy SEAL, Chris had surely heard worse—even from me—but he was completely caught off guard.

"I'm not hiding anything!" he protested when he realized from my tirade what I was mad about.

I continued to let him have it.

"The kids can hear you," he said finally.

"Good!" I screamed.

On and on—it was a good rant, let me tell you. I completely and totally lost it. Chris got up and left, wisely seeing that as the smart thing to do.

I was still frothing. My dad came in, no doubt wondering why his daughter had turned into the Wicked Witch of the West. I showed him some of the messages.

"Look at this! Look at this!" I shouted, as if my father were Chris's defense attorney. "What do you think of this? Why would he do this?"

"These are no big deal," said my dad.

"It is a big deal. This how it starts."

I was furious. If I hadn't had the one experience with the old girlfriend, maybe I wouldn't have gone so ballistic. In any event, I just saw red.

To his credit, my father remained calm, quietly pointing out that the evidence showed Chris wasn't doing anything more than responding in what by any interpretation was an innocuous manner.

I left the house and went over to a friend's, explaining what had happened. By the time I finished, I felt embarrassed, and had finally realized that—well, obviously nothing was going on and, yes, okay, I did totally overreact.

I called Chris and apologized.

"Please come home," I told him.

He did. Later on, we talked. I let myself be vulnerable and honest, admitting that I still felt some hurt from the entire affair (or non-affair) he'd had with his old girlfriend. We talked about trust and how hard it was for me to completely let go of my fears, even though I knew he was at his heart an honorable man and faithful husband.

"I'm sorry," I told him. "I don't want you to think that I'll never let it go."

He turned off all the messaging on his Facebook account and took other steps on the others. "I don't need this," he told me. "I'm sorry that it hurt you."

Over the next few days, we talked about other things, things I'd been carrying around for a long time.

"Chris, I think you slept with that girl," I told him finally, referring to the old girlfriend. "You just didn't want to admit it."

He listened. He didn't say yes. He didn't say no. He just listened.

"I can do better for you," he said finally.

Somehow, the strife made our marriage better. We got back to holding hands and making out on the couch, touching each other during the day, and cuddling in bed.

We'd been distracted by everything, and now we returned to what was important. We laughed; we had fun. I felt again like we were made for each other.

There is a point for everyone, I think, where physical attraction is everything, and it can lead to love. A person looks beautiful to you, and therefore you love them. Beyond that, as you grow with them, as your love deepens, your perception of beauty starts to deepen. At that point, what you love becomes beautiful—or rather, you are better equipped to recognize the inherent beauty.

We were there. Chris would gaze at me in the mirror from the bedroom as I was getting ready for bed, and his eyes would be filled with love. I would lie next to him on the bed and just feel loved, secure in the knowledge that the most amazing man in the world had me in his arms.

And yet, there was a little part of me, a nagging part, that told me I didn't deserve all this happiness. I remember calling a girlfriend around this time and raving about how our marriage seemed to have gone to a new level: *Amazing.*

Then I added, "But I feel like something bad is going to happen to one of us. Because it's just too perfect."

Sometime in the fall of 2012, Chris told me he had found out some things that the two other principals in his company, Bo French and Steven Young, had done.

He knew they had started another company, this one called Craft International Risk Management (CIRM) LLC; it had been registered as a company in August of 2011. In his opinion, the two corporations were interrelated, except for one thing: Chris wasn't one of the owners of CIRM. That seemed very unusual to him, but he nonetheless agreed. Subsequently, though, Chris told me he was surprised and hurt to discover that they had borrowed money from Craft to start CIRM without telling him. He also worried that some contracts might be moved from Craft to CIRM.

Chris talked to them and they assured him it was always their intent to add him to the company and that they were paying back the money. (They later told me that they had paid back a little more than half.) They also told him that there were contracts they couldn't get because of having an American sniper on the paperwork. Some people in other countries they might want to work with would be averse to supporting an American sniper; this, they said, was the reason for the new company.

We talked about it quite a lot. It really bothered him; I wasn't sure what to make of it myself.

After a lot of thought, Chris told me he didn't think the arrangement was right. He was going to tell his partners in Craft that he needed to be officially a part of the new company. And it needed to be done immediately.

It was a major change for him. In general, Chris operated on a handshake, and was always willing to take people at their word. The fact that he might not get a contract for months after being told something never bothered him; he just trusted that people would do the right thing.

Coming from the pharmaceutical world, I looked at things quite a bit differently. But the business was his.

CHRISTMAS

A couple of days before Christmas 2012, I stood in the kitchen baking batches of cookies. Angel and Bubba were helping and playing with Chris at the same time; at some point, we spontaneously began singing Christmas carols.

It had been an incredible year. Chris's book had come out and become an international sensation. He was famous, not just in our house as a great dad but around the world as a hero. He'd been on the top television news programs and starred in a reality series. Corporations and organizations were vying to get him to speak. There was a movie in the works, another book, and talk of maybe another TV series and a string of endorsements. We'd traveled across the country and even to Europe.

For me, it had been a hectic and even harrowing twelve months. I'd seen a lot of the bad side of people, but also experienced much more of the good. Talking to people who came to the book signings, I'd had my faith in patriotism and our country renewed.

But for me, the best thing that happened that year was all of us standing in that kitchen, singing and laughing.

My husband was back. He was whole. The love of my life was once more a true partner in our marriage and a father who could romp with the kids and teach them everything we held dear.

It was a perfect, perfect moment, everything I had envisioned when we spoke those vows on the boat, everything I had hoped for when I clamped my arms around Chris when he returned from his last deployment.

Oh God, I thought, let this moment go on forever.

FOUR

SHATTERED

February 2, 2013, was a Saturday like many of our Saturdays. Until it wasn't.

WORRIED AND WORSE

Around two thirty that afternoon, a friend called and asked if we wanted to join her and her husband for a birthday dinner at an area restaurant.

"I don't know if we can," I told her. "Chris is out and—"

"Call him and ask if he wants to come."

"I don't want to bother him," I said, explaining that he and Chad Littlefield were with a veteran and probably in the middle of talking to him about how hard it can be to adjust to civilian life. They'd been gone a few hours, and I didn't expect them back for a while more.

"Oh, go ahead, call. He won't care."

I knew she was right, and so I called.

Chris answered pretty quick.

"How's it going?" I asked.

"Fine."

I could tell it wasn't.

"I'll make this quick," I said. "I just called to know if you wanted to go out for Cheryl's birthday tonight."

"Yeah, that's great."

"All right. I'm going to let you go."

"Yup." He was irritated about something for sure.

Around four, Leanne Littlefield called me. She and Chad had planned to take her dad and mom out to celebrate her father's retirement from the fire department.

"Have you heard from Chad or Chris?" she asked.

"No."

"Chad said he'd be home by now. And he hasn't answered his cell."

"The reception out there is bad sometimes," I told her. "I'll call Chris and see if I can get him."

"All right. Call me back."

I texted Chris, but didn't get a response. I went and picked up Bubba, dropped off Angel's friend, and came back home.

"Guess what, guys," I told them. "We're gonna go out to dinner with Cheryl and the family!"

"Awesome," said Bubba. "This is the best day of my life!"

We cleaned up and got ready. It was unusual for Chris not to answer my text. Still, there were plenty of reasons he might not, starting with bad cell reception.

Chris's terse reply earlier made me think that the veteran, Eddie Routh, might be in crisis mode, maybe even ready to hurt himself. Suicide was a horrible side effect of the war and PTSD. Chris had talked to a couple of guys close to suicide before. It was heartbreaking to think about young men ready to throw their lives away because they weren't getting adequate care. It could take quite a lot of persuasion to get them off the ledge and seek the help they needed.

Leanne called again. "Have you heard anything?"

"No."

"Damn it—I have to leave now to get to Dallas. He's going to be way late."

"I'm sure they're okay," I said. "Maybe they busted a tire in a no-reception zone."

That was bordering on wishful if not desperate thinking. By now it was getting dark. It was unlike Chris to be this late without calling or texting. I went outside and sent him another text.

Are you OK? I'm getting worried.

I knew if he got that, he would text right back that he was fine. I hated to share my fears with him. But today . . .

I waited, but there was no reply.

Finally, I decided the best thing to do would be to take the kids and let him join us at the restaurant later. Four other neighboring families had been recruited for the impromptu party. We all happened to go out at roughly the same time, and stopped to chat out on the driveway.

I had just gotten the kids in the SUV when a police car drove down the road. It was Mark, a friend of Chris's, who often stopped by to say hi and pass the time.

"Hey, Mark," I said, going over to him as he pulled up. "Everything okay?"

"Have you heard from Chris?"

"No. Mark, what's going on?"

"Have you seen his truck?"

"No."

Externally, I was very calm. But inside I could feel myself starting to panic. These were not normal questions. No way.

"What's going on?" I asked again.

"I need to know where his truck is."

"Mark, what is going on?"

"I've heard he's been hurt," Mark told me. "I need his license plate number."

A hard breath. "Okay." Another hard breath.

I went across the street to one of our friends. As she came over, I felt the panic and fear and emotion surging inside me.

"What's going on?" she asked.

"I—I think Chris has been hurt."

I caught myself before I lost it. I could see the rest of the neighbors looking over. A tear or two slipped past my guard.

"I want you with me, okay?" I told her.

"Yes, of course."

"Just you."

"Yes, wait."

I took out my cell phone and called another friend. "Could the kids spend the night with you?"

"What's wrong?" she asked.

"I just need you to do that."

"I'm on my way." She was eight and a half months pregnant and had four kids, but she didn't even waste time asking for details. She must have heard something in my voice that said I needed her. She was there within five minutes.

I went in and grabbed the kids' PJs.

"Hey guys," I said coming back out. "You can have a sleepover!"

"Mom, is everything okay?" asked Bubba.

"I don't know," I said. "I think so. I just have to work on some things."

"Okay."

"Mom, is everything okay?" Bubba asked again.

"I think it is."

My friend came and the kids left. I went inside with Mark and found the information about the truck.

"And you haven't seen it today?" he asked again.

"Not since Chris left."

"I want you to stay inside."

"Chris has been shot?" I said. I don't know why.

"That's what I heard."

Repeating these memories make them fly back. Time compresses, and I am once more in my house in February, fearing the worst but not willing to admit it. My time as a SEAL wife had taught me that you never to go to that worst place emotionally, until you are forced to.

Even in the most deliberate telling, the memories never run cold. They always burn, shaking my voice and curdling my chest.

I called my mom.

"Mom, I can't talk, okay?" I said quickly.

"Okay," she answered.

"Chris has been shot. I don't know where he is. I want you to pray for him. Dad, too. I just need you to pray."

"Oh my God. OK, honey, we will be praying."

"I'll call you when I know something."

"Okay."

I got off the phone. My cell phone began exploding with text messages and calls from people asking what was going on. I didn't know what to answer, and so I didn't.

Okay, he's been shot, I thought. Probably in the stomach. Gut wounds are terrible, but he'll make it. This sounds really bad, but it's survivable.

I knew if he'd been shot in the hand or the leg, I'd have heard from him by now. So it had to be something a little more serious— but not *too* serious. I didn't think, or didn't allow myself to think, that it would be anything worse. I just couldn't.

We can get through this, Chris. We've gotten through so much already.

People started coming into the house. Three men I didn't know walked into my kitchen.

Who are you? Why are you here?

I found out later that they were pastors from local churches. I'm sure someone told me, but it didn't register, maybe because that would have led to the inevitable conclusion that Chris was dead.

I floated along for a while in something like denial. Harsh reality pounded at the doors and every window, but I refused to acknowledge it.

Sorrow telescopes time and rearranges it. Things that happened quickly seem in memory to have taken ages. The order becomes jumbled—which thing did I do first, which next, what then?

I called Leanne. She was at the restaurant, still expecting Chad to show up any moment.

"Leanne, Chris is hurt. His truck is missing. I don't know what's going on."

"Oh my God, Taya," she said. "What's happening? Where's Chad?"

"I don't know. I'll call you as soon as I find out."

"I'm leaving Dallas right now and coming home."

"Okay."

The phone rang as soon as I hung up. It was Debbie Lee, Marc Lee's mother.

"Hey Debbie, what's up?" I said. She had texted, and was now calling. I didn't want to be rude, but I knew I needed to keep the line open.

"I—I heard about Chris, is it true?"

"What have you heard?" I asked.

"I heard . . . bad things."

"What bad things?"

"Uh . . ."

"Damn it, Debbie! What have you heard?"

Debbie took a deep breath. "I heard he was killed."

"Okay. Well, I hadn't heard that. I'll let you know if I hear."

I got off the phone angry— How dare people say that! You NEVER go to that place. Until . . .'

Chris is dead?

A friend came in. "Taya, Mark wants to talk to you."

"Okay."

I went down the hall, where Mark and another police officer were waiting.

I had heard so many times before about people who got horrible news falling to their knees or passing out, and I wondered how I would react. Now here I was.

"Mark?"

I looked at him. From what I remember, his eyes were down-cast; he stood strong in his uniform, and yet he looked crestfallen, defeated.

He nodded his head. "I'm sorry."

"He's dead?" I asked. "Chris is dead?"

He nodded again.

The tears started. "Mark, are you sure?"

"Yeah. Sorry."

The tears came in a downpour.

"Mark, Mark, I'm sorry. But I have to know—are you one hundred percent sure? Is there any way you are wrong? Any possibility you are wrong? Before I go down this road—are you one hundred percent sure?"

How many other times had I stared at this scene from afar, thinking that Chris was dead or dying? How many times had I rehearsed myself for the possibility of the deepest, darkest sorrow?

But that was ages ago, another lifetime. The time of danger had passed. We had gotten to a place where the only thing before us was happiness and fun and growing old together.

But it was now that my deepest fears had come true. Now that I stood in the hall, grief welling inside me, tears flowing.

"Are you one hundred percent sure?" I demanded. "Are you one hundred percent sure?"

"They wouldn't have me tell you if there was any doubt," said Mark.

"Okay," I whispered, leaning against the wall. "Okay. Okay."

Much later, Kim, my good friend who was with me, described the scene as the police told me what they knew. "It was like you went into business mode," she said.

Outwardly I was calm, in charge—I would let no one see the utter emptiness inside me. I would not share my despair, but rather take charge and get things done. I was strong.

Inside, I was desperate and weak and screaming.

I walked back to my kitchen.

"All right," I said. "Let's say a prayer."

We all held hands in the kitchen. Tears fell down my face.

"Pray for Chris," I said, struggling to push the words out. "I know exactly where he is, but I want you to pray that his transition is going okay."

One of the pastors said a general prayer about the passage of the soul to the afterlife.

"Okay," I said when the prayer was over. "But I want to pray for Chris, the man. I want to hear his name."

Another pastor started another prayer, this one a little more personal. I looked down at the floor as we finished.

"Thank you," I told them. Then I asked Kim to have them leave. Priests and death were in my worst nightmares while Chris was deployed, and I just couldn't deal with them there.

I called my mother and told her Chris was dead.

"Oh my God," she said. "I'm so sorry."

"I know, I know," I said. "I have to go, though—"

"I'm on my way."

I hung up. I called Chris's dad.

"Wayne, I have to tell you something. Are you somewhere sitting down? Where you can talk?"

"I'm at the police station," he told me.

"Oh." He knew.

"We'll be heading up there soon," he told me.

"Thank you."

I called Karen, a good friend in San Diego who's a doctor. Anything big that happens in my life, she knows, usually ahead of time.

She was having dinner. She stepped away and answered.

"I have to tell you something and then I have to go," I said. "I can't talk. You remember I told you Chris was taking a veteran shooting this weekend? Okay, okay, okay—he shot and killed Chris."

"Oh!" Karen said.

"I have to go."

After I hung up, I realized that she would try and come out to be with me. She'd just had back surgery, and I was sure the flight would be extremely painful—at that point, she couldn't even sit in a car for twenty minutes without excruciating pain.

I called back.

"I'm coming," she told me, even before I could object.

"But—"

"I'm coming," she insisted. "I already have my flight."

"You can't fly! Your back."

"Taya, I'll be there soon."

I found out later that she stood up for nearly the entire flight.

My sister called. Friends called.

Leanne again. "Taya, what's happening?"

"Where are you?"

"Up by the soccer fields," she said. It was five minutes from my house.

"Leanne, just get here, okay? Get here safely."

"Taya, tell me what's happening? Is Chris okay? Is Chad okay?"

"Leanne, pull over."

"Okay."

"Chris is dead," I told her. "I don't know about Chad. Please, get here safely."

She pulled into the driveway a few minutes later. Inside, she sat on the couch. I went over and sat on the coffee table, grabbing her hand. By now, we knew that two bodies had been found, though Chad had not yet been identified as a victim.

"We don't know what happened," I told her.

She started to break down.

"Don't do this," I said. "We don't know what's happened."

"They found two bodies—it has to be Chad."

"We don't know," I insisted.

"Why do they know it's Chris and not Chad?!"

"I don't know. But it could be anybody. Hang in there until we know."

"He's got tattoos! I can tell them about the tattoos!" Suddenly she looked at me. "Oh, my God. You've just lost your husband. How are you comforting me?"

"It's okay," I insisted. "We're going to get through this together."

I called the friend who was watching the kids and talked to her husband, telling him what had happened. "Chris was killed. Tell your wife when the time is right. Please keep the kids until the morning, but don't tell them. I'll tell them when I get them."

"Oh my God. Of course."

"Make sure that they have a good meal in the morning, because it's going to be hard for a while."

"Yes."

"Call me when they wake up in the morning."

Leanne's friends and family came in. By now the house was filled with people. I stood up.

"Guys," I said to a few of our friends. "I'm going for a walk. You want to come?"

"Are you sure you want to do that?" asked someone.

"I'm just doing it. You don't have to come."

I got up and went to the door. Five or six men followed. Outside, I walked to the end of the driveway, and then I just started to run. I ran and ran until my lungs started to hurt.

It was dark. The neighborhood was calm and quiet, as if nothing had happened, as if the world had not turned itself upside down.

We walked around to the street behind my house. I saw Wayne's truck pull up on the street behind the house. I managed to meet him outside and collapsed into his arms.

We were still hugging when someone said they'd just positively identified Chad.

God, I thought, horrified that I wasn't there when Leanne found out. I turned and ran up the driveway toward the house.

Leanne came out and saw me. We collapsed together, both bawling.

"I'm going to go to my house," she said. "But I'm here for you."

"I'm here for you," I answered.

"I was mad at him for being late."

"Of course you were. Don't do this to yourself."

"I love you."

"I love you."

Inside the house, people crowded in. They kept coming, friends, people I didn't know. Time stood still, yet sped on. People came; eventually they had to go home, exhausted. Wayne and Deby went into the guest room to rest. My friend Kim drifted off on the couch.

Another friend, Clint, laid his head on the kitchen counter and promptly fell asleep.

I found myself on the couch, the last one awake.

"What happened to you, Chris?" I asked. Maybe aloud, maybe not. "What happened?"

I got the sense that he was there with me, trying to comfort me.

Did this really happen? Is this really it?

How am I going to tell the kids?

If he was there, he couldn't tell me.

TELLING THE KIDS

Somehow, it became the next morning.

I don't remember sleeping. I just remember walking to the kitchen and finding Wayne already up. He asked how I was going to tell the kids and offered to do it with me. I thanked him, but told him it was something I had to do alone.

"I'm going to tell them outside," I said. "I don't want that horrible memory to be inside the house."

I was improvising, still forming a plan as I spoke. I thought maybe I would go to a park and meet them there. But when they came over to the house with our friends, I realized I didn't have the energy or the heart to leave our home. I met them outside on the lawn, trying to act as if nothing was wrong.

"Hey, Mom," said Bubba.

"Did you have a good time?" I asked.

"Yes . . . yes."

"I need to talk to you, actually." I sat down on the lawn. They sat with me. "Sit on my lap, okay? Both of you?"

Bubba sat on my right knee and Angel on my left. I took a deep breath.

"Um." I was already crying. "Daddy's hurt," I told them.

They looked at me. I closed my eyes.

"Is he dead?" blurted Angel.

I opened my eyes and nodded yes. She let out a cry that came from her gut. Bubba's eyes glassed over and tears poured out. I held them both close. "I'm so sorry, guys. I'm so sorry."

We stayed there for minutes or hours. Finally, Bubba asked if we could go inside.

"Yes," I told him.

Inside, everyone had given us space; the living room was empty. We sat on the couch and I told them what had happened.

"Daddy was helping someone," I said. "There was something really, really wrong with that person and his brain. He shot and killed Daddy and Mr. Chad."

"Why would he do that?" asked Bubba.

"I don't know," I answered.

"Daddy's heart didn't work?" asked Angel.

"No."

"Why can't they give him another heart?"

"I . . . they can't."

We cried in silence. Finally, Bubba got up. "Can I go?" he asked.

"Yes. Do whatever you want."

Bubba started running and playing. He played nonstop for the next several days, going and going, doing his best to keep the deep sadness at a distance.

SEEING CHRIS

From the moment I heard Chris had been shot, I wanted to go to him. The police insisted that I not go to the murder scene, and they kept me from the autopsy as well. They kept saying it was better that I not see him; I kept insisting that I had to.

Had to.

"You can't go," two or three police officers told me. All were good friends.

"I'm trying to be a good sport and respect the process," I told them calmly. "But I have to go."

"No."

"Yes!"

"You don't want to see," said one of the officers.

"Don't tell me what I want!"

Their faces were stern and adamant, but I'm sure mine was, too. Finally I exploded, talking to my good friend Rich, who's with the Dallas PD and had seen Chris when he was brought in for the autopsy.

"Goddamn, Rich!" I yelled over the phone when he called. "Why do you think it's okay for you to see him and not me? I've been patient! Enough is enough! I'm driving to Dallas and I'm not waiting."

"He looks—"

"I don't care what he looks like!"

I went on. I'm sure I used other profanities. Finally, they gave in and agreed to take me to the funeral home where Chris was to be brought at the end of the autopsy.

Was I wrong to insist that I needed to be with my husband? I'd always loved him no matter what, and was willing to see him at his worst as well as his best. Maybe I was being irrational, but I had a deep emotional need—and if you'd asked me, I would have insisted that he needed me there as well.

I knew it wasn't pretty. I knew they cut him open with a saw. I got that he was murdered.

I still needed to be there.

Our close friend Vincent—"V" for short—went with me. V had been with us on the book tour at different points and was a Dallas policeman; he was a calm, reassuring presence. Silent and watchful as he drove me to the funeral home, he waited with me outside as the white van pulled up. Someone had found a pair of blankets that had American flag motifs and covered both Chris and Chad with them. It was a thoughtful gesture, but it also meant I couldn't see my husband's face, or more than the bare outlines of his body as he was carried past.

"Give us five minutes," said someone as I started to follow the gurneys inside. "Five minutes."

"I don't want him prepared," I said. "I don't want him cleaned up."

"Five minutes."

I stepped back.

We waited—I don't know, probably less than five minutes, but it was all I could stand. I went inside, determined, unstoppable.

The funeral director met me. "I didn't do as much as I wanted. His hands are dirty from the fingerprinting."

"His hands were always dirty," I said.

Inside the room, Chris lay on the gurney, chest covered with the blanket. I bent to his face, tears pouring from my eyes, and kissed him.

How many times? A thousand. Not enough.

Never enough again.

I don't remember all of the details, or everyone who was with me as that day turned into night. I don't mean to slight anyone; it's just that my memory has twisted itself so deeply with grief and pain that teasing out the details is a herculean trial, something more than I can manage.

Wayne was there, and Deby. V. At some point, I'd told Wayne that I wouldn't have trouble seeing Chris; my difficulty would be leaving. And so it was: after hours had passed, Wayne came and told me that I had to go.

"Five more minutes," I pleaded.

He nodded and faded back. I stood by Chris's body, knowing he was no longer here, yet feeling his presence as strongly as I'd felt anything ever.

"It's time to go," Wayne said gently a half hour later.

"Five more minutes."

Once again Wayne stood back. How much time passed, I don't know. It felt like only a few seconds.

"You do have to go," Wayne said again. This time, he put his hand under my elbow. V did the same on the other side.

"I can't leave him."

"Your kids need you. It's night."

"I can't," I said. I thought about wives in other countries who lay down next to the casket all night. Why couldn't I do that?

"The kids," he said.

"The kids."

We left. My legs buckled but with their help and against all reason I kept moving. My heart kept beating and my lungs kept breathing, all against my will.

By the time I got home it was dark. The house was filled with people but I was alone, numb; the world now was a silent, distant thing, far from my body and far from my thoughts. I went into my office and sat in my favorite chair—a big, soft recliner far from the door. It was my refuge.

Four or five of my friends came in, sifting through the distance that separated me from the world, entering my pain. They knelt next to my knees, and one by one put their hands on my legs and my arms. Tears began rolling down my face.

Words came—a few, then a torrent. I recounted what the last hours had been like, seeing Chris dead, seeing the unbelievable, the unimaginable, the thing that I always dreaded and yet never thought could happen. Sometimes I whispered.

I got to feel his hair. His body was soft. I kissed his face. I told him I loved him. He wasn't all cleaned up. I was glad—I was glad. I could see his eyes, his set jaw. I could see, I could touch . . .

We sat there together, my friends around me, all of us wrapped in my tears. They said nothing, yet their powerful presence was more eloquent to me than any words can describe. It was one of the most beautiful yet saddest moments of my life. My friends didn't speak, but they understood.

How long we stayed like that, I have no idea. If I had needed them to stay for a hundred years, they would have.

People talk about how important women friends are; that night I understood.

FRIENDS, AND MORE FRIENDS

People started flooding back in, doing what they could. Marcus Luttrell and his wife Melanie were among the first to arrive from out of town. They ended up staying for days, even though they'd driven up from Houston with only the clothes on their backs. I didn't know Melanie very well, but over the next few weeks we would form a friendship that has bonds of steel. She has a quiet, calm presence and a grace that is contagious. Laughing or crying—anytime I'm around her, I feel calm.

The house filled up with active-duty and retired SEALs whom I hadn't seen in years. The military even pulled a few men who'd been close to Chris off deployment, flying them in to be with us. Southwest and American Airlines donated flights for family and close friends; someone else donated a tour bus to park on the street, giving people a place to go outside the house. The kids used it as a makeshift playhouse; we used it for meetings about the funeral arrangements and other business.

There were countless donations, large and small, of items for the funeral, food, and even cash for whatever expenses we had. People pitched in in ways I would never have imagined. The street was blockaded, and police put up a 24/7 watch.

There were many media requests—all very polite—for interviews and statements. Chris's brother Jeff took on the burden of speaking for the family, and he did so eloquently, with a simple dignity that would have made his brother proud.

I was too shattered to talk to the press, let alone appear on camera.

We took the kids to see Chris's body the next day.

He'd been cleaned up a lot. Leanne had suggested that we have a photo book with pictures of Chris; it was a brilliant idea, a way of putting their good-byes in a better, if not exactly happy, context.

Before going in, I told them they were going to see their father's body without his soul. Their dad was now in heaven; all they were going to see was the body God had loaned him for this world.

How much comfort that was, I don't know.

Bubba stood near him for a bit, then decided he was done. At some point he told me he didn't like to cry. "It hurts too much when I cry." Instead, he would run hard, play hard. The thing about grief is, we all do it in our own way, in our own time, kids included.

He went out with V and they sat together on a couch, looking at the book. Within a few moments I heard V's deep voice boom; laughter echoed in the hall. Bubba was telling him stories about his father, reminding him and all of us of who Chris really was.

Angel and I stayed with Chris.

"Can I touch his hand?" she asked.

"Yes."

There was a flower in the room. She put it on him.

In the immediate aftermath of Chris's death, Bubba dealt with his grief by playing. He played all the time, with anyone and everyone who came to the house. It was his way of staying busy and not focusing on sadness.

Angel, younger, was a little more direct, though quieter. She often looked toward her brother as her spokesman and maybe test case: his emotions guided hers. She expressed her connection with her dad directly, mentioning that she often felt him still close to her. I came to take that as a comfort and reassurance: Chris walked with us still.

Over those first few days, people continuously brought the kids toys and games. They were showered with gifts but for weeks and months. It was a touching, natural gesture, an attempt to do something tangible for them to ease their pain. But after a while, it became problematic. They got so many things that they couldn't possibly play with everything. And I was afraid they might get spoiled. There were signs of that—an expensive tablet computer left carelessly around, piles of neglected toys scattered in every room.

Even as a young'un, Chris loved
the Wild West . . .

. . . while I was a Big Wheel
Mama growin' up.

Dad and his girls—Ashley *(middle)*
and I enjoy the Oregon coast.

Chris as a
cowboy—love
those chaps!

Our wedding was like nothing I'd envisioned growing up.
Yet it was perfect.

Chris kitted up and ready to fight during his first tour in Iraq.

Preparing for battle in the desert, 2003.

Chris with a chestful of his medals in 2008, celebrating his SEAL Team's twenty-fifth anniversary.

Chris with his second family: his SEAL teammates—their faces are blacked out for security reasons.

A father and son snooze-fest before Chris had to leave for his first deployment as a sniper.

Like father, like son . . .
zzzzzz . . .

A family Christmas in Alpine.

The family inheritance—Chris introduced Bubba to horses during an early visit to Texas.

Body paint and tattoos also ran in the family.

The kids check out Daddy's flying steed on a base family day.

Number one. The publication of Chris's memoir in January 2012 would change our lives forever.

Whether in Texas, California (like here), or just about anywhere in America, book signings brought out crowds of people to meet Chris.

Throwing out the first pitch at a Rangers game gave Chris one of his all-time highs.

Another came when he met one of his lifelong idols, Randy White. The former Dallas Cowboy brought a book to be signed, and penned his name on Chris's souvenir jersey.

Here we are in Europe to promote the Polish edition of *American Sniper*, enjoying the traditional *tatanka*, aka "frisky bison," which can be made only with Żubrówka vodka.

Chris and Chad Littlefield while watching the premiere of *Stars Earn Stripes* on TV. Chris's friends made up T-shirts to celebrate the show.

One of my favorite photos. Chris's arm around me always felt reassuring.

Chris and Bubba enjoy a moment of fishing at the dock at Rough Creek Lodge. I don't think they caught anything, but there were still smiles all around.

Who better to learn to swim from than a SEAL—even if he hated being in the water.

Dad always looked the kids in the eye, whatever it took.

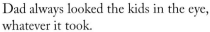

Chris loved helping the Easter Bunny do his job.

At the memorial. *(© Larry W. Smith/eps/Corbis)*

The outpouring of patriotism and condolences warmed my heart on the ride to the cemetery . . . *(Courtesy of Rob Kyker)*

. . . literally thousands braved the rain to line the highway to say good-bye to my husband. *(RK)*

Chris's fellow SEALs were an important and very moving part of the burial service. *(RK)*

Good-bye, Daddy. *(RK)*

The Patriot Tour has given me an opportunity to carry on what Chris had started. *(Team Never Quit)*

Then came *American Sniper*, the movie. Bradley, Clint, Sienna, and screenwriter Jason Hall all did a spectacular job bringing our story to the screen.
(Dave Allocca/Starpix)

American Sniper has now been translated into twenty-four languages—from Chinese to Serbian. *(Motion picture artwork © 2014 Warner Bros. Entertainment, Inc.)*

The kids sharing a happy moment together at Rough Creek. With God's grace and perseverance, we carry on and manage to find moments of joy.

Eventually, we came up with the idea of sharing some of the toys with other children. We filled up a laundry basket with brand-new things, then gave them to a local charity. We've continued doing that since: Lego sets, video games, dolls, action figures—more toys than the kids could have played with in ten years have gone to other children, hopefully providing them with some comfort and happiness.

I would never have thought generosity might have its negative effects. But I also learned that it shouldn't—and that I was the one who had to do something about it. Other people's kindness taught the kids how to be generous toward others.

There was much kindness and generosity toward us in those dark days. I'll never forget some of my friends doing dishes at my sink. Some were there until eleven or twelve at night, day after day. Little things were major things at the time. I remember a few days after Chris's death realizing that Angel needed to change. I went to her dresser drawer, desperate to find something—anything—she could wear that was clean. I hadn't had a chance to do the wash, so I cringed when I opened the drawer . . .

Only to find the dresser stuffed with freshly laundered clothes. Two of my friends had washed and dried all of our laundry without a word.

I can't list everything people did for us. Husbands as well as wives pitched in. They didn't ask—I would have told them, *NO! I don't need help!* They just did it. They knew, because they were moms and dads, too. They knew.

Angel mentioned to my sister that we had let her release helium balloons to send to the kids in heaven.

"I want to send some to my dad," she said.

My sister and some friends went and got a huge batch of red, white, and blue balloons. That evening, the kids and the adults went outside. There must have been 150 people there—neighbors, relatives, friends, Team guys. Someone said a prayer, and then everyone released them.

They floated up, slowly vanishing in the distance. Angel stayed and watched until the last one was out of sight.

Friends did more than help; they shared their grief. Some talked about it. I talked about it—I needed to know.

The conversations were as deep as our grieving. They didn't follow the simplest scripts you might read in book on grieving, because grief is a difficult and twisted emotion. Faith helps, but it's neither a cure-all nor a balm to anesthetize the wounds. It helps you get through, but it tests you at the same time.

I remember talking to Kelly, Ryan's widow. I especially valued her perspective because she knew what it meant to lose her husband unexpectedly.

"It's not going to be easy," she told me. There was no reason to sugarcoat the truth, or ignore the pain. "This is going to suck for a long time."

"God knew this was going to happen?" I asked, half questioning, half stating. "This is part of His plan?"

"I've always thought, in grief, God is crying with me."

How true. Whatever we think of God, whether what humans do is part of His plan or not, surely He would weep for our sorrows.

"I feel so blessed that the kids had time to be with Chris," I told her. "And it's so sad for your daughter, not having time with her dad."

"She has a very real relationship with her father. We have pictures and we talk about him a lot."

I marveled at her strength and quiet will. Would I achieve that? It surely felt impossible.

"Is it ever okay?" I asked. "How do you make it okay?"

"I can tell you that my life with Ryan now feels like a different life," she said. "Time has a way of stealing the pain from you."

I fell apart. I didn't want to lose any more of Chris, even if it meant stopping the pain.

POLICE BUSINESS

A few days after the murder—I'm not really sure when—our friend Sean came to me and said there was a Texas Ranger outside who wanted to talk to me.

"Why?" I demanded. "What's there to say? That guy murdered two people. What can I possibly say?"

I guess I was worried that, in some way, someone would try and turn it on Chris. Somehow they would try and make a case that he was responsible for his own death.

Looking back now, I see how ridiculous that is. But at the time, I didn't trust anyone. I was adamant: I wasn't talking to him.

Sean offered to go with me. "His name is Danny, and he's the lead investigator. I've talked to him," he added. "I trust him."

"You trust him?"

"Yeah," said Sean. A former SEAL, Sean now worked in law enforcement himself. "I'll be right there with you if you want."

I relented. "All right."

We walked out to the bus where the Ranger was waiting. I don't know what I must have looked like. I spent that whole week wearing Chris's camo jacket over a pair of yoga pants and a T-shirt. If

I remembered to brush my hair at any point, it had to have been because of divine intervention.

Chris's parents were already inside.

"I, uh—can I grab your hand?" I asked Sean, stuttering as I prepared for the worst.

I squeezed his hand hard as we talked. I squeezed so hard I might have broken bones.

Danny was the lead investigator on the case. I'm sure when he's dealing with criminals he's an undoubted bad-ass, but talking to me he was the kindest, gentlest man you could imagine. We spoke for quite a while. He started by asking me about how Chris had met Eddie Routh, and what had happened prior to the murder. We talked like two human beings who had met in the worst circumstances, yet somehow had to work together and even care about each other. Intermingled with the questions about the case were more personal ones, and just regular conversation. It was a two-way street: I learned a lot about his family, and I got a strong sense of respect and responsibility.

And I found out Sean has really strong hands.

Holding hands, whether it was a friend's, my father-in-law's, or even a stranger's, seemed to steady me somehow. I always needed that reassurance in the days right after the murder.

I told Danny that I hoped there was some way the accused could be released into the general prison population. I told him that because I was sure he would be brutally beaten and hurt, and maybe killed.

I know they didn't do that, and I know they couldn't do that, and I know they wouldn't do that. I also know it was not exactly a very Christian thing to hope for.

But it was what I wanted.

A couple of months after the murder, I asked Danny if he would take Leanne and me to the murder scene. While we were there, I asked if he had any pictures that showed what had happened.

He did. But that wasn't *really* what I wanted.

"Can I see them?"

He was reluctant, but by this time he knew me well enough to realize that the more information I had, the better I would feel. And so he showed me those horrible pictures, and in a way it made the murder not easier to accept, not easier to understand, but different in a way that was important to me.

The logical side of my brain took over. I talked to Danny about how it must have happened, where they'd been, where the murderer moved, the sequence of shots. I was very scientific, very far from the emotions I felt. It was as if re-creating it in my mind might somehow control the horror and sadness.

We walked around the range. Leanne put her fingers into the wood divots where the bullets had hit. She cried.

When we were leaving, a man came out who said he was the first on the scene.

"I used to be a paramedic," he told me. "I want you to know I did everything I could do for him."

"You're saying he wasn't dead?" I asked.

"There was definitely electricity going through his body."

"Are you saying he wasn't dead?"

"I think if I'd have had paddles [for resuscitation], I could have saved him."

"Oh."

I knew by then that Chris had died instantaneously, and that no one could have saved him, even if they had been there instantly, not an hour or more later. There was no reason for the man to feel like he could have done more, but there was also no way for me to relieve whatever guilt he felt, or assuage whatever impulse led him to tell me the story.

"Please don't say anything to the Rangers," he said. "I wouldn't be very popular."

"Sure."

Another man called us over a few minutes later. He told me he had seen Chad first and grabbed his hand and said Hail Marys out loud, over and over.

"Then I saw the other man and I did the same thing," he recalled. "If that brings you any comfort."

"Oh, thank you," we told him. "Would you say it with us now?"

"Oh, I don't know if I could do it now. I was so in the moment."

I went home confused, and not just because of the different stories. I'd thought going to the scene would solve something, but it didn't provide real peace. Nothing could. And the questions it answered were replaced by new ones even harder to satisfy.

Why, God? Why?

PEACE WITH GOD

Friends ask if I was mad at God for taking Chris from us so early.

No. Not with God. Not to this day.

I'm angry with the murderer—beyond angry.

But Chris's death brings the question: If God is all-powerful, why didn't He stop it? Why did He let someone kill Chris?

The answer that keeps coming to me is as hard to accept as it is simple: God didn't stop it because He has a plan. It's difficult sometimes to remain optimistic about that plan, but in the end, that is what faith means: trust in the plan.

I think God knows what's in our hearts. He has given us free will and the ability to do right and wrong. I don't know at what point God knows for certain what will happen, but I think we do have choices and we are responsible for our actions. We may suffer because of others, but He will take care of us no matter what. We will never be alone.

Whatever questions I have about faith, I know for certain that Chris himself is in a place where he's happy. I deeply believe that. It's the people he has left behind who suffer, not him.

And I know that life goes by in the blink of an eye. I have no doubt that we'll see him soon.

I do have anger, great anger. I get mad that someone could murder two men who were trying to help him. I get mad that Chris had to fall on his face. That he was caught off guard, shot from the side and back. That in his last moments, he couldn't do what he lived his life to do, protect someone dear to him.

I get mad at all of those things and many others—but that is not the same thing as getting mad at God, or even doubting His plan.

So many people were changed by Chris's life. Many others were changed by his death. I saw much good and charity from others as a result. So if it's true that there is great evil in the world, and that evil was responsible for Chris's murder, then I have to recognize that there is great good as well, and that I witnessed it even in the darkest depths. That doesn't excuse the evil, much less make up for it. But it does mean that evil need not prevail, and will not prevail, as long as we can perceive the good even at the worst times.

I struggle to be at peace with the fact that it hurts like hell to lose my husband. It hurts like hell for our kids. But ultimately, God's plan is not about me, or even them. It's about the deeper mission of our lives.

Many people say they've changed the direction of their lives because of Chris's example—Team guys, servicemen, people who read the book and heard about his death. It is of great comfort to know that their reactions are part of God's plan. I see beauty rising from ashes.

And there is this other thing I keep coming back to. My faith tells me that I will see Chris again. I cling to that. If I didn't think I could touch him again, hold him in his perfection, and my perfection, in the glory of the afterlife—then truly I would despair.

What was remarkable to me in retrospect was the kids' attitude toward God.

As far as I could tell from their prayers, they weren't angry with Him that their father died. Instead, they told God they were thankful that He had given them Chris to be their father.

They said it without crying, without anger, and without prompting.

The faith of innocents is truly a blessed faith.

COINCIDENCES?

Do we know the future somehow, even before it happens? Are things just coincidences, or unconscious expressions from some sort of pre-knowledge of what will happen to us?

I mentioned earlier that Chris had been thinking about getting rid of his truck; the truck turned out to be somehow related to the crazed motive for the crime, at least according to what the murderer told his sister. I mentioned Chris saying, out of the blue, that he thought Chad would take a bullet for him. He thought about giving up dipping, as if feeling that he should do something to keep his life going longer.

Those can certainly be explained as coincidences, as can other things: The day before he was killed, Chad had lunch with his parents, something that he did rarely. When he was leaving, he walked down to his vehicle, then suddenly turned back and gave them another big, heartfelt hug: their lasting memory of him, I would guess.

Maybe they aren't coincidences; maybe God grants us some moments of pre-knowledge. I don't know. Maybe God puts things on our hearts and gives us a little push. Or it's possible those of us left behind simply remember what we want to be significant when we experience loss.

I do know I am glad Chris and I had that Christmas. I'm comforted by the weeks right before he died where our marriage reached a state of near perfection. And I'm glad that I have so many good moments from our days to remember.

My world had stopped, but the outside one kept going. On Saturday, one week after the murder, Bubba had a basketball game. He wanted to go. I wanted him to go, too.

And if he went, I was going, too. Even though I hadn't been out of the house except to go to the funeral home.

A friend picked Bubba up early so he could get there for the pregame warm-up. When it came time to leave to watch the game, I decided to run rather than drive. It was five minutes by car, and I thought it wouldn't take long to trot over.

I was wrong about that.

Four or five of the men at the house accompanied me, including my brother-in-law Jeff, who had just gone through an operation and was still recovering. I'm sure his rehab plan didn't include running alongside a half-crazy woman, but he did anyway, without a complaint or even a "Hey, slow down."

We got to the church gym just in time for the game. I felt such pure joy watching Bubba play. It was one of the very few times that whole month that I was able to completely forget my grief and feel fully myself. They were fleeting moments, but they loom large now in my memory, little islands of relief in a sea of dread.

We all walked home. The men tossed a ball back and forth with Bubba. They couldn't replace Chris, but they provided an enormous, unstated reassurance to Bubba that he would never be alone.

Just as my path through grief was varied and unpredictable, at least to me, so too were the paths that others took. Some people reacted in very odd ways. A few were even destructive.

No one, of course, blamed me for Chris's death. But at times they felt I was interfering with their memory of him. They wanted to be the ones preserving his memory, or what they thought his memory should be.

I've heard from others who have lost loved ones that there can be bad feelings among people who were close to them, pseudo-competitions for the dead person's love. Family members get jealous; it's easy to misinterpret statements in the heat of emotion. Anything might mean a person loved the dead man less; any odd gesture might indicate they could have done more to save him.

Another thing I noticed—far more benign—was that everyone's memory of Chris came from not only a different place but a different time. He knew so many people, but only a very few knew him in every phase of his life. He changed over the years, as we all do. Some of the things that changed him were big: marriage, war, fame, fatherhood. Others were just the course corrections we all experience as we bump and bruise along. But each one of us claimed the Chris we knew as being the "true" Chris.

When I stand back and look at things objectively, I know even I didn't know the *entire* Chris. Sometimes, I wonder if even he did.

CLOTHES

Melanie Luttrell pulled me aside one day and asked if I had something to wear to the services that were being planned for Chris and Chad.

"I don't know," I told her. Clothes were the furthest thing from my mind. "I'm sure I have something. There's no way I'm going shopping."

"Of course you're not going shopping," she said. "Tell me what you'd like and we'll get it here."

"What do you mean?"

"Do you have any idea of what you might like?" she asked. "We'll have clothes delivered to the house."

"You can do that?"

"There's a service that will do it at the mall in Dallas."

I didn't even know these kind of things existed. More importantly, I did not quite understand why I needed a new dress at a time like this.

Melanie explained that I needed a proper *black* dress for the funeral—I didn't have one.

Oh. Of course. Widows wear black. And I'm a widow.

A store had contacted some of my friends and offered to supply one. As we talked, Melanie sensed my restlessness and suggested that I get out of the house for a while—I could go to the mall with my mom or a friend and pick out something.

"Okay," I told her finally. "Will you come with me?"

"Don't you want your mom or sister or—"

"If you don't mind, I'd like you to be the one with me. You're so calm and decisive, and that's what I need."

"Okay."

The owner of the mall met us in an underground parking area I hadn't even known existed. He gave me a package of gift cards from stores in the mall. I was floored by the generosity and kindness. We went to a clothing store, and they took us into a private back room to show me some dresses. They even gave me a little wine.

While we were waiting for them to bring the clothes in, I started going through the playlist on my phone, thinking of what I wanted played during the ceremony.

"This is one of my all-time favorite songs," I said to Melanie, showing her a Randy Travis song. "It's not for the memorial, but it's one of my all-time favorite songs."

It was "Whisper My Name."

I played it and started bawling. The song perfectly captured who Chris was for me.

"You think we could get Randy to sing it?" I asked Melanie.

"We'll definitely reach out to him," she said.

They did. And before I knew it, Randy was going to perform.

Meanwhile, the store attendants brought some beautiful clothes in. They were all wonderful—and expensive.

"Are you kidding me?" I said when I saw some of the price tags.

"Stop," answered Melanie. "They've all been donated."

"Donated?"

"Yes."

Wow. To this day the generosity floors me. I chose an elegant black jacket and skirt, very tailored and formal yet feminine at the same time. Unfortunately, it needed a few alterations to fit. I hesitated, thinking it would take weeks to get it ready.

"Take it," said Melanie. "The alterations will be done and delivered tomorrow. Don't worry."

"Tomorrow?"

In my world, alterations take forever, even if you're not the one doing them. Appointments, measuring, fitting, refitting . . . This was a whole different experience.

"They don't even know my size," I protested.

"I sent them a picture. They know your size."

And they did. The outfit came as promised, and it fit perfectly.

The woman at the boutique gave me a beautiful necklace, an angel's wing with pearls. I can't even describe how her kindness, and the kindness of so many strangers who helped me in those days, still touches my heart.

It wasn't only my clothes I had to pick out. I had to choose Chris's.

I didn't really want to have an open casket, but the Team guys who were at my house said that an important part of closure involved seeing the body. I realized as I listened to them that an open casket would help everyone pay their respects.

I won't go into the details of the injuries or what the morticians had to do to make Chris look presentable. I will say simply that Chris looked at peace.

But what should he wear?

I thought about having him laid to rest in his uniform. But the truth is he hated wearing it. He really needed to be dressed in something he was comfortable in.

And that wasn't going to be in a suit, either: he hated being in a jacket and tie even more than in a uniform.

Tie? *Ha!*

I got a pair of his best pressed jeans. They had a nice crease in the pants leg, just like he liked. I found one of his plaid button-down shirts, another favorite.

Kryptek, which produces tactical gear and apparel and was one of Chris's favorite companies, had presented him with a big silver belt buckle that he loved. It was very cowboy, and in that way very much who Chris was.

"You think I can pull this off?" he'd asked, showing me how it looked right after he got it.

"Hell, yeah," I told him.

I made sure that was with him as well.

But if there was any item of clothing that really touched deep into Chris's soul, it was his cowboy boots. They were a reminder of who he was when he was young, and they were part of who he'd been since getting out of the military.

He had a really nice pair of new boots that had been custom made. He hadn't had a chance to wear them much, and I couldn't decide whether to bury him in those or another pair that were well worn and very comfortable.

I asked the funeral director for his opinion.

"We usually don't do shoes," he said. It can be very difficult to get them onto the body. "But if it's important to you, we can do it."

I thought about it. Was the idea of burying them with Chris irrational? The symbolism seemed important. But that could work the other way, too—they would surely be important to Bubba someday. Maybe I should save them for him.

In the end, I decided to set them near Chris's casket when his body was on view, then collect them later for our son.

But Chris had the last word. Through a miscommunication—or maybe something else—they were put in the casket when he was laid to rest. So obviously that was the way it should have been.

I thought about putting some tobacco dip in his casket. It had been a big part of his life. But since he'd decided to give up dipping a few weeks before . . . tobacco was out.

There was a part of me that wanted the mortician to arrange his fingers so he was flipping people the bird. Chris would have *loved* that. And many of the people who knew him would have roared at the joke—it was very Chris, a last practical joke.

But I'm sure some of the older family members wouldn't have seen the humor. Discretion won out.

Still, I couldn't send him off without *some* sort of off-color humor. Profanity and pranking were just *too* Chris to be ignored. So I went into his closet and found a gag T-shirt, the one that read, DO I LOOK LIKE A @#$#$!@ PEOPLE PERSON?

He wore that to his grave under his plaid button-down shirt, a silent last guffaw.

CHAD'S FUNERAL

Chad was laid to rest first.

Leanne wanted to have a simple ceremony, in keeping with the way Chad had lived his life. I'm sure she would have wanted it to be quiet and small as well, but under the circumstances that was impossible. The local Baptist church hosted a ceremony that drew hundreds of people; so many packed in that many had to watch on a video feed in a nearby room.

The service beautifully reflected Chad's life, with memories and poems recalling his vitality and thoughtfulness. He was a kind, quiet man without airs or pretensions, and his service honored those beautiful qualities.

It happened that I was with Chad's parents when they saw him laid out for the first time. His father grabbed him by the shoulder and said, "You go rest high on the mountain, son. Rest high on the mountain."

I'm still moved to tears by that memory. His dad said it with conviction and pain, affirming both faith and, ultimately, life.

The kids came with me to the church. It was the first time they'd gone to a funeral of someone they knew well.

Tears flowed down Angel's face as the ceremony came to an end. We slipped out together to the restroom before going on to the cemetery.

"Mom," she said, leaning against the stall. "Daddy keeps saying he's sorry. Why does he say that?"

"I don't know, honey." I had no doubt she was hearing her dad—their connection was so strong it surely would survive even death. "I don't know if he's sorry that he can't hold you, or that he's not here. But I'm glad you're hearing him."

"Yes."

The Patriot Guard Riders showed up as a personal gesture, honoring Chad and his family and escorting them to the grave.

He died just shy of his thirty-sixth birthday, having left a quiet but important mark on his community, his family, and his friends.

We miss him still.

THE LONG GOOD-BYE

And then it was our turn.

For the longest time, Chris had talked about wanting to be buried at Arlington National Cemetery, the country's foremost military cemetery, near Washington, D.C. But toward the end of his life, he'd begun to rethink that.

Soon after Chris's death, Marcus Lutrell, a good friend of Chris's, suggested that Chris be buried in the state cemetery in Austin. Located near the state capitol, the cemetery is the final resting place of notable Texans, from Revolutionary War veterans to recent governors. It's a frequent destination for school groups and tourists; beyond that, it's a lovely setting, quiet and serene.

But I just didn't know. Marcus said it would be appropriate for any number of reasons, starting with Chris's love of Texas.

"Trust me, it's gorgeous," he said when he saw me hesitating. "It'd be perfect."

Governor Rick Perry soon joined in, maybe at Marcus's suggestion, encouraging me to have Chris buried with other legendary Texans. I told him that I couldn't just decide without seeing it.

The next thing I knew, someone volunteered their private plane to fly the family there. The kids, my parents, Chris's parents, his brother and his family all came along to help me decide.

In a way, it didn't feel like my decision, or even the family's. It was really Chris's. Or should have been. When we were on the plane, I asked everyone to pray with me. "I want to hear Chris's voice and see what he thinks about the place," I told them. "I want to hear his wishes."

The governor and his wife picked us up at the airport. Mrs. Perry took my parents and the kids to their house for lunch while the rest of us went with the governor to tour the cemetery. The main entrance reminded me of the Alamo, a place Chris had always loved. His fascination with history seemed to fit perfectly with the place. School kids came regularly to learn about our history, something I knew would appeal to him.

It just felt like Chris.

Still, I had to be sure. I excused myself and took a walk away from the others, moving down the hill to a spot where I could see the immense flag.

"Okay, babe," I said. "If you can talk to me, tell me what you think. I don't know."

Bad-ass.

The words flew into my head, bypassing my ears.

Bad-ass. Bad-ass. Bad-ass.

Over and over, I heard those words in my head. It was as if Chris was there, telling me yes, this is where I want to be buried.

There were plenty of logical reasons to choose Austin—it's much closer to the family, and I can be buried next to him when my time comes. But I truly felt that Chris had spoken at that moment to me.

Walking back to the family, I felt his arm around me and his gentle lips on my temple.

"Okay, babe. Austin."

When you feel things like that, physically or mentally or somewhere in between, you wonder sometimes if you're making it up.

But you don't want to question it—the feeling is too intense, and too welcome.

Having decided on the cemetery, we still had to pick a place for the funeral. That proved harder.

Funerals are usually very private affairs, with only a few friends and family involved. But in this case, there was such an outpouring of sympathy from the public that I felt people had a right to help send him off. Chris's parents agreed. Together with other family members and close friends, we tried to figure out how to accommodate them all. We thought about holding the service at an outdoor rodeo arena—appropriate for a former cowboy—or some other place that could hold a lot of people. But we couldn't find anyplace free on such short notice. We brainstormed possible alternatives.

"I'm just trying to think of all the things Chris liked," I said, my mind drifting. "He loved the Cowboys . . . Why not Cowboys Stadium?"

"Chris did love the Cowboys," said Jeff.

"That would be great," I said. "But . . ."

"Why not?" asked Wayne.

"Well, it's *Cowboys Stadium* . . ."

They convinced me we could ask.

I don't know exactly what happened, who asked, or how it worked. All I know is that in what seemed like no time at all, Jerry Jones had given us permission to hold the memorial there.

More than that, Jerry volunteered to provide *everything*—the building, the staff, the security. His incredible generosity floored me.

"It's an honor to do it," he said when I tried to thank him.

Chris would have been floored at the idea of being given a service in Cowboys Stadium—though I suspect he might have tried offering Mr. Jones some advice on how to run his football team when he met him.

While others did the work putting the ceremonies together, I made two strong requests: I wanted to hear the song "Amazing Grace," and I wanted bagpipes.

We got both, and more.

Sometime that week, Angel came to me at bedtime.

"Mama, can I tell you something?"

"Yes, of course."

"I keep hearing Daddy say, 'I love you, baby girl.'"

"You do?"

"Yes," she said. "His voice sounds a little different, though."

"I know, honey."

"I keep trying to make him laugh. He's laughing—but his laugh sounds a little different than when he was here."

I tucked her into bed.

Chris was the only person who really understood Angel's humor. Her face would light up when he laughed. It was part of their special connection, and they still had it, even with him gone.

Hours before the actual ceremony was to begin, a private gathering was held in a downstairs club area of the stadium. It was quite an affair, with an elaborate buffet and bar. Chris was laid out elegantly in a room at the side where people could pay their respects. There was a long line to view the casket.

I came a little while before the memorial ceremony was scheduled to begin. As I walked from the car to the private suite, I caught a glimpse of the huge screen that hangs over the middle of the field. There was a picture of Chris and me, seventy-two feet high, 160 feet wide.

Something caught in my throat.

I'm not going to do this now, I thought. I am not going to break down.

I kept walking to the room.

People were lined up in the hall, waiting to get in. The place suddenly fell silent.

"Thank you," I told them as I passed. "Thank you. Thank you."

There were so many close friends I hadn't seen in years, or I had seen and just hadn't been able to connect with. I wanted to touch and connect with each one, but the circumstances didn't allow it.

I went to the casket to check on Chris, to make sure he was okay. It sounds silly, I know, and yet it was the most natural thing, as if we had come to a party at different times: I was arriving late, and the first thing I had to do was go and check on my husband.

We spent a few moments together, he and I. The others gave us space, just as they would have if he'd been alive. Then I went back into the room, hugging people, holding myself together. At different points my lip would begin to quiver and I would feel myself starting to slip, but I quickly got it back in control.

I will not be weak. People will not see me break down.

The minutes slid away. Finally, it was time for the formal ceremony. They needed to close the casket and take Chris out to the field.

It was my last chance to be with him, face-to-face.

Whatever we believe about spirits surviving, I thought, however strongly I still feel Chris beside me, whatever happens in heaven, this will be always my final chance to look at him as I know him now.

I went over to the casket. I touched his face and stroked his hair.

"This is it, babe," I whispered.

My knees weakened.

Don't do this! You're going to cause a scene.

I want to feel this. How do I do this?

I stood back, empty. I wanted to impress it all in my brain, this one moment and our lifetime together. I wanted it preserved. But the emotion was so overwhelming it threatened to obliterate me.

I started talking to Chris in my head.

Look at this, babe. Cowboys Stadium!

All these people! Isn't this great?

Can you believe this? Who would have thought?

The one-sided conversation, such as it was, pulled me together. I took a deep breath, and gave him a kiss on his head, then turned away.

I stopped after a few steps, glancing back.

Walk! Just walk!

If you don't walk now, you never will.

Walk!

I turned and walked away, this time for good, never to see my husband's face again in this lifetime.

The area around the fifty-yard line had been set up with a stage and seating. The kids held my hands as we went to the elevator, ready to go out.

"Can you believe we're in Cowboys Stadium for Daddy?" I asked them, trying to rally my spirits as well as theirs. "He would be so blown away."

I think they nodded.

The elevator opened. We got in. The car went down, and suddenly we were walking onto the runway that led to the field.

Pay attention to what's around you. This is unbelievable!

The bagpipers began to move, the tap of their shoes on the concrete apron echoing loudly. The cadence centered me. The pipes began to mourn and my spirit swelled, the music propelling me forward.

The casket was marched out and placed front and center.

The pallbearers and Navy honor guard stood at attention.

I was moving in a cocoon of numbing grief and overwhelming awe. There was a prayer, speeches—each moment moved me in a different way. The easy jokes, the devotional hymns, each had its own effect.

I began to float.

When I'd asked people to talk about Chris at the ceremony, I'd made a point of reminding them of his humor and asking if possible to add some lighter touches to their speeches, roasting him, even; it was all so Chris. But now some of the light jokes tripped a wire:

Don't talk bad about him! Don't you dare!

Then in the next moment I'd realize he would have been leading the laughs, and it was all good again.

I couldn't force a smile, though.

One of the things that I've always felt missing from funerals and services is the voice of the man or woman who was the deceased's partner in life. I've always wanted to hear from the person who'd loved them more than anyone. Biblically, the two become one flesh—the spouse is their other half. It has always seemed to me that his or her voice was critical to truly understanding who the deceased was in life.

I also felt that *American Sniper* had told only part of Chris's story—an angry part in much of it. There was so much more to him that I wanted the world to know.

People said Chris was blessed that I hung in there during his service to our country; in fact, I was the one who was blessed. I wanted everyone to hear me say that.

Beforehand, a friend suggested I have a backup in case I couldn't finish reading my speech—a "highway option," as Chris used to call it: the way out if things didn't go as planned.

I refused.

I didn't want a way out. It wasn't supposed to be easy. Knowing that I had to go through with it, that I had to finish—that was my motivator. *That* was my guarantee that I would finish, that I would keep moving into the future, as painful as it surely would be.

When you think you cannot do something, think again. Chris always said, "The body will do whatever the mind tells it to." I am counting on that now.

I stand before you a broken woman, but I am now and always will be the wife of a man who is a warrior both on the battlefield and off.

Some people along the way told Chris that through it all, he was lucky I stayed with him. I am standing before you now to set the record straight. Remember this: I am the one who is literally, in every sense of the word, blessed that Chris stayed with me.

I feel compelled to tell you that I am not a fan of people

romanticizing their loved ones in death. I don't need to romanticize Chris, because our reality is messy, passionate, full of every extreme emotion known to man, including fear, compassion, anger, pain, laughing so hard we doubled over and hugged it out, laughing when we were irritated with each other and laughing when we were so in love it felt like someone hung the moon for only us . . .

I looked at the kids as I neared the end, talking to them and only them.

Tears ran from their faces. Bubba's head hung down. It broke my heart.

I kept reading.

Then I was done.

AT THE CEMETERY

The burial was scheduled for the next day in Austin. Dallas to Austin is close to two hundred miles, a several-hour trip even when there's no traffic and the weather is good.

We had a police escort, so traffic wasn't a problem. The weather, on the other hand, didn't want to cooperate—I woke to a light but persistent rain.

Appropriate for a burial, maybe.

I got the kids dressed, got ready myself, and went over to the school where everyone was to meet the hearse for the trip south.

The Patriot Guard Riders—a volunteer organization of motorcycle enthusiasts formed to "ensure dignity and respect" at memorial services—were there, along with a massive bus for friends and family. There were also dozens of private cars, friends waiting to drive in the long, improvised parade to the cemetery.

There was only room for one person to ride in the hearse, so I went alone with Chris. Road trips were kind of our thing. We did a lot of them. Here was one more, our last.

A helicopter passed overhead. I noticed one of the men sitting at the side in overwatch position, his own silent tribute.

I reached my hand up in thanks. I knew they wouldn't see me, but somehow I felt my gratitude would be communicated.

The crowds were tremendous despite the drizzle. They lined the highway in clumps of hundreds, holding signs, waving flags.

"Chris," I said. "Look at what they're doing for you. Look."

I don't think it was all just for Chris, not that I don't think he deserved it. The gratitude people expressed as they shook his hand during book tours and at appearances hadn't been solely for him either. Then they were thanking all servicemen and -women through him. They were doing the same this morning. Their patriotism was a message to all who served:

Thank you for your service. We truly appreciate it.

We got to the cemetery around noon. Over two hundred Patriot Guard Riders were lined up at the entrance, waiting with their flags.

All through the memorial and the burial ceremonies, I kept trying to focus on what was going on around me. I wanted to make my eyes into a camera, recording, remembering. I didn't want my emotions to interfere with my appreciation of the honor that was being done for my husband.

That was the one thing I allowed myself to feel—admiration for the honors being bestowed on him. Other, darker emotions tried to elbow in. I fought against them.

One by one, Chris's fellow SEALs walked to the casket and pounded their Tridents into the cover, a tribute to their brother.

Before they were done, the casket glittered in the sun, which had just peeked through the clouds.

When the last man had put his badge in, the SEALs gathered in a circle on one knee. With heads bowed, they called his name, one last time. Twenty-one guns fired, their echo sad in the stillness. A flight of F-16s crossed overhead.

Gone.

I was handed the folded flag. Twenty-one bullet casings were included in the folds, commemorating the twenty-one-gun salute that had seen him off.

I gave it to Angel.

"Momma, what does the Trident mean?" she asked.

I turned to Walt, one of the SEALs who had been close to Chris and had been a comfort to us since his death. "I think Walt would be the best person to explain that."

He got down on his knees and pointed out the different elements of the SEAL symbol. When he was done, Angel reached into the flag and pulled out a bullet casing.

"Is this the bullet that killed my daddy?" she asked.

Walt winced. "No, honey. That bullet's in heaven."

With the ceremony over, people began drifting away. I went to the casket with the kids. I had them touch the wood to say good-bye.

Standing didn't seem right. I knelt.

Good-bye.

Good-bye, good-bye, good-bye.

FIVE

DESPAIR

Funeral over, Chris buried, friends gone back to their own lives . . . the kids and I struggled to find our way. The world around us was familiar, yet completely foreign. Their dad's laugh was gone; my bed was cold.

The old rituals—prayers at night, dinner together, cuddling on the couch—were still there, but they were all different. We felt Chris's presence every day, but we felt his absence more acutely.

SHOWER ONCE A WEEK

Personal hygiene takes a hit when you're struggling to get through the week. My goal after Chris died was to take a shower every five days. No makeup, my hair in a bun—I was a mess, and knew it.

It used to be that before I would walk out of the house, I'd at least dab on a bit of lipstick and fix my hair—or hide it under a baseball cap. Now I gave that up. And no one cared. Or at least they didn't say it.

There's a lesson in that, though I didn't realize it at the time. I have come to realize friends don't judge you based on your lipstick or makeup—or if they do, they're not really your friends. It's a simplistic thing to say, yet for many women I'm sure it's a profound revelation. We're raised so much to care for our "looks" that we have a hard time believing the exterior is really secondary to the interior.

I kept my tears in check as much as possible. I didn't let myself cry, for fear that I wouldn't be able to stop.

Jeff and his wife had had a baby just before Chris died. Shortly after the funeral, it was time for her baptism.

As Christians, we believe in baptizing children into our faith. It's a joyous occasion, a time of celebration—but I didn't feel much like celebrating. Standing in the pew, I felt the tears starting to come. A flood had built up behind the lids of my eyes; there were enough tears to keep Texas green for a full year.

I felt them starting to trickle out. My face began to twitch, the rest of me tremble. I fought to keep control—if I let go, if I let myself go, I would lose everything.

My throat choked closed. I could feel the dry heaves starting deep in the pit of my stomach.

Chris! Chris!

If only he'd been here. If only he were alive.

How can I go on without you?

I clenched my fist.

No. I am not going to lose it.

I closed my eyes, held my tears back, and somehow made it through the ceremony.

There was work to be done. A lot of it.

Chris had been in the middle of several important projects when he died. One was the movie based on his life, and another the new book. Had he lived, Chris would have acted as a consultant, filling in the screenwriter and others on specific details to make the movie more realistic. At the same time, his death changed the direction of the movie—it seemed obvious that they had to deal with it in some way.

Would there be a movie at all? Hollywood being Hollywood, movies were shelved for far less important reasons than the death of their subject. But Bradley Cooper quickly made it clear that he wanted to proceed, sending a personal message through the screenwriter, Jason Hall.

Coincidentally, Jason had finished the first draft of the script the day before Chris died. Shaken by Chris's murder, he flew out from Los Angeles to attend the memorial. We formed a bond almost immediately. We started talking regularly by phone as he reimagined the ending of the film and restructured the rest as well. The calls soon became a lifeline for me, a way to talk about Chris and what I was going through; I'm sure Jason helped me far more than I helped him.

An even more immediate problem was *American Gun,* which was already behind schedule when Chris died. The manuscript was far from finished and needed considerable work. I felt a real duty to him to get it right, even though there was next to no time to do that.

Fortunately, Jim DeFelice, who hadn't been involved in the project, agreed to help revise and pull it together. We were able to do a job I'm sure Chris would have been very proud of. Jim leaned on a lot of friends, both his and Chris's, for anecdotes and stories to round out the tales, and I'm extremely grateful for all their help.

Plans to create a memorial edition of *American Sniper*—a project of love for all concerned, myself included—took additional time and attention. There was also the question of Chris's charitable efforts, which I didn't want to stop just because he had passed away.

Then there were the "normal" widow or widower duties: sorting out the estate, getting finances in order, untangling the bureaucratic knots a sudden death can cause. And of course I had to do my real job as well: taking care of the kids.

I threw myself into everything, often going until three in the morning. Then I'd get up at five to be with the kids.

The kids missed a lot of school at first; there was just no way that they could slide back into the routine of classes, especially given the (indirect) connection between the school and what had happened to their dad. Accused killer Eddie Routh's mother, who'd asked Chris to get involved, still worked there.

We tried home schooling at first. I thought having them home would mean less pressure for them. I didn't have the time myself, but my mother was with us and she volunteered to try.

Mom was a good teacher, but we soon realized there was a problem. Bubba verbalized it best: there was a conflict between the roles of grandmother and teacher. Teachers have to stay focused and lower the boom when necessary. Grandmothers, on the other hand—well, that's not their job.

"I want to have fun with my grandmother," he said. "It's just confusing."

Uneasy about sending them back to the school where Routh's mother had worked, I spoke to a good friend who was a principal at a different school in our district about the possibility of having them transfer there. With her blessing, I went to the superintendent and talked to him about the transfer. He made it very easy for us.

Angel spent another week taking lessons at home before starting at the school. I drove her in on her first day.

"Mamma, I feel like Daddy's with us in the car," she told me. "He never missed my first day."

"You're right," I told her. "I'm sure he is."

Jesse Ventura announced that he was going to pursue his lawsuit, even though Chris was dead. So in effect I "inherited" a lawsuit.

Many witnesses supported Chris's account, and I was confident in the case. Still, it wasn't easy. And what was really galling were the slanderous attacks on Chris. (Since the law says you can't slander a dead man, it wasn't technically slander. People could say whatever hateful thing they wanted.)

Among the many things that baffled me was the claim that Chris had accused Jesse of "treason." That was absolutely not true. Chris accused Jesse of expressing his opinion—an opinion that Chris didn't agree with, but one that was hardly treasonous.

It was just one more bit of nonsense in an ocean of craziness.

Before Chris passed away, I'd volunteered to coach Angel's soccer team in our local recreational league. It was a commitment I vowed to keep. I was determined to show those little girls how to succeed on the soccer "pitch," as the field is sometimes called.

I may have gone a little overboard. I mean, how many six-year-old girls have the misfortune of being coached by the wife of a SEAL?

Day One:

"We start by running!" I shouted enthusiastically. "Everyone run around the park. Let's go."

"The soccer field, Mrs. Kyle?" asked a player.

"No! The *entire* complex. Come on!"

I'm guessing it was maybe five or six times as far as they'd ever run before—or maybe ten or twenty—and a good deal farther than many teams with considerably older players ran. But the girls were good sports about it. We built endurance and worked on drills, and we had fun—you never knew when the coach might grab one of the players and twirl her around enthusiastically for doing a good job.

"I'm taking goal," I'd say when shooting practice wasn't going well. "Anyone who can hurt me gets an extra piece of candy!"

I gave out a lot of candy that afternoon.

We were a young team and a little rough at first, but we got better as we went. It was fun to watch the transition many of the girls made over the length of the season—they not only got in better shape and learned to play soccer better, but they seemed more confident as well.

I will guarantee one thing: they slept pretty well the nights after practice.

The first Easter Chris was gone, I stayed up late Saturday night to hide the Easter eggs. We got up early, and I watched as Bubba and Angel went to work finding them. You can't help but smile at kids who are just alive with the fun of it all. For a few moments I was so absolutely into their happiness that I forgot how tired I was, and didn't think of Chris or the fact that we were missing him so badly.

Finally, after all the eggs and candy were gathered, I told the kids I was going to take a shower and get ready for the rest of the day. I was feeling great—until I closed the door behind me.

The sense of loss that I'd been screening out hit me. It drove me to my knees, and I began crying uncontrollably.

There was a knock on the door. Angel opened it and looked in. I did my best to smile. "Hey, what's up?" I asked.

"Are you okay, Momma?"

"Yes."

"You miss Daddy?" she asked.

I nodded.

Angel came in and gave me a hug. "You know he's still here with us, right?" she asked.

"Yes. Yes, I do."

SMOKING

There were plenty of times when grief washed up like a tsunami and threatened to drown me. Tears would suddenly come, and I had no control over them. I wanted control—I wanted to present a hard face to the world. Earlier in our marriage, when Chris was deployed, I would do anything to keep him from thinking that I was worried about him. Now I was trying to do the same thing to the world: I wasn't going to show them my vulnerability, my real emotions. I was going to bury myself in work. I was going to help the kids. I was determined to carry on like the brave, heroic mother I felt I had to be.

Even though inside, I was falling apart. My core was despair, all despair.

I needed to do something to keep myself from losing control. I found it in smoking.

Cigarettes gave me something to focus on. I'd excuse myself, go outside, light up. Everything about the cigarette was comforting.

Momentarily.

Smoking kept me from falling down a hole, but it quickly became a crutch, and then an addiction. I craved nicotine, even though I knew it wasn't good for me.

I tried quitting.

I hadn't been a big smoker before, but I had smoked during different periods of my life. I'd quit several times. I was good at it. It was almost a science: I'd go cold turkey. Day One I'd be miserable. Day Two, I would be irritable.

Day Three: Sleep.

Day Four: Sleep.

And that would be it. I'd quit.

For a while.

Months, sometimes; even years. Then, for whatever reason— usually nothing in particular, just the chance that a cigarette was nearby—I would start again.

This was the first time that I couldn't quit. I tried several times, but couldn't get there. Weeks went by and I'd realize I was no longer trying to stop. Feeling guilty, I'd give it a shot again. One day, two . . . then a cigarette would somehow come back into my hand and I'd be smoking again.

The rational part of me tried to reason cigarettes out of my life. I analyzed when I smoked, and saw I was using them to remain calm. There are other ways of staying calm, I reasoned. Rather than smoke, I decided I could substitute a few minutes of prayer.

An excellent idea. Until I tried it. My calm kept getting interrupted.

You can always find reasons to smoke. And no matter how rational you are, you can excuse away the obvious health risks.

Chris chewed tobacco and it had nothing to do with his death: when it's your time, it's your time. So why not?

I had a great-aunt who lived to be a hundred and smoked all the time. But she paid for it—the last decade of her life was filled with health problems. The rational part of me argued: the lesson *isn't* that we all die when it's our time to die, but rather, the quality of your life is up to you. God will determine when you die; you will determine how you spend that time, in misery or health.

It was a great insight, but it didn't stop me from smoking.

A lot of healthy impulses and habits took a beating in those months. My resolve to make healthy dinners slid out of sight. We'd always tried to avoid fast food when Chris was alive. Now, if there wasn't time to make dinner—fast food was there.

We're hungry. What does it matter?

It took months to get past that and start eating healthy again.

Even then, smoking remained. I have to confess, cigarettes were a good excuse for a lot of things. If I was at a business meeting in New York or doing something where I just needed to take a break, a smoke got me out without questions or comments. No one looks at you funny if you excuse yourself to grab a smoke. Imagine the reactions if you say, "Hey, I'm going to go grab a five-minute prayer. I'll be back."

Or worse, "Hold that thought. I just want to go cry a minute."

Excuses are easy. Quitting is much harder.

MEDICATION AND COUNSELING

But cigarettes are a distraction, not a cure. As I struggled with grief and tried to put our lives back into some sort of order, I began to feel the unmistakable signs of depression.

Clinical depression is a disease, and a devastating one. If you haven't lived through the awful sense of worthlessness it can be hard to understand. It's like being at the bottom of a very, very deep shaft with no way out. You try clawing up the sides, but eventually your fingernails break and your hands bleed, and you fall back even deeper into the pit. It's beyond sadness, and deeper than grief.

You can be as positive as you want, you can change your mentality, but if your chemicals are depleted and your body stops working the way it's supposed to, all the positive thinking in the world isn't going to change your body chemistry.

I recognized the symptoms, since I had had the ailment once before. Still, I didn't want to admit that I needed help. I told myself a lot of things, none of them very convincing:

I don't need it. Toughen up. Grow up.

I'm a failure. I'm worthless. How pathetic.

I'm tough! I don't need it.

These are exactly the things that depressed patients often tell themselves. It's a strange kind of feedback loop, where your illness ends up encouraging itself.

"If you had diabetes and needed insulin, you'd take the medicine, no questions asked," a physician told me finally. "So stop fooling yourself, and get help."

And so I did. I went to a doctor, who prescribed antidepressants, and I started talking to a variety of counselors, each of whom helped me in their own—or maybe my own—way.

One of the most helpful things I did was talking regularly with a counselor who had seen me back when I was in school. He still lives out on the West Coast, but Skype made regular sessions with him as easy as clicking a mouse.

One of the advantages of talking with him was his long knowledge of who I was. Basically, I couldn't BS him.

"This has always been an issue for you," he could say, with great authority, if I tried to put something off to grieving. At the same time, his ability to work with families gave him a perspective not only on grief but on how the kids would deal with it, which has been of great value to me.

One of the most difficult issues to deal with was the kids' desire to know what was going on. Not just about my grief, but about the different court cases and other trials and tribulations I had to deal with. Some of those things were not only beyond their understanding, but also the kind of problems that kids should never really have to think about.

No one should.

"I know you want to know everything I'm going through, honey," I told Bubba one day. "But I don't want to rob you of your childhood."

"But Mom, don't you think if you tell me all this stuff now, that when I'm an adult and I have really bad stuff, I'll think it's no big deal?"

I looked at him and thought, Why should you have to know?

"The thing is, Taya, they're smart," my counselor told me when we discussed it. "It's really uncomfortable for them to not know what's bothering you. I'm not saying tell them everything that's bothering you. But tell them enough to let them know."

And so I started, a little at a time. I found it's hard to open up to your kids without scaring them or making them feel bad—which would only make me feel worse. There were many poignant moments. I know the kids have been changed by Chris's death. They've learned about evil at an age when no child should have to.

COLOR THERAPY

We also started working with another form of therapy that, though unorthodox, helped us with more than just grief. Called color therapy, it uses color as a starting point for interpreting different psychological conditions. It was the sort of thing I might have thought was nonsense until I witnessed its effect myself.

To summarize very roughly, the underlying theory holds that before we know words, we know emotions, and we tend to associate these with colors before we have a vocabulary to explore them. That association stays with us, and offers a way for us—and the therapists who help us—to examine the emotions we feel but can't talk about, or talk about inefficiently.

I originally contacted the counselor, Lana Allen, because a friend's daughter had raved about the work she was doing with her. Lana has a special way with children, managing to connect on their level. Interestingly, she's not a grief counselor or a children's counselor per se; her therapy is more wide ranging.

In a basic session, Lana would show me a screen with different colors. As I stared at the screen, one color would come to dominate. I could try not to see that color, or to see less of it, but gradually that color would take over.

When I first started, the color would suddenly diminish, pulling back to the size and strength of the others. All of this happened without any conscious intervention from me; it was like watching a movie, if movies consisted of blocks of color that got bigger and smaller.

Lana theorized that the changing size of the colors corresponded to a fight in my psyche between my emotional side and my logical side. When the emotion—grief, sadness, anger—started to get strong, the logical side of my brain would take over so I wasn't overwhelmed by it. The two sides of my brain—left and right, one primarily emotional and one primarily logical—worked together to keep things in balance. I needed that balance to continue to function.

The color therapy gave me insight into how I function, and why I acted so rationally and calmly when I got the news that Chris was dead. It was a survival instinct. The emotion was too much to take in, so the other side of my brain simply took over: *You shut up, so we can deal with this.*

Of course, the emotional side couldn't be denied or submerged forever. The longer problems were suppressed, the more they would exert themselves in unhealthy ways.

Working with the colors, we explored my emotions and what I was feeling in my body—the knots and tensions. It's amazing the connections that come out once you begin.

With the kids, Lana translated complicated concepts about the body and stress into terms they could understand. The brain is like an alarm center, she'd say, and there are highways that send different emotions to different parts of our body. The pain you feel in your chest or the tightness in your neck is there because the alarms have overloaded your body.

The therapy gave the kids ways to talk about different emotions without fully understanding them. Directly and indirectly, the colors were windows into what they were feeling. They could deal with different emotions without having to relive them.

I've come to understand that there is really a very strong link between the mind and the body. And the therapy provided many insights, a good number of them seemingly random.

Can I make a pun about these coming "out of the blue," or would that be too much?

One day Lana was talking about different emotional states and shocks, and she mentioned the word *"terror.* I realized that word described almost perfectly what I'd felt since Chris died—sheer terror. It was like being scared that the worst thing would happen all the time.

Which it had.

Terror. It was more than grief or feeling scared. It was as if the fight-or-flight mechanism we hear so much about was stuck in overdrive.

Logically, I knew that the *worst possible thing* had already happened; I didn't have to be scared about it anymore. Emotionally, though, I was stuck in that phase.

Understanding the sensation didn't put it to rest. I still felt incredibly pressured, as if a twenty-ton weight were about to fall on me. But it was an important insight, and it did have an effect— maybe the weight slipped to fifteen tons.

Other things helped me relieve stress: massages, chiropractic treatments, even acupuncture.

The parent of one of Bubba's friends is a practicing acupuncturist and chiropractor. He offered to give me a treatment one day. The first few needles got my attention, though I can't really say they hurt.

Then he pushed one in that released something mentally: I began crying and couldn't stop for maybe five minutes.

They say there are many different stages of grief and mourning. Denial, bargaining, acceptance. Everyone goes through these, according to the experts.

I don't know that my grief could be easily divided. It was impossible to separate it from the turmoil left in Chris's wake—

the lawsuits, the overdue work, the need to find a way to make a living, the demands of raising children as a single mom. But there certainly was disbelief and denial.

There was also, at times, a reserve so steely that I felt like a different person.

After the initial shock and tumult, I entered a stage where I felt as if I were walking through mud up to my chin. My life in those first months went from complete chaos to semi-controlled but overwhelming disaster. It was progress, though not much.

The more I struggled, the slower I seemed to go. I pushed toward the future, trying to resolve each issue, or at least get through them, but progress was at a snail's pace while the pain remained deep and constant.

I thought to myself, I want to get out of this mud. I want to reach a place where I can swing my arms and legs and feel free.

But inevitably, a question would occur to me: When I am beyond the mud, will I be completely free of grief?

And if so, will that mean I no longer love Chris? Will he no longer exist for me? Will our marriage and everything we had together be completely negated?

I asked Chris's brother, Jeff, "Will it ever get better?"

"I don't think it does," he told me. "I think you just learn to live with the pain."

Can you do that and still move forward? I try, every day, but I have yet to know for sure whether it is possible.

BIRTHDAYS AND TALK

I thought I was doing well as Chris's birthday approached in April.

A friend called up with tickets to a Rangers game. That sounded like a nice way to spend the day; it was something he would have loved to do. Chris's father came with us and I tried to think of it all as a celebration of Chris's life.

Look, baby, we're at the Rangers game just like you would have wanted. And they're winning!

But I kept nodding off. I was so exhausted by everything—work, grief, just getting through the days.

What is wrong with me? Why am I so tired?

On the way home, I talked to Bubba and fell asleep at the same time. Half dreaming, the words came out as gibberish.

"What'd you say, Mom?" he asked.

"I . . . I'm just tired," I said finally.

It was too much. My body just shut down. Fortunately, I wasn't the one driving.

I went to bed as soon as we got home. The next day I got up, just keeping on.

Helping the kids deal with their father's death was a constant learning experience. I felt—still feel—I was always taking some new turn I hadn't expected.

As the days went on, Bubba's anger began to emerge in fights with his sister. Finally I took him aside to talk.

In the bathroom, of all places. I can still see him sitting on the tub.

"I know you're angry," I said. "And it's okay."

"I'm not angry," he insisted.

"You're not angry that Daddy is dead?"

He insisted he wasn't. I insisted back.

"It's okay to be mad," I told him. "You have to let it out. Otherwise it will come out in bad ways. Like getting mad at your sister. I'm not going to force you to cry," I added, finding my way as we spoke, "but I am going to ask you about things you miss about your dad. And you're going to have to tell me, even if it means crying. Because it's okay to cry. If you try to hold it in, you'll self-destruct."

I know that for a fact—I've come close myself.

"Well, okay," he said.

Not exactly convinced, I'm sure.

Later that night, we cuddled together in bed.

"Tell me something you miss about Daddy," I said to him softly.

"Do I have to?"

"Yes. You don't have to talk a long time."

"I miss the way he played with me," he said.

The tears started. I held him.

CHARITY

If there was one thing that helped me survive the first months of grief—and in fact continues to make things easier for me to this very day—it was the kindness of strangers. The outpouring of love and charity after Chris died was surely a miracle.

Almost as soon as the news got out that he had been killed, people started raising money to support us. The size of the outpouring really hit home for me when Glenn Beck asked me to come into his studio to hear a tribute to Chris. Chris had been on the TV show when the book came out and took an instant liking to Glenn; the feeling turned out to be mutual. Glenn was genuinely moved by Chris's death, and shared his grief both privately with his family and publicly with his audience.

Glenn called me into the office and presented me with a beautiful wooden box. A SEAL Trident was emblazoned on the front.

It opened up into a binder, which contained letters that people had sent to Glenn's Mercury One charity about Chris.

I looked at it and just felt like crying. "I don't know what to say."

Then he gave me a check.

Tears slipped from my eyes. We went to a studio to do a quick video thanking the charity's board; I choked up.

"You're giving me more than money," I told them when I managed to steady my voice. "It's the opportunity to collect myself and come from a position of strength."

One of the prizes on *Stars Earn Stripes* had been a Ford F-150 Raptor, a souped-up pickup. Shortly after the series ended, Chris mentioned to a friend that he'd been impressed by the truck and had hoped to win it and give it to me. As they got to talking, he confessed that what he really wanted to do was get me a new Ford Expedition—a Texas-sized SUV. We've had a series of SUVs in the family, and I love the vehicles for their versatility and usefulness, but all of the ones we've had were older, typically with eighty or ninety thousand miles on the odometer before we got them.

The week after Chris died, the friend who he'd been discussing the SUV with went to a cousin who owned a car dealership and arranged to buy me a new Expedition. I actually don't know the financial arrangements—everyone asked to be anonymous. The dealer threw in a warranty and service contract. When they presented it to me, I was floored. The piece of mind of driving a brand-new vehicle wasn't exactly hard to get used to.

At the same time, I kept the old SUV I'd been driving—I lend it out to others when they visit or to friends who need a truck.

The only thing we owned that was bigger than the Ford was our house.

After Chris died, Kyle Bass sent me an email and then came over to the house in person detailing his plans to forgive the house mortgage as a gift. It was a very generous offer—one matched by a few other friends—but I felt embarrassed, and even overwhelmed, when he told me to stop paying the mortgage. I thanked him profusely. I also thanked the others for their offers and generosity, explaining that Kyle Bass was taking care of us. I kept paying the taxes and other expenses, of course, but not having to write a mortgage check every month was a welcome relief.

The biggest thing these gifts have done for me is relieve stress. I didn't have to worry about putting food on the table. I could devote my energy to my kids and to projects related to Chris. It was an immense blessing, but with that blessing, came guilt. Did I deserve it? Did I deserve a new truck, or money to pay for food? Did I deserve luxuries?

That summer, the neighbors decided to sell their six-year-old Mustang sports car. I decided to buy it. It was not a necessity, and while I could argue that it got much better gas mileage than the Expedition, my reason for buying it was far more selfish than that. It was more fun to drive than the big trucks I'd driven since we had kids. I got a ridiculously good price because it belonged to a neighbor. But there was a certain twinge inside when I decided to do it. It was not the most prudent or responsible thing for a widow to do.

Was I abusing the kindness and charity I'd received?

I talked to different people about the donations. They told me unanimously that they had given me the money with no strings attached. On the contrary, several told me to have fun with it, to enjoy it in the spirit in which they had offered it.

But while I was grateful for that opportunity, it wasn't really me. I decided to put a portion of the money away as a special fund in case the worst happened—if I die, it will be there for my children. But I felt that I owed the people who had donated so generously something.

And I owed Chris as well. He had wanted to do so much good—he had already done so much good—that I felt obliged to continue that.

The generosity of all these strangers seemed to urge me to reach for a new goal:

Pay it forward.

The idea of doing small things for people was something Chris deeply believed in, and I did, too. But paying it forward was hard work.

I considered simply donating the money to different charities. But that wouldn't really fulfill Chris's ideal. I wanted to continue his legacy—and the only way to do that was to put together a charity specifically to carry on the things we had valued together.

People often start charities related to things they've lost or suffered through. I'm no different, and as I was looking for a focus, I came back again and again to the idea of supporting marriages and families under strain. I didn't want to focus just on veterans; from what I've seen, the families of first responders have very similar stresses and strains.

As I learned firsthand, our struggles in life affect more than just us. There is a ripple effect to our spirit and to others that isn't always obvious. The more I thought about it, the more I realized that by helping a marriage, we help the family that is united by it. It was a truth I knew in my heart, but it was also something that has rarely if ever been the focus of a charity: there are no foundations that encourage veterans' and first responders' marriages.

Here was my mission.

I wish I had understood more fully the effects trauma had on Chris. I wish I could have him here to love differently and with more understanding. I did my best, but maybe I could help others do better.

I looked to other groups as models. I am personally very impressed by organizations like the Gary Sinise Foundation that go the extra step. One thing (out of many) they do is build homes. They don't just build cookie-cutter houses; they build homes for specific families and their needs. And then there is Troops First, which also builds homes, sets up networks of support, and does unique things like the Proper Exit program, where they fly wounded vets back to the scene of their injuries and let them leave on their own terms.

I was also very impressed by the Boot Campaign. They're a nonprofit group that does a lot to promote patriotism and help veterans; I especially like their emphasis on supporting veterans' families. They have an awesome, hardworking board. I learned a lot from talking to them.

The last thing you want to do as a charity is to make a mistake that people believe was intentional. The more balls you have in the air, the more potential there is for mistakes. Missing a detail that seems unimportant at the time could easily lead to disaster. I started studying up on it. More importantly, I reached out for others to help.

Even though I went into it with both eyes open, it was a process that turned out to be even more complicated than I thought.

CREDIT WHERE NONE IS DUE

So much good followed Chris's death that I don't want to focus on the negative. But it does deserve to be mentioned that many people came forward and took credit for things that they had no right claiming credit for, inflating their roles in his life to make themselves look good.

A few people seem to have gotten into their heads that they could make a living off of Chris.

Of course, that happened before he died, too.

Some people felt entitled to go against the family wishes even at the funeral services because they had made donations or had some other excuse. It's too bad. I can't be hateful, but I am reminded often that some things are simply not for sale, and can never be bought.

Sad to say, I heard reports about money being raised under false pretenses; people used Chris's name to sell something or other. It was impossible to keep track of this, especially at first. Eventually we arranged for intellectual property lawyers to shut down the use of Chris's name, likeness, and logo except in the very few cases where it was authorized. But it was a little like Whac-A-Mole—one would be shut down, two others would pop up.

Chris's death spawned a number of articles and even books purporting to celebrate his life. I haven't read any of them. Some of them seem to have done a decent job; others, I'm told, are crass rip-offs, cynical attempts to make a quick buck at the expense of a hero's life.

Unfortunately, there's little I can do about most of these. As long as they don't violate Chris's copyright or break some other law, the authors have the right to say and do what they want. Freedom of speech and the press are important freedoms. Chris fought for those rights. It may be ironic that his memory is abused because of them, but that's the way it goes.

More hurtful, though certainly also allowed by the First Amendment, have been the strange and usually anonymous comments about him online. I'm not talking about reviews of the book or Facebook comments disagreeing with his politics. I mean hateful slander about his character. I suppose it's understandable when supporters of Jesse Ventura say outrageous things, but even a famous politician thoughtlessly said he deserved to die because he'd been a sniper in the military.

Bizarre.

More bizarre were the comments from alleged friends who gossiped to others about some foible or failing of Chris's—and then threatened to reveal all to me. As if I didn't know my husband better than anyone, his few faults as well as his blessings.

Chris used to say that he would spend a lot of time in the woodshed when he got to heaven, but believe me, if St. Peter takes him back there at all, it will be for the briefest of moments. The good far, far outweighed whatever bad there was. We're all human, of course, and none of us are perfect, but Chris was far above the average part of the spectrum.

When you don't have to look someone in the eye, it's a whole lot easier to diss them. Online, there are some miserable people who just want to spew hatred. And then there are other people who don't believe what they're saying at all, but are hoping to provoke a reaction.

Even the professional news media more and more emphasize things they know will get a reaction: fear, scandal, and things we can hate. We have negativity and fear broadcasting 24/7.

There is something about human nature that seeks that out. There can be five hundred good comments about something, and one negative. Which one do we focus on?

THE RIGHT PEOPLE AND THE RIGHT MOMENT

Being positive isn't always easy—and it can be even harder to do the right thing.

That summer, still trying to figure out how to carry on Chris's legacy and start a charity, I was invited to a networking event. While I was in the audience, a man who'd met Chris got up and started talking about how they'd met at Shot Show, how they'd gotten along, and how he knew they'd instantly become friends. It was that way with a lot of people: they just couldn't help but be friends with Chris, and vice versa.

"Then I heard about his death," said the speaker. "And I know this sounds awfully selfish of me to say, especially with his wife in the audience, but I felt as if I'd been robbed. I'd lost a great friendship before it even had a chance to begin. I've never cried the way I cried when I found out."

Then he invited me up—the people there had put some money together and gave me a check for $25,000.

It was more seed money for the charity. Better, the networking event provided me with contacts for dozens of people with experience running charities. I felt like God was telling me, "I got this."

I know you feel as if you can't do this, but I can. And I will.

Similar things happened as the year went on. I happened to mention the need for a website with Jennifer Lee, V's wife, a friend who had drawn even closer following Chris's death. The charity would need a designer and graphic artist; I had no idea how you went about finding one.

"Taya," she said, "you do know what I do for a living, right?"

"Uh, well—"

"No?"

"Um, no," I admitted.

Jennifer is a vice president of a corporation; included in her responsibilities was overseeing a team of designers and website creators.

Duh!

"I would love to be a part of this," she said. "Let me set that up."

Great!

We talked about other things, including the fact that *American Gun* was due to be published shortly. The publisher wanted me to help promote the book, which meant a lot of television appearances. I was willing to do anything I could—but nervous about being on TV. Chris had had some media training before his book tour, but I hadn't.

"You don't know any of those kind of people, do you?" I asked.

She shook her head.

But God was listening. A few days later, Jennifer called me from Ohio, where she had gone to visit some relatives.

"You're not going to believe this," she said. "But about that media trainer . . ."

Her sister-in-law and a friend had recently started a company that helped charities and nonprofits in various ways, from marketing to media training.

I just felt like it was divine intervention. God was putting the people in front of me I needed. The charity—which would eventually become the Chris Kyle Frog Foundation—started to take shape. There was still a lot to do; over the next several months I would be ready to quit many times. But every time, God put someone in my face to help.

I encountered my share of people who looked at me as "the little woman" who should say "yes" to whatever business they proposed, then go back to the kitchen. That attitude was most acute in the business world, but I encountered it in plenty of "normal" life situations as well. Proving I could walk and chew gum at the same time was never enough; I had to do it with a PowerPoint and perfectly coifed hair—while taking care of two kids as well.

There's an unfortunate tendency to look at a stay-at-home mom and conclude that she isn't interested in "serious" things. Business sense? Forget it. I hate to say it, but I think that stereotype is especially applied to the women who are married to military guys. A lot of people seem to think that we don't have the intelligence, or the experience, to be able to handle business. It's hard for people to understand that we're *choosing* to stay home; a lot of us—myself included—were quite successful in the business and professional worlds before devoting ourselves to our families.

I was most surprised to see that attitude among some of the people working with me on the charity. I guess I thought they'd be more enlightened.

Now, the truth is, I couldn't handle all the things Chris was involved in, let alone the charity, on my own. But no one could have. Chris would have had to hire and involve a lot of people as well.

Unfortunately, I didn't realize how true that was for quite a while. I kept pushing myself to do more, to prove that I was worthy, and to turn my grief into something useful. There was so much to do that even when people stepped up to help, I tried to keep most of the burden to myself. I kept feeling that I had to do more, and that it all had to be perfect.

After several months of nonstop work, a friend offered to let the kids and me stay with his family for a few days. It was the first vacation we'd had since Chris died.

His house is located on the coast in a beautiful, parklike setting. It was very peaceful, and with his family around, I felt a load off my shoulders. For the first time in months, I could sleep for ten, twelve hours, not worry about the kids, not worry about anything.

But amid all the peace, I couldn't entirely escape my sadness. One morning I was out walking and suddenly felt as if I were being pushed down into a hole. My friend's adult daughter happened to see me and asked what was wrong.

"I just realized that Chris doesn't really belong to me anymore," I told her. Tears were rolling down my face. "He belongs to everyone, and I've lost that part of him that was mine."

"I have chills all over my body," she said. "This has never happened to me before, but I feel Chris wants me to tell you something. *He'll always be yours.*"

While we had buried Chris, one important task related to his grave remained: picking a headstone.

That turned out to be harder than I would have imagined. There were so many choices that finding the exact right one became a daunting task. It wasn't just me I had to satisfy; the kids had to have a say.

"Mom, Daddy's stone is going to be big," said Angel. "I want it really big."

Maybe she was concerned that it would be on the ground and she wouldn't be able to see it, or find it easily. But she really didn't have an explanation; she just knew what she wanted. And if it was important to her, it was important to me.

To help us get an idea of the different possibilities, the officials at the cemetery took us across the grounds. I was impressed by Coach Tom Landry's stone, which was navy blue with silver specks that sparkled when hit just right by the sun. Not only was it beautiful; Landry was a legend among Cowboy fans—something Chris would have appreciated.

Still, there was something about the color that didn't quite suit Chris, and I began to worry that it might be too close to Coach Landry's. So when Gilbert Beall, the artist who would prepare the stone, offered to show me some other possibilities, I gladly accepted. We went to another cemetery where he pointed out a somewhat similar stone in dark green. Like Coach Landry's, it's from Scandinavia and has a subtle sparkle. It's a handsome, stately rock. Dark green was Chris's favorite color; it reminded me of hunting and nature, which of course Chris loved.

It was also very expensive. But of all the things I might spend money on, my husband's final resting place was the most deserving.

The design—it hasn't been finished as I'm writing this—has elegant trim work that reminded me of the trim on our house. But it also has a simplicity to it that for me speaks of humility. The artist is doing a relief of Chris, based on Chris's favorite portrait of himself: in camo in Iraq atop rubble. It was one of the few pictures of himself he actually liked. On my side—not to be occupied for many, many years—there will be a relief of the kids' and my hands together. It will be a lasting symbol of our lives together.

Little things assume immense importance when they are associated with death. You focus on things that seem irrational—except at the moment.

We had to choose a specific location and position for his grave. There was a beautiful spot on the hill that would have let him face the flag, but the arrangement would have meant placing his head below his feet.

I couldn't do that.

I ended up choosing a spot at the bottom of a hill, on a piece of flat land near a stream.

Still, not everything was perfect. A politician was going to be buried nearby.

"Could you make sure there's someone between Chris and the politician?" I asked. "He really wasn't fond of them."

You just want to keep taking care of the person you love.

As the months went on, I couldn't shake the feeling that Chris was still somehow with us. Maybe it was the depression; maybe it was grief. Maybe something else.

Feeling down and empty, I chance to look across the room and think I catch a glimpse of him.

I go to a restaurant with the kids and sit at a table. A while later I look up and swear Angel is sitting on Chris's lap.

I take a walk and from the corner of my eye see him in his camouflage jacket walking beside me.

He's in a crowd, or standing across the parking lot, or lurking nearby in the shadows.

TELLING CHRIS'S STORY, AND OURS

American Gun was scheduled for publication around Father's Day 2013. Meeting the deadlines was an incredible effort—toward the end, we were working around the clock, every day of the week. But finally we finished. The only thing that remained was the selling.

The publisher had originally planned for Chris to do publicity, much as he had done on *American Sniper*. But without him there, they asked me to fill in. While they expected some interest in the book and its tales about American history, they knew that the media would be far more interested in my story—how I was coping with Chris's death.

I felt honored that people cared.

I'd done some interviews with Chris when *American Sniper* came out, but this was different; I was on my own. It was a coming-out party, in a way, the first time I'd spoken publicly about Chris for any length since his death.

I wanted the book to do well, not only to honor Chris but to earn back the advance the publisher had given him for it. But I also saw the promotion efforts as a chance to talk about different issues facing veterans, especially PTSD. I wanted to make it clear that, barring special circumstances, veterans with PTSD are not threats to the rest of us. And I wanted to spread Chris's idea about small gestures of support meaning a great deal to veterans who have come home from war.

The publisher thought I could use security to accompany me, and we turned to V, who'd been on the first book tour. I talked about the plans for the media and book tour with Jennifer a short time later; she'd helped arrange for some media training to prep me for the more emotional points.

She asked if I was okay.

"Yes," I said. "I feel really confident."

"Good. I'm going with you."

"No, no, I'm fine."

"Of course you are. I'm still going with you."

It became kind of a running joke with my friends that summer—I'd tell them I was fine to do something on my own, and they'd show up for support. Then I'd turn around and thank them profusely when I was done, because truthfully I couldn't have gotten through without them there.

The arrangement was tricky for V and Jennifer—normally a bodyguard won't travel with someone related to them, because they tend to be a distraction. But there were no incidents anywhere, including New York, where I was joined by Harper publicist Sharyn Rosenblum and Jim for part of the time.

Sharyn had handled the arrangements for *American Sniper* and developed a deep connection with Chris and me. By now she was more friend than publicist, and I was glad to have her along as an advisor.

Bill O'Reilly agreed to have me on, in a kind of reprise of Chris's appearance. Bill had defended Chris after the Jesse Ventura suit was filed, and I think he was genuinely distressed by Chris's death.

That didn't make it any easier to do the show. I mean, *Bill O'Reilly.*

We arrived early. In makeup, I kept telling myself to be confident. The others kept giving me thumbs-up signs, and Sharyn was very positive, but when the producer came to get me, I felt my throat tighten.

I'm losing it, I thought while walking out of the green room.

I stopped in the hall and waited, trying not to show my panic to the producer.

He disappeared into the studio. I stood there, breathing

slowly—or rather, trying to breathe slowly. Mostly, I wasn't breathing at all.

Sharyn appeared next to me.

"Take an extra water in with you," she suggested, handing me the bottle.

I'm not sure why she thought that would work, but I nodded.

"One minute," said the producer from the doorway.

At that instant I absolutely could not go on. I couldn't even move—which was fortunate, because if I could have moved, I would have run out of the building, probably all the way back to Texas.

The producer prompted me again, gently adding that I could take my time; they were going to tape rather than air the spot live. Somehow I managed to move myself in the direction he was pointing. I entered the studio and saw Bill sitting at his television desk, waiting. That psyched me up—for half a second. Then the urge to run was joined by other, even less attractive urges emanating from my stomach. I clamped my mouth shut and walked silently to the guest's chair.

Bill is not chatty before interviews, but that was a good thing—my mouth still wasn't working. The producer must have seen something in my face—sheer panic, most likely—and he hopped over to calm me down. I have no recollection of what he said or did, or how my mouth finally started working. I just know I took some sort of breath, turned to Bill, and said something along the lines of "I'm ready."

Or maybe he said that. Someone started a countdown, and Bill O'Reilly snapped into Bill O'Reilly mode, talking to the camera and introducing me.

Go, girl!

He asked about the book, about guns, about Chris's murder. I answered. He kept asking. I kept answering.

He was very kind and accommodating. We talked about history, guns, and Jesse. I'd like to say that it got easier as I went, but the truth is, I don't remember if it did. I don't remember much of anything, except that I was very glad when it was done.

I was on *Fox & Friends,* MSNBC, Glenn Beck's show, Anderson Cooper's show—so many that I can't remember. So much of media is cold, but the feelings I got from nearly every interviewer were warm and genuine. They were truly sorry for the tragedy of Chris's death, and I felt that many wanted to do as much for all veterans as I do.

Then, just as I was starting to get used to the routine, it was over. The book was on its own.

It was an instant bestseller, a tribute to Chris and the people around the country who'd decided to support him.

FILM THERAPY

People say that work can be therapy. In the case of the movie, I think it literally was.

Jason Hall and I stayed in very close contact as he revised the screenplay. I don't know how many hundreds of hours we spent talking. He did it because he wanted to get the script right, but also because I was grieving and he wanted to comfort me. He became a friend and almost a counselor as we discussed not only Chris's life but different aspects of loss and grief. I appreciated not only his efforts, but what all of those hours of work must have meant for his wife Elisha.

There were a lot of times when I choked up and couldn't talk. At those moments he turned from writer to friend, telling me it was okay to let my emotions out.

I told him about my niece's baptism, about how horrible it would have been to let go.

"Why?" he asked.

"It would have caused a scene."

"So?"

"People would have looked at me like I was a poor widow. They would have been pitying me. I don't want that."

"It's real," he insisted. "It's raw. No one's going to judge you on that."

"But—"

"You better let it out," he said. "Or you'll end up being a bitter, raw old woman."

I knew the kind of woman he was talking about. There's a difference between a grandmother whose life and love shine through the wrinkles on her face and the unpleasant old woman who wears a scowl as a scar of her battles against the world and herself.

"You gotta let it out," said Jason. "Let it out."

He was right, but I was still afraid. More and more, I feared falling into a deep depression. As the grief stubbornly remained with me, I began dreading the crevices I knew were ahead.

"Let yourself go," urged Jason. But I was too afraid to do that. And so what I feared became more and more a reality.

I thought releasing my emotions would mean I'd let go of Chris as well. As long as I hurt, I had proof he was still there.

If I allowed my tears to flow and my body to heave, surely there would come a time when they would be exhausted. I would not have enough tears to fill a lake or green all of Texas, but if I did—if I let myself loose and simply cried for hours and days and weeks—then there would eventually be an end. There would be a finish to the physical expression of my grief, if only because of exhaustion.

And if my crying was done, then my memory would be over. My love would be gone. I would lose my husband for good.

If all I had of him was grief, then so be it—I could at least hold on to that.

SPIELBERG AND CLINT

With the script nearly done, the studio and Bradley Cooper's production company looked for a director. They didn't want just any director, and that summer they announced they were moving ahead with a big one: Steven Spielberg.

Wooo-hooo! I thought when I heard.

Saving Private Ryan was one of Chris's favorite movies, and he loved *Band of Brothers*. He would have been honored at the idea of Spielberg making this one.

Spielberg was interested in seeing some of our home videos and photographs so the designers and director could get an idea of how things should look.

One of the people in charge of props told me: "It's not my job necessarily to make things look exactly as they were in real life. But I want [the movie] to look so authentic that when you see it, you'll think it's part of your own personal history. It will be your life to hold onto."

That attention to detail—and that care and dedication—moved me, and I did everything I could to help them. Still, I didn't want to just put my memories in the mail or FedEx. To put me at ease, the studio offered to use a team of couriers so that the material would be in someone's hands each step of the way.

They sent a driver out one day. He was a big, hulking fellow who filled Chris's office the way Chris would have.

"I just have a few more things to pack up," I told him. "If you could just wait a second."

"Sure."

Bubba came in, still wearing his jammies. "Hey," he said to the guy. "You play darts?"

"Uh—"

By now Bubba was so used to people dropping by and playing with him that he didn't even need to ask who they were.

He'd also become pretty good at darts.

I wrapped up quickly, sparing the poor fellow the humiliation of losing to a kid whose voice wouldn't change for several more years.

Some things were just too difficult to do.

Bradley Cooper wanted to know more about Chris, and I decided to send him some of the emails I'd saved while he was deployed. I sat down and read the first one, and started to cry.

This is silly.

I tried a few times, but couldn't go on.

A few days later, I tried again.

Once more, I had to stop.

I sent them to Bradley and to Sienna Miller without reading the rest.

Unfortunately, things didn't quite work out with Spielberg, and he ended up detaching himself from the project that August. But his replacement may have been even better, at least from Chris's point of view: Clint Eastwood.

I couldn't help but think back to the conversation Chris and I had had about Eastwood possibly directing.

"Still doing your magic, huh, babe?" I said the day I found out, glancing toward heaven.

One of the things I'd always admired about Clint Eastwood as a director was his ability to tap deep undercurrents of meaning in his films. His movies don't show and tell everything in an obvious manner; they get their message across in subtle ways, but make you feel it.

From practically the moment the movie was announced, people asked me whether I was excited. The truth is, I wasn't.

I was scared.

I was the person left to make sure it was right, and it was up to me to make sure that Chris was represented accurately, even though that was really out of my hands.

I wanted so much for the movie to show *all* of Chris, not just the part of him that had to go to war. Certainly his service to our country was his life's calling. But I wanted—want—people to understand who he was, the whole Chris: father, husband, friend, as well as warrior.

How do you take someone's whole life and shrink it into a couple of hours? I don't think you can.

As good as I felt about the efforts Jason was making, and what Bradley and the studio were doing to get things right, I began to feel apprehensive. What if they didn't get it right? What if the movie made Chris out to be arrogant? Or simply missed him entirely?

I couldn't express my doubts to the movie people. They were trying too hard. But the more I kept them in, the bigger they grew.

My computer is tucked into an armoire, whose doors fold out to reveal the desk. Before Chris died, I'd covered the inside with photos, mostly of him and the kids.

I didn't realize at first, but the photos pounded my heart every time I worked. The happy memories they represented were shards of fractured steel, perforating my soul.

Eventually I realized I had to take them down. I cried as I did. Then I put them back, and cried some more.

An hour later, I took them down again. This time I put them into a drawer, where at least I could take my pain in doses.

After Chris died, the National Rifle Association decided that they wanted to honor him at the NRA national convention. So they called and asked me to attend and represent him.

"I don't want to just stand there and get an award," I told them. "I feel as if I have to contribute something."

They agreed—I think reluctantly. Maybe they were worried that, since my husband had been shot, I would be anti-gun. On the contrary, I didn't blame the weapon; I blamed the man who did the killing. And maybe saying that publicly was part of the reason I wanted to speak.

> It is an honor to be with you today. America needs people like
> you who are willing to stand up and fight for part of what makes
> America great. In the next few minutes, I want to share my
> personal perspective of what you are doing when you expend time
> and energy to protect our freedoms—not just those protected by
> the Second Amendment, but all of them.

I'm sure you know the reason I'm here speaking to you today, instead of my husband, Chris Kyle. I challenge anyone to tell me there isn't evil in this world. From the days of Cain and Abel, we know all too well, there will always be evil.

But that evil shouldn't take away our freedoms. In fact, the only way to defeat evil is by taking advantage of those freedoms. And so, let me talk about some sides of Chris that maybe you don't know, and use his experiences to highlight why our freedoms—and the responsibility to do good that comes with them—are so important.

Giving the speech helped convince me that I could honor Chris's memory by taking the stage. And that led to another idea: if people were willing to listen to me, they might be willing to support the charity as well. The two could go together.

Instead of simply organizing the charity, I could work for it as well. That would give me a meaningful though unpaid job, and give it a way to continue growing. It was a way of paying it forward.

I certainly believed in the message; the only question was whether I could believe in myself.

I don't like to be the center of attention, which may be an odd quality for someone who is interested in public speaking. But going onstage felt different. There, I wasn't the focus; the focus was on the message—how Chris changed my life, how ideas like "paying blessings forward" and the "ripple effect of kindness" can make all of society better.

The idea was still tentative—but then again, so was everything in my life.

THE FROG AT DISNEY WORLD

Chris and I had purchased a flexible time-share around the time Bubba was born, hoping that we would have a family vacation tradition. It had never gotten the kind of use we wanted—whose does?—but when it was used, by us and other family members, it did provide a lot of fun.

In the year after Chris died, a friend organized a trip for the kids and me to use the time-share at Disney World in Florida. I felt exceptionally lonely the night we arrived in our rental car, exhausted from our flight. Getting our suitcases out, I mentioned something along the lines of "I wish we had Dad here."

"Me, too," said both of the kids.

"But he's still with us," I told them, forcing myself to sound as optimistic as possible. "He's always here."

It's one thing to say that and another to feel it, and as we walked toward the building I didn't feel that way at all. We went upstairs—our apartment was on the second floor—and went to the door.

A tiny frog was sitting on the door handle.

A frog, really? Talk about strange.

Anyone who knows the history of the SEALs will realize they trace their history to World War II combat divers: "frogmen" specially trained to infiltrate and scout enemy beaches before invasions (among other duties). They're very proud of that heritage, and they still occasionally refer to themselves as frogmen or frogs. SEALs often feature frogs in various tattoos and other art related to the brotherhood. As a matter of fact, Chris had a frog skeleton tattoo as a tribute to fallen SEALs. (The term *frogman* is thought to derive from the gear combat divers wore, as well as their ability to work both on land and at sea.)

But for some reason, I didn't make the connection. I was just consumed by the weirdness—who finds a frog, even a tiny one, on a door handle?

The kids gathered round. Call me squeamish, but I didn't want to touch it.

"Get it off, Bubba!" I said.

"No way."

We hunted around and found a little tree branch on the grounds. I held it up to the doorknob, hoping it would hop on. It was reluctant at first, but finally it toddled over to the outside of the door jam. I left it to do whatever frogs do in the middle of the night. Inside the apartment, we got settled. I took out my cell phone and called my mom to say we'd arrived safely.

"There was one strange thing," I told her. "There was a frog on the door handle when we arrived."

"A . . . frog?"

"Yes, it's like a jungle down here, so hot and humid."

"A frog?"

"Yeah."

"And you don't think there's anything interesting about that?"

"Oh my God," I said, suddenly realizing the connection.

I know, I know: just a bizarre coincidence.

Probably.

I did sleep really well that night.

The next morning, I woke up before the kids and went into the living room. I could have sworn Chris was sitting on the couch waiting for me when I came out.

I can't keep seeing you everywhere.

Maybe I'm crazy.

I'm sorry. It's too painful.

I went and made myself a cup of coffee. I didn't see him anymore that week.

I didn't want the kids to know I was smoking, so instead of taking along cigarettes, I brought along some of those nicotine lozenges.

That turned out to be a bit of a mistake. I snuck one while we were standing in line for It's a Small World.

Great idea, right? Try that with a cigarette.

Except . . . within minutes I felt as if I had to heave.

"Stay in line," I mumbled to the kids. I ran to a nearby garbage can, unburdened myself, and returned.

"Mom?" asked Bubba.

"I'm fine."

I ended up buying a pack of cigarettes and smoked them on the balcony of the room that night while I returned some business calls.

At one point I looked down at the corner near the railing.

The frog was there.

"I'm not buying it," I told the creature.

I went back to making calls. When I was done, the frog was still sitting in the same place. I walked over and took a few pictures. It didn't seem to care.

I *do* think that Chris was and is with me, but whether that has anything to do with the frog—I have no clue.

I don't seem to have any control over the odd occurrences, let alone the feeling that he is with me. So in the end I have to accept them. It's a kind of faith in reality beyond easy explanations, acceptance of things that neither make sense nor can be reduced to anything except what they are in themselves: like a frog on a door handle.

BUBBA'S BUCK

Among the many people Chris met while doing charity work was Randy Cupp, who invited him and Bubba out to shoot with him come deer season. When Chris passed away, Randy made it clear to me that the offer not only still stood, but that he would love to give Bubba a chance to kill his first buck.

With deer season upon us, the kids and I decided to take him up on the offer. Angel, Bubba, and I went out to his property on a beautiful morning. Setting out for the blind, I felt Chris's presence, as if he were scouting along with us. We settled into our spots and waited.

A big buck came across in front of us a short time later. It was an easy shot—except that Bubba had neglected to put his ear protection in. He scrambled to get it in, but by the time he was ready, the animal had bounded off. Deer—and opportunities—are like that.

We waited some more.

Another buck came out from the trees not five minutes later. And this one was not only in range, but it was bigger than the first: a thirteen pointer.

Chris must have scared that thing up.

"That's the one," said Randy as the animal pranced forward.

Bubba took a shot.

The deer scooted off as the gunshot echoed. My son thought he'd missed, but Randy was sure he'd hit him. At first, we didn't see a blood trail—a bad sign, since a wounded animal generally leaves an easily spotted trail. But a few steps later, we found the body prone in the woods. Bubba had killed him with a shot to the lungs.

Like father, like son.

While Bubba left to dress the carcass, I went back to the blind with Angel to wait for another. She was excited that she might get a deer just like her brother. But when a buck walked within range, tears came to her eyes.

"I can't do it," she said, putting down her gun.

"It's okay," I told her.

"I just can't."

"Do you want me to?" I asked.

She nodded.

I took aim. Even though I was married to a hard-core hunter, I had never shot a deer before. I lined up the scope, walking him into the crosshairs. A slow breath, and I squeezed the trigger. The shot surprised me—just as Chris said it should.

The deer fell. He was good meat; we eat what we kill, another of Chris's golden rules.

"You know, Angel, you're going to be my hunting partner forever," I told her later. "You're just so calm and observant. And good luck."

We plan to do that soon. She'll be armed with a high-powered camera, rather than a rifle.

LEGAL ENTANGLEMENTS

Now that I was in a position to, with the estate, eventually own or control 85 percent of Craft, I tried to get a clear understanding of what was going on with the company. I knew that before he died, Chris had expressed concerns about being shut out of Craft International Risk Management or CIRM, the apparently related company.

Beyond that, I was worried about Craft's general viability. Its financial struggles had led Chris to stop taking a salary in August 2012, and I saw no reason that things had improved.

The LLC Agreement included certain provisions likely intended to prohibit a spouse from participating in ownership or management of the company. But as a beneficial owner, I thought it only fair that I be allowed to look at the books. I offered to involve one of my relatives, a business expert, to help examine the operations and offer restructuring advice for free, something ordinarily worth about $50,000. But the request was spurned, and while Bo and Steven later contended in court papers that I was given full access to Craft's financials, my lawyer countered that we only received data showing general income and expenditures.

What started as a friendly inquiry as I attempted to get a handle on the estate's finances became a serious conflict as time went on. Until this point, I had cautiously thought of Chris's business partners as friends. Now they were adversaries. It was a bizarre and baffling turn of events. I couldn't understand why I wasn't being given complete information about the company. Worse, Bo and Steven insisted that they had the right to use Chris's name and likeness for the company's business. That didn't seem right either.

The bad feelings were palpable.

The Ventura lawsuit was an even heavier weight, a sort of torture I'd never encountered before. Even forgetting the effects of the negative publicity, it is amazing how much work and strain are involved in a lawsuit.

I should point out that both my husband and I tried to reach an amiable and just agreement without animosity or going to court. It takes two sides to agree, however, and no acceptable compromise could be found. Each party's position remained the same through the trial.

As the year went on, I felt I was handling my grief and depression better, but the pressures kept piling up. You don't really ever feel "comfortable" being a widow. You endure, maybe get through it, but you don't ever truly own it.

And still, a part of me didn't want to get beyond it. My pain was proof of my love.

One night I went over to a friend's house and just started bawling. I had been going through photos of Chris when he was in his twenties and thirties.

I'm going to be an old woman somewhere, and he's going to be young.

So many other emotions ran through me every day. People suggested that I might find someone else.

"No," I'd tell them. "No one will ever take his place."

School forms would ask about the kids' family situation. Were their parents married, divorced?

I'm not a single mother. I'm raising the kids with my husband! Even if he's not here. I always think about what he would want to do.

One night, alone in my bedroom, I picked up the laundry basket off the treadmill. I suddenly felt as if Chris was there with me, somehow hovering two feet off the ground.

He grinned.

"I'm working on something for you," he said. And I knew he meant he was trying to hook me up with a man.

I jerked back. Had I really heard that? Was he really there?

The room was empty, but I had the strongest feeling that he was there. I could feel his grin.

I became furious.

"How dare you!" I screamed in my head. "I don't want anyone else. I want you! What's wrong with you?"

I walked out of the room.

I blocked him out for a while, partly because of that incident, partly because of how overwhelming the emotions were. Finally I realized

I didn't want to do that. And one night toward the end of the year, I said aloud, "I'm sorry. I didn't mean to block you out."

The room was empty, but I sensed he might be with me.

"I am so sorry!" I repeated. Then I started bawling. I felt as if he came over and put his arm around my waist.

I'm sorry. I didn't mean to hurt you.

His voice, in a whisper, but one I felt rather than heard: *I didn't want to hurt you.*

I cried and cried. I felt a million things—sorry, crazy, insane.

I finally glanced up and looked in the mirror. I was alone.

"I'm not losing it," I told myself. "What little I have left, I'm not losing it."

I slumped off to bed, exhausted.

SIX

FAITH

Michael Ainsworth/Dallas Morning News

As much as I tried to keep my emotions in check, they found ways to escape and overwhelm me. They got worse instead of better. I'd be in the bathroom getting ready and would suddenly start to cry. One morning it went quickly to dry heaves.

Within moments I realized I couldn't stop.

I grabbed my cell phone and called my friend Karen, the doctor. I was too close to hysteria even to take an antinausea pill. Luckily, she guided me through some breathing exercises, and I finally got myself under control. But I lived in fear that I might lose it and not be able to stop.

Nearly ten months had gone by since Chris and Chad had died. Grief was a black hole in my chest threatening to consume me from the inside out. I needed an iron will to keep it at bay; eventually, even an iron will wasn't nearly strong enough anymore.

Christmas was approaching. I'd gone through nearly a year without Chris, and if anything I was feeling worse. I was completely tapped out.

The truth is, if it weren't for my kids, I'd rather have been with him.

TAPPED OUT—DECEMBER 2013

The worst thing: I wasn't taking care of my kids the way I wanted.

For any mother, that has to be the most damning thought. We can fail at business, even at being a wife, and go on. But fail our children?

One day I looked at them and realized they had grown without me even knowing it. And yet I was spending a lot of time with them: I'd be waiting when they came home from school to monitor their homework, play, and make dinner—all the time trying to ignore the constant stream of texts and emails arriving on my phone. I'd wait until after they went to bed to work—often until two or three in the morning.

That showed in the mornings, when I'd sleep through two or three alarms and had to rush to get the kids up and out.

I was working at the house with a friend when one day she looked at me very seriously.

"Are you all right?" she asked.

"Yes, of course," I said. "Why?"

"You're constantly grabbing at your neck."

I looked down and saw that my chest was red. I'd somehow developed a nervous habit—possibly, it turned out, as a strange, psychological side effect of the medication I was on. I did it without even knowing it.

There were other symptoms. My temper was shorter and shorter, and at times I felt as if I was going to have a heart attack. On the outside, I was calm. On the inside, I felt like I was just going to explode.

I think in that moment, as I unclutched my hand from my chest, I finally realized what it must feel like to return home from combat. The adrenaline and the shock to the system must be completely overwhelming.

It made me feel closer to him. I realized that he must have felt pressed on from all angles. He would have had to struggle to keep himself balanced, whole. I wish I had understood that better at the time.

I went to see a psychiatrist.

"How are you?" he asked when I walked into his office.

"Great," I said.

"That's an answer I don't get very often."

We talked some more. He started asking questions. As I answered them, I began to cry.

"Your husband?" he asked.

"He was murdered."

"Oh . . ."

We adjusted the medication. The clutching at my chest stopped. The pain stayed.

CRAFT ULTIMATUM

Around mid-December, I went to New York to attend the premiere of the movie *Lone Survivor*, about Marcus Lutrell's moving ordeal in Afghanistan. Shortly after I arrived, I got an email from the Craft principals seeking to sever my interest in Craft. They indicated they would buy me out for $12,500. But I had better make my mind up quick.

I can just imagine how Chris would have responded to that. The offer was, in my opinion, ludicrous. Further, my understanding of the agreement, and the position taken by my lawyers, was that an offer to buy me out—even a legitimate one—should have been made months before.

We had reached an impasse, or maybe something worse. It seemed clear to me that Bo and Steven were not going to cooperate with me. If I wanted to find out what was going on—and if I wanted to make sure that Chris's name, likeness, and logo were only used in ways that he would approve—I had to take legal steps.

On December 13, I filed suit. I asked to see the financial records of Craft to determine whether Craft had made unauthorized payments or loans and whether Craft International Risk Management, the company Chris thought he had been shut out of, had usurped any business opportunities of Craft. The suit asserted claims for breach of fiduciary duty, fraud, and conversion, to name a few.

The conflict got worse. Just before Bo and Steven were to be deposed in the lawsuit, they declared Craft bankrupt. They also insisted that they had the right to use Chris's name, likeness, image and his skull logo for company business. That seemed outrageous to me. If the company was bankrupt, then surely the company should no longer control Chris's name and trademarks.

If the principals were Chris's friends to begin with, why had they not included him in the new company? And why all the BS now? If the business was worthless, so be it—let everything drop.

They suggested at one point that Craft should receive money from the publication of *American Sniper.* Craft benefited from *American Sniper* in several ways. For one thing, the publisher contracted with them to provide security for Chris during the book tour, an unusual move. More importantly, Chris's new fame helped raise the company's profile; he wore the logo at almost all of his appearances, at least partly at their request. But there was no specific connection between Craft and the book.

I don't know what to think. Maybe the idea was to procrastinate and make me spend more money on lawyers. Maybe they just lost touch with reality. Who knows?

I do know this: Dealing with Craft and worrying about the Jesse lawsuit at the same time caused a lot more stress than anyone could handle under any circumstances, let alone mine.

CHRISTMAS

I tried not to think about the fact that this was going to be the first Christmas without Chris. I didn't want to ruin the holiday, or all the days leading up to it. I wanted to celebrate the season and let the kids have fun.

I'll feel what I feel that day, I told myself.

It was a great day for the kids. My parents, sister, and brother-in-law were all there. After they opened their presents, the kids went and played with friends; they said it was the best Christmas ever.

But for me, it felt empty. True, I felt some joy watching them, but it was as if in between the happiness and me was a thick layer of Lucite that bent and distorted the emotion, reducing it the way cloudy plastic reduces light.

My sister Ashley and brother-in-law Stewart flew in from Australia for the holiday, but they ended up doing far more than celebrating. Stewart especially was a godsend. He just started pitching in on the many business issues involved in the foundation, helping me understand what had to be done and then making sure it was followed through. His guidance as well as my family's love really helped get me out of the metaphorical hole I'd sunk into and rededicate my efforts to the foundation.

Did God send my family to my side exactly when I needed them?

In late January, a friend pointed out that there were flags all through the neighborhood.

"Taya," she asked, "what national holiday is coming up?"

None that I could think of. Then I realized that it was to honor Chris—our neighbors and the local Rotary Club had gotten together and put the flags up in Chad and Chris's memory.

I wondered what I should do to mark the anniversary of his death. I thought of going to the cemetery. But then I realized that I shouldn't celebrate the day he died—there was no way I was going to honor his end like that. Instead, I treated it as a normal day, or at least as normal a day as I could muster. I wrote about my feelings and posted them on Facebook, pouring my heart out and crying as I hit enter on the keyboard.

ALL OUR BURDENS

Late that winter, there was a hearing for Chris's accused murderer, Eddie Routh. The hearing was important; it gave him the option to plead guilty and avoid the death penalty.

The courthouse was an hour and a half away, but I felt I had to be there to bear witness for Chris. Chris's mom and dad and his brother Jeff felt the same way. My brother-in-law Stewart, my friend Vanessa, and some other family friends also came along for support.

Thank God they were all there with me. I went in thinking that I was fine, only to find my strength sliding away as the proceedings began. Occasionally one of my friends or family would put their hand on my back and help ease my anxiety. I tried to do the same for Jeff, who was sitting beside me; I could feel his anger seething.

A lot of our friends were hoping Routh would plead guilty and spare us the ordeal of a trial. I didn't really have an opinion. Part of me wanted things over with, but another part wanted the man judged.

Tears rolled down my eyes for much of the proceedings, even though from a legal point of view they were routine. In the end, Routh didn't plead guilty. A date was set for a May trial.

So be it, I thought.

I was standing on the aisle as court was dismissed. Routh's family had taken seats on the other side, and I caught a glimpse of his mother as she got up.

Somehow I realized she was going to come over and try and talk to us.

I wasn't ready to deal with that. There had been reports in the media that her son had threatened people with violence, something I doubt Chris knew. That doesn't make her responsible for what happened, but I have to wonder if things would have been different had Chris realized how severe her son's problems were.

I caught the prosecutor's eye as she started toward us.

Help!

He walked down to intercept her.

"I just want to say something," said the woman.

The bailiff stepped in, keeping her away.

"I just want to talk to them," she said tearfully. "This is just as hard for us as it is for them."

What a weird thing to say, certainly at that time and place. Her son was still alive; my husband was dead. As hard as it was for her, things were far more difficult for us.

Maybe some people will wish I could have taken a different, more generous view. It's not that I don't understand her pain; it has to be brutal. But I don't know what I could have said, let alone done, that would have assuaged it.

I know as Christians we need to show mercy and forgiveness, just as we will one day ask the same of God. But at that moment and place, I would have had to be a saint to do any more than tremble as I walked from the courthouse.

My stance on the death penalty is one of the many things that I have had to wrestle with since Chris's death.

As a Christian, I know that judgment is God's. Yet I want justice for my husband.

I believe that, if we have faith and repent our sins, we will be forgiven when we get to heaven; the Bible says as much. On earth, things are more complicated. In Texas, the alternative to the death penalty is life without parole. The prison where murderers serve out their sentence is truly a terrible place, and there is no hope of parole.

I've thought quite a bit about it, and come around to the view that life without parole may in fact be a worse punishment than death. It does provide protection for society as well as justice for a person who has murdered. I haven't changed my mind about the death penalty—I think it is an appropriate punishment for certain crimes—but I have come to see life without parole as an appropriate punishment as well.

Can a criminal redeem himself in the eyes of God by asking for forgiveness? That's for God to judge and decide.

As a Christian, I hope he can. But at the same time, forgiveness does not mean that they are absolved of the consequences of their actions on earth.

Asked by the prosecutor, I said that I was good with whatever they decided to seek as a penalty, provided he didn't walk the earth as a free man again. Otherwise, I deferred to anyone else in the family with strong feelings. That was as far as I could go toward forgiveness.

A few months later, the trial was postponed until early 2015 because of a new law that required comprehensive DNA testing and processing. Every bit of DNA material found in Chris's truck, for example, had to be collected and analyzed—a process that would take months under the best circumstances. So any hope of closure had to be put off for a year.

I don't have post-traumatic stress disorder, but Chris's death and the things that followed brought me a little closer to understanding what it must be like. Simple things can catch you off guard.

Parents' Back-to-School Night, for example.

I went to one recently. Pretty much your routine, suburban middle-class experience. But walking in one of the hallways I began feeling very sweaty and panicky. The walls didn't close in, exactly, but there was a certain unease that I couldn't classify, let alone get rid of.

There was no reason for me to be panicky in that moment, but I was. I saw people I knew and should say hello to, but I just couldn't make the effort. All I could do was stay in my corner.

I know PTSD has become a very overused term; in some ways it's the disease of the week. Still, I do have a lot of sympathy for people who have it.

But I need to make it clear: having PTSD does not make you schizophrenic, or a murderer. Plenty of good people have PTSD, and the only ones they harm are themselves.

The diagnosis is not, and should not be, a Get Out of Jail Free card. It can't excuse bad behavior, let alone criminal behavior, even if it can give us some understanding of people's conditions. Even people who are hurt or injured are responsible for their actions. From everything I have heard, PTSD doesn't change your core character—it doesn't turn you into an evil person or sociopath.

I know it's a difficult balance. We have to be sympathetic toward the victims of PTSD while not letting them use it as an excuse. We can't risk putting a black mark on anyone who has the diagnosis, or even has trouble readjusting to normal life after experiencing trauma.

GOD

I know for a fact that my life with Chris changed my relationship with God.

I was raised Episcopalian—Sunday school and all that. I always felt, from the time I was young, that God was real. There were times when I doubted if Jesus was the only way to God—people all over the world believe in God, so why does there have to be only one way to find salvation? I've come to a place now where I've accepted Jesus as my savior, but I also wouldn't be prepared to tell others that they're wrong for taking another path to God.

If I am going to believe in God and Jesus this strongly, my faith should be able to stand the test of examination. And I think it has.

Soon after I moved to Texas, I read *The Case for Christ*. The author, Lee Strobel, says that he approached the topic of Christ's divinity and existence with great skepticism; he even considered himself an atheist at one time. He interviewed a series of expert witnesses and proved to his satisfaction that Jesus was in fact real.

For me, that's important. I need more than faith to believe.

The churches that I have always liked are the ones that I call "come as you are." They bring the Bible to you, interpreting it for everyday situations. For me, they make faith relevant as well as real. More than one of my favorite churches has referred to their congregation as a "motley crew"—and I think that's a good thing.

Chris could readily reference certain parts of the Bible that applied to war and fighting. But his knowledge and beliefs went far beyond that.

We were talking about religion and the Bible one night while he was deployed. I don't remember exactly the conversation, but I do recall being surprised that Chris was able to talk about the Bible in such depth. Maybe misinterpreting my surprise, he told me I could look up what he was talking about in the Bible myself.

"I have one in the truck," he said.

"You do?"

"I always have one with me."

It was something I'd never known. He was not the sort of person who made a big deal out of religion. I guess he lived it more than proclaimed it.

During the nights of Chris's first deployment, I would pray to God that He would protect him. The prayers were deeply personal, and as I prayed, I sensed the weight of what I was asking settle on my chest like a physical thing. In that weight, I felt God's hand. It was a connection I had never known before.

Some people say God hears you most strongly when you need Him the most. I came to believe this during Chris's time in Iraq, and that faith has strengthened over the years. But what I needed to believe after Chris's death was that God has a plan for us. More important, I had to accept that His plan is the best plan. Even if I didn't like it. Maybe it is less about the best plan for an individual and more about others—the ripple effect of life and faith.

During the war, I was constantly afraid Chris would die. What made it worse was that he told me many times that he wanted to die on the battlefield.

Let me refine that.

He didn't *want* to die, but if he *had* to die, then he couldn't imagine anything better than dying on the battlefield. It was part of his sense of duty: dying on the battlefield would mean that he had been doing his utmost to protect others. There was no higher calling, and no higher proof of dedication, for Chris. So there was no sense fearing death in combat. It would be an honor.

That idea hurt me. I knew my husband wasn't reckless—far from it—but in war there is a very thin line between being brave and being foolish, and when Chris talked like that I worried the line might be crossed.

I started going to church more during his first deployment, and eventually went to women's Bible studies to learn more about the Bible. But fitting the idea of God and faith and service together was never easy. What should I pray for? My husband to live, certainly. But wasn't that selfish? What if that wasn't God's will?

I prayed Chris would make the right decision when it came time to reenlist or leave the Navy. I wanted him to leave, yet that wasn't exactly what I prayed for.

Yet I was disappointed when he reenlisted. Was I disappointed with God, or Chris?

Had my prayers even been heard?

If it was God's plan that he reenlist, I should have been at peace with it. Yet I can't say that I was.

Right after he made his decision, I took a walk with a friend whose faith ran very deep. She knew the Bible much better than I did, and was far more active in the church. I cried to her.

"I have to believe this is the best thing for our family," I told her. "But I don't know how it can be. I'm really struggling to accept it."

"It's okay to be angry with God," she told me.

That caught me short. "I—I don't think we're supposed to be."

"Why not?"

"Well . . . Jesus was never mad at God, and—"

"That's wrong," she said. "Don't you remember in the temple with the money changers? Or in the garden before he was crucified, his doubts? Or on the cross? It's okay to have those feelings."

We talked some more.

"I do believe that if Chris dies," I said finally, "God must be saying it's still okay for our family, even if I don't know how."

She teared up. "I'm in awe," she confessed. "I don't know if I could say that."

Now, years later and no longer a stranger to death or grief, the doubts I expressed were stronger—and so was my anger, though not with God or Chris.

I knew accepting God means accepting that He has a plan. But did that mean I must trust, somehow, in that plan?

Even if I hated it?

As a parent, we often have to make difficult decisions. We have to say no to our kids, even when it disappoints them. We tell them they have to do certain things for their own good, regardless of whether they like it. I think God is like that, in a way: making certain things happen for our eternal good. Even the suffering on earth, which will somehow be redeemed in heaven.

Does He say: *Yes, you have to suffer, but you're going to be okay. I have your best interests at heart. And you have something to learn.*

At my darkest times, I struggled to believe this. I tried to remember that, even when things don't go the way I'd hoped, He's still there. And that maybe we need great disappointment to appreciate the good, and to better appreciate the meaning of God in our lives. I've come to realize that part of faith is opening yourself up to free will and knowing God will bring beauty, even in the midst of evil.

It's one thing to say all this. To believe it every day—to live it and not despair—that is a struggle.

Driving my daughter to a friend's house one evening, she asked me about God.

"Why doesn't God stop bad things from happening?"

I glanced back at her in the seat. Her eyes were big, her expression pensive.

"I'm sure he could, but that would break his promise to us," I said, working the answer out. "Because he promised to give us free will, and that means that we are free to do bad things as well as good."

"But other people?"

"Other people, too. All people have free will." I worked to explain it, not just to her but to myself. "God promised not to leave us alone," I said, coming back to an idea that has often comforted me. "It doesn't mean we'll always be happy. But He will always support us."

Angel was thinking about her father and his death. I wondered if she was going to cry.

"It's okay to cry," I told her.

"I'm not going to cry," she said. "I have a lot of questions about God. But I can't think about them now."

"You can always ask."

"I know."

"Are you angry with God?"

"No. He didn't do this to us."

"It's okay to be mad at God," I admitted finally—to myself. "He can handle it."

FAKING IT

At different points over the past two years I've lost complete track of time. I don't mean the hours—that, too, but I'm sure we all have those days where we think it's ten in the morning only to discover it's really four in the afternoon. I'm talking bulk. I've found whole months flying by without my really noticing—I took the garbage out one night and stopped myself in the driveway, wondering why it was so darn hot.

Of course it's hot, I realized. *It's June!*

My therapist pointed out that losing track of time is common for people who have gone through traumas. And losing your husband certainly is a trauma.

Chris's death is a time marker when I think back; I tend to date everything from then, before and after. I have trouble placing dates to things that happened since he died; I have to work hard to pinpoint them.

Sometimes, surviving has been mostly a matter of faking it.

One afternoon we went to a friend's house. It was a bit rainy, but not so bad that the kids couldn't play outside. At some point, they started having a mud fight.

Their faces were pictures of sheer delight. Lost completely in the moment, they giggled and laughed and slid all over the place.

I forced myself to laugh, too. They were having so much fun that it would have been a crime not to. Yet inside I was feeling horribly oppressed, by the court cases and trials as well as Chris's absence.

I think we all do this to some degree. Business travelers, for instance, can't let the fact of a long jet flight hurt their presentation. A salesman won't let the fight he just had with his wife prevent him from making a new sale. Inspirational ministers talk about the glory of God rather than the toe they stubbed on the way up to the pulpit.

I knew I had to be happy for the kids. If I couldn't be genuinely happy, then I at least owed it to them to be fake happy.

Could they tell the difference?

PATRIOT TOUR

My interest in trying more public speaking received a boost when Marcus Luttrell and his wife Melanie invited me to join the Patriot Tour.

Marcus had thought up the idea of a tour with Chris and Chad Fleming, an army veteran who lost his leg in the War on Terror. The idea was to have a small group of veterans travel around the country, telling people about their sacrifices and encouraging them to be patriots themselves. Rock bands tour; why not patriots?

My own story wasn't much. Instead, I focused on Chris and the meaning of small gestures. I talked about how kindness can have a ripple effect. I did my best to do what Chris would have done, highlighting others. The more I talked, the more comfortable I felt, and the more confident that I could combine it with the foundation and make a living doing it.

In a lot of ways, Marcus was a trailblazer for Chris and me.

I've watched him slowly heal, physically and emotionally, as time has gone on. I've also seen how strange things can get for a public person. They happened to him before they happened to Chris, and while there's nothing that can truly prepare you for the windstorm that is fame, at least we were able to glimpse a little bit of the craziness before it actually hit.

Marcus is a wonderful, complicated person with a warm heart and, occasionally, a gruff exterior. His wife Melanie is the perfect balance. In his speeches, Marcus gives her full credit for saving his life as he recovered from his wounds, and she surely deserves it.

One thing I learned from watching Marcus on tour was how important a tight group of very trusted friends can be. He still has close relationships with people he knew growing up. That's a real luxury. Not having to explain yourself to your friends, being accepted for who you are, not being judged by media images—those are all difficult once fame hits.

Even before.

Being on the tour for a few weeks was like traveling with an extended family. Not only are Marcus, Chad, and people like David Goggins, Billy Wagasy, and Pete Scobell inspiring speakers and performers, but in "real" life, they're inspirational as well. They're kind men and warriors at the same time, not only willing to do anything for you, but capable of pulling it off. And the idea of what they're doing—sharing themselves with others, talking about veterans' experiences, inspiring people with real-life stories about perseverance and overcoming hardships—is so much of what I want to do that joining the tour felt like being home.

While we were traveling one day, Chad took out his phone and showed me a picture.

"Look at what we got!" he exclaimed proudly.

His two-and-a-half-year-old daughter stood in a ballerina dress holding a tiny little animal.

A pig, actually.

A pig?

Her name was Miss Sprinkles. It was the cutest thing I've ever seen.

"Is that real?" I asked.

"Sure," said Chad. "My wife's mom bred them. There are more. I'm sure she'd give you one."

"Well . . ."

"They're miniatures. They only grow to be twenty pounds. They potty-train. They are so easy."

"Potty-train?"

Long story short—I ended up getting one for Angel. I suggested we name her Hammy Wynette. Angel picked Roxie instead.

When she's bad, it's Baby Bacon.

People tell you that pigs are the fourth-smartest mammal, that they're affectionate and easy to live with. But what they don't say is that they squeal as loud as a freight train when they are little.

What do you do when life isn't crazy enough? Get a pig!

ENERGIZING

I was visiting Marcus and his wife when a friend asked if she could talk to me alone. Teresa was the spouse of a Team member who'd served with Chris. We hadn't spent a lot of time together, but we'd always had a connection.

"I have something I want to give you," she said. "I don't know if it's going to seem corny to you or what, but I kind of want to do it for me."

She pressed a medal into my hand. I looked at it—it was the medal she'd received for completing the Boston Marathon.

"You and Chris kept me going," she explained. "It was almost eerie how, when my legs were tired and I wanted to quit, Randy Travis's song came on the iPod. It was the one he played at the memorial. My iPod was on random shuffle but it was always at just the right moment. I would hear that song and it would spur me on."

Maybe Chris was somehow behind that. People have told me of other inspirational incidents; each one, from simple to grand, has touched me with its beauty.

The kids helped keep me together as well. One day they came in from playing after dinner, and I told them I was just completely exhausted by work and everything else. I said I'd take a shower as soon as I finished up; then we'd read and get ready for bed.

They warmed up some towels in the dryer while I was showering and had them waiting for me when I was done. They made some hot coffee—not really understanding that coffee before bed isn't the best strategy. But it was just the way I like it, and waiting on the bed stand. They turned down the bedcovers and even fluffed my pillows.

Most of the time, their gifts are unintentional.

Angel recently decided that, since the Tooth Fairy is so nice, someone should be nice to her. My daughter wrote a little note and left it under her pillow with some coins and her tooth.

Right?

The Tooth Fairy was very taken with that, and wrote a note back.

"I'm not allowed to take money from the children I visit," she wrote. "But I was so grateful. Thank you.'"

Then there was the time the kids were rummaging through one of Chris's closets and discovered the Christmas Elf.

Now everyone knows that the Christmas Elf *only* appears on Christmas Eve. He stays for a short while as part of holiday cheer, then magically disappears for the rest of the year.

"What was he doing here!" they said, very concerned, as they brought the little elf to me. "And in Daddy's closet!"

I called on the special brain cells parents get when they give birth. "He must have missed Daddy so much that he got special permission to come down and hang out in his stuff. I wonder how long he'll be with us?"

Just until I could find another hiding place, of course.

What? Evidence that Santa Claus doesn't exist, you say?

Keep it to yourself. In this house, we believe.

This reminds me of a funny Chris story.

Back when we lived in California, Easter was coming up and Chris was home with the kids. I forget exactly what the children did, but they got out of line and Chris decided rather than disciplining them, he'd use a little daddy logic on them.

Daddy logic, as expressed by a SEAL sniper.

"I'll tell you, you better behave," he said, "or I'll keep the Easter Bunny from coming."

"How?" one of them wondered.

Daddy logic met kid logic and raised the ante through the roof.

"I'll sit on the stoop and I'll shoot him when he comes," said Chris. Somehow he kept a straight face. "You'll ruin it for everyone, not just yourselves."

We had great behavior for weeks.

It's different living with a sniper as a dad.

Then there are other stories, touching ones, that don't belong to me.

The other day a friend related a story he'd heard from one of Chris's old schoolmates. Back in high school, a student who didn't particularly know Chris had found the only open seat at the "cool" lunch table.

"What are you doing?" said one of the kids. "You can't sit here."

"Uh—"

Chris walked up and sat down. "Have a seat," he told the young man.

He did. And no one bothered him at school the rest of the year.

I've talked to people who felt very strongly that Chris has done things for them since he died. The stories move me, even though I don't really know what to think about them.

I guess if you think of how Chris acted as protector during his life, and how he wanted the people he loved to be happy, it makes sense that he might spend some of his energy in the afterlife to keep doing that. I could easily see him talking God into letting him come back from time to time to take care of things down here.

I'm sure there are rules to follow—but knowing Chris, if there's a way around them, he's figured it out.

VISITORS

Where do the biggest movie star of his generation and a revered director (and great actor in his own right) stay when they are visiting someone?

Would you believe the local Holiday Inn?

Hoping to forge a better connection to Chris, Clint Eastwood and Bradley Cooper came to see me and the rest of the family in early spring of 2014, before they started filming *American Sniper*. The unpretentiousness of their visit and their genuine goodwill floored me. It was a great omen for the movie.

Bubba and I picked them up at the local airport and brought them home; within minutes Bubba had Bradley out in the back playing soccer. Meanwhile, Clint and I talked inside. He reminded me of my grandfather with his courtly manners and gracious ways. He was very funny, with a quiet, quick wit and dry sense of humor. After dinner—it was an oryx Chris had killed shortly before he died—Bradley took Bubba to the Dairy Queen for dessert.

Even in small-town Texas, he couldn't quite get away without being recognized, and when someone asked for his photo, he stepped aside to pose. Bubba folded his arms across his chest and scanned the area much as his dad would have: on overwatch.

I guess I didn't really understand how unusual the situation was until later, when I dropped them off at the Holiday Inn. I watched them walk into the lobby and disappear.

That's Clint Eastwood and Bradley Cooper! Awesome!

The next morning, I went over to pick them up. I'd spent the night thinking of more things I should tell them—everything about Chris I thought they needed to know.

It was all too much.

"I don't know how to tell you everything," I confessed to Bradley as he got into the car. I started to cry. "There's so many things and we have such a short amount of time."

"Just being here is all we need," he said. "I'm not an imper-sonator. I'm just here to feel Chris's life—I feel him here with me right now."

Bradley put me at ease and I calmed down. Back at the house, he and Clint became almost like family. Little bits of their personality came out as well—and I saw a glimmer of Clint's famous Dirty Harry character later on in the day when I had to leave to go to Bubba's basketball game.

They'd talked about coming with me—which frankly would have created an impossible circus. But I did give them the option. As they stood trying to make up their minds, I snapped into anx-ious mom mode.

"All right," I told them both. "You're welcome to come. But if you're coming, we're leaving now."

I guess my tone was a little too strident.

"So you want to get tough with me, huh, lady?" said Clint in his best Dirty Harry voice as he raised his eyebrow.

It's amazing how threatening a simple facial tic can be.

I left them home to study some of Chris's replica guns and gear. Our town already had its ample share of lawmen.

When they were first casting for my part in the movie, the produc-ers asked if I had any suggestions.

"I'll tell you what I don't want," I said. "I don't want someone in their early twenties who's never had any heartbreak or gone through anything difficult."

I heard later that Clint thought he'd have a hard time casting me. I hope that was because I'm such a complex but soulful person, though you never know.

When he settled on Sienna Miller, he hit it on the head. The first time I talked to her, it felt like I was speaking to an old girlfriend. She *got* everything. Whether I explained how it felt the first time Chris kissed me, or how it felt when he held me, she completely understood. She's a woman with deep empathy as well as a great actor.

My part—*her part*—in the movie isn't very big, but it's important, and I felt it was in good hands. She knows what it's like to be a mom, and she knows how it feels to worry about someone and to live through situations you can't control.

Still, I remained nervous: What if, despite all their efforts, they didn't manage to convey what Chris was all about? The director, the actors, they were all at the top of their field, but that was no guarantee that they could pull it off.

One thing the prep for the movie made me realize: Chris and I had gone through a lot in our short time on earth. We'd known war, we'd known the joys of birth—and the tremendous hurt of death. Hard times, defaults, large checks, big taxes, and fame. We'd run the gamut.

And we'd been in love the whole time. The last month of his life was the best of our marriage. The year leading up to it was the best we'd ever had, outside of our first. We'd started on a high level and moved up.

How many people can say that?

I'm not saying the good times would have gone on forever. I'm sure there would have been difficulties and other trials, dark clouds. But to have had those moments of seemingly perfect love and happiness—I was truly blessed.

JESSE

That was my life—veering from high to low, from appreciation and acceptance back to depression, from something less than jubilation to something more than grief. I mounted a great show for casual friends; those close to me, like Stewart, saw the ongoing toll not only of Chris's loss but the work it took to maintain the façade of happiness.

Still, I knew there were better days ahead. I knew if I could push far enough away—get through enough mud—I might achieve something close to peace. Or at least I hoped that. My road veered left and right, up and down, but surely there must be a point where it would straighten out. Maybe that would be a Road to Damascus moment—a point when, like Paul, I would understand everything and be relieved of the worst of the pain.

Summer came. Jesse loomed.

If there were to be a moment when my burdens could be lifted, then the trial presented the best chance. I was confident, as Chris had been. We would put on all the witnesses we could find, either in person or by deposition. I felt the evidence was strongly in my husband's favor; we had a persuasive case. I was sure all would be well in the end.

Jesse's lawyers called me as their first witness, which I guess was a surprise. Maybe it was meant to lessen the sympathy for a "widow." But that comes with the territory.

I think if Chris had been there, he would have sat back in his chair, cool and calm. I think the jurors would have seen that, and been very much influenced by his confidence.

But of course he couldn't be there.

No, he was. With me, and on video. He'd been deposed months before he died, and parts of that testimony were played at the trial, as were excerpts from some of the news shows he'd been on.

Watching them was painful in so many ways.

How can anyone attack this man?

How can anyone think this man was lying about anything?

I lost my composure only once, putting my head down as grief overcame me. I recovered quickly.

A parade of witnesses—SEALs and non-SEALs (some of them fans of Jesse Ventura)—testified either in person or by deposition to parts of Chris's version of events. There had been words, a conflict, a punch. The other side claimed nothing at all had happened. Nothing.

And that the primary reason people bought the book was because of Jesse's name, which wasn't even in the book.

I was listening and thinking: This is perfect. The jury is going to hear this and see it is at odds with the testimony. They'll have to find in favor of my husband.

The judge gave the jury instructions, and they went off to deliberate.

And deliberate.

And deliberate.

When I first headed to Minnesota, I thought I would go home to Oregon each weekend to see my kids, who were staying with my parents. But I ended up so drained by the first week of testimony that I realized those quick visits would have been too much, both for them and for me. So I stayed in St. Paul. Work didn't stop at four or five o'clock when the jury was sent home. I'd go back to the hotel with the attorneys and help if they needed something, or just discuss different aspects with them. It was where I felt I had to be.

After the closing statements, we felt that the verdict might come pretty soon. I was thinking in terms of hours if not minutes.

But then it didn't.

I kept missing my kids, and finally, on the third day, it was too much. I booked a plane to go see them.

Meanwhile, the jury continued to deliberate behind closed doors. Finally, it became clear that they couldn't reach a unanimous verdict. We decided to accept a split vote to break the deadlock; the alternative would have been another trial.

It goes without saying, I thought the vote would be heavily in our favor. The facts of the trial, as far as I could see, were clear. If anything, I was baffled that anyone could be holding out. Eleven people testified that they saw or heard things that supported Chris's account. The accounts differed slightly, which of course makes sense: no two people ever remember things that happened six years later the same. People describe the battle of Fallujah differently, but that doesn't mean there wasn't a battle of Fallujah.

So I was very confident. But God has a purpose for everything.

Tuesday, July 29, some three weeks after the trail had started, I was back in Oregon with the kids and my mom when the lawyers texted me, saying they should have the verdict within ten minutes.

I waited.

Finally my cell phone rang. It was the legal team on a conference call.

We had lost. The vote was 8-2 against.

I was stunned. I don't think I breathed, let alone spoke, for nearly a minute.

The lawyers told me the terms. The jury had ruled in favor of

Jesse on the defamation case, awarding him $500,000. This was covered by the publisher's insurer. But adding insult to injury, the jury had awarded Jesse $1.3 million for unjust enrichment, which the insurer said it would not cover.

Tears came to my eyes. Paying off the verdict would take all that we had made from the book, and more. My mom was standing nearby. "Where are your car keys?" I asked her. I was still on the phone with the lawyers.

She gave them to me. I tapped Angel on the head. "I'll be back, honey."

As I walked out to the driveway, I thanked the lawyers and hung up. Then I drove straight to a grocery store and bought a pack of cigarettes, even though I hadn't touched a cigarette for five days. I stood outside and smoked.

I don't know how many.

"All right. On to the next," I said finally, crushing the cigarette and heading back to my parents' house.

I did not talk to the media after the trial, since I knew I was likely to appeal. And truthfully, what could I say that would make any difference?

I gave a very brief statement through the lawyers, and otherwise turned down opportunities to provide my side of the argument. It hurt, even if from a legal point of view it was the right thing to do. Since then, I have tried to ignore not just what Jesse says but also what other people say in general about the situation. It's not worth my time or my emotions.

But it's hard to ignore everything. And sometimes it's important to know what people are saying about you, if only because it gets back to your friends, who then start to wonder.

At the end of the day, more than enough witnesses came forward to support what Chris had said. Why the jury chose not to believe them or Chris—I can only shake my head. Would the result have been different if the trial had been held anywhere other than St. Paul, where Ventura's portrait hangs in the state capitol? The experience has been an interesting introduction to our legal system, not to mention the world of haters and their hangers-on.

What did cheer me, though, was the outpouring of support and even outrage after the trial. Many people still believed in Chris, no matter what the jury said.

Thank God. He'd lived his life as an honest and open man. Unfortunately, the jury never got a chance to look him in the eye and realize that.

The decision on whether to appeal was a fraught one.

I prayed about it a lot. I looked through the Bible for various phrases, without really arriving at a good decision.

Sometimes you just have to cut your losses and go—but this didn't feel like just a business issue. There were principles involved, primarily doing the right thing by Chris.

Late at night, I was sitting on my back patio talking with a friend.

"What do you think I should do?" I asked.

She answered with a question of her own. "Taya, what do you always say?"

"Stand up for what you believe in?"

"Right."

"But we might lose."

"Then remember what Chris said when going up against someone: *You may win, but you will remember you fought me.*"

I realized that making the decision didn't mean that I had to win. The important thing was to stand up for what I believed in. If people were going to try to abuse Chris, they were going to have to fight me. They might win, but they'd go away with scars.

My lawyers filed post-trial briefs immediately after the verdict came down explaining that the amount of the unjust enrichment award exceeded the Estate's total net royalties on the book. Between money due to Scott, the agent, and Jim, we received maybe half the royalty earnings. And we still had to pay taxes and expenses for everything from stamps to lawyers, and you see that conjectures about revenues were wildly optimistic.

Because the case is under appeal, I cannot comment in depth about it. Many have suggested that the attorneys could have been more aggressive in countering statements and claims they felt were misleading. Hindsight, of course, is 20/20. We will see what the future holds.

I wonder sometimes if, between negative campaigning and social media and plain old gossip, our society has just gone too far to the negative. You have to make a personal decision not to spread bad news about people—and it can be a tough decision when you're involved in a fight. Holding back from criticizing people who are attacking you is very, very difficult. Trust me—even writing this book my tongue is bleeding.

It's a societal problem, I suppose. Taking the high road sounds good, but is it possible? More importantly, does it work?

You hear people ranting and you wonder, how can we have a fair society at all?

CHAIN-SMOKING

After the verdict was announced, I took a few days off to recover, but then had to get back to work. I'd agreed to a speaking engagement in California, and while they offered to cancel it, I felt I would be better off keeping it.

Slog on, Taya. Push through the mud.

There were other things to focus on besides lawsuits. Losing the trial was heartbreaking, but if you really want to hurt a mom, tell her the babysitter she has counted on for years is going off to college. That is a crisis to beat any lawsuit.

Honestly, losing our babysitter Rea at the end of the summer was a difficult blow. She'd been really like one of the family, and the kids and I missed her instantly. Her loss did more to unbalance us than a thousand Jesses could have.

Not that she or Jesse or anyone but myself was to blame for my smoking, which escalated at the very end of the summer.

I might have stopped after the first cigarette, or the first day, or the first week. But I didn't. Instead, I found myself smoking more and more. I couldn't get enough nicotine.

I could easily rationalize it. In the scheme of things, it wasn't the worse vice in the world. It was better than drinking, which would mean I couldn't drive the kids and surely could have horrible consequences. I didn't want to take tranquilizers, because they would leave me tired. There are hundreds of things worse than cigarettes.

Smoking was something I could get away with, and why not?

It spiraled. I couldn't sleep because I'd smoked so much during the day—so to calm down, I smoked. Then I needed to smoke more during the day to stay awake.

I tried to hide it from the kids, even turning off the security cameras so they couldn't see me when I'd go outside. But they were on to me, Bubba especially.

The little sneak caught me one day, coming around the car when I was outside puffing away.

"I was wondering what you were doing," he said, spying me squatting behind the truck.

He'd nailed me, but the look on his face made it seem as if our roles were reversed—he looked as if he were in shock, as if I'd just slapped him.

When I went back inside, I found he'd taped signs to the walls:

DON'T SMOKE!

I laugh about it now, but not then.

"Why are you so devastated that I'm smoking?" I asked when I found him.

"Because. I already lost one parent. I don't want to lose you, too."

"I'm sorry, I'm sorry," I told him. "I'm going to stop."

But of course it wasn't nearly that easy. As horrible as I felt, I was deep into the habit. I would quit for a while—a day, an hour—then somehow a cigarette would find its way to my mouth.

I continued to rationalize, continued to struggle—and Bubba continued to call me out.

"I'm trying," I told him. "I'm trying."

He'd come up and give me a hug—and smell the cigarette still on me.

"Did you have one?"

"Yes."

"Hmmmm . . ." Instant tears.

"I'm trying, I'm trying."

One day I went out to the patio to take what turned out to be a super stressful call—and I started to smoke, almost unconsciously. In the middle of the conversation, Bubba came out and threw a paper airplane at me.

What!!!

My son scrambled back inside. I was furious, but the call was too important to cut short.

Wait until I get you, mister!

Just as I hung up, Bubba appeared at the window and pointed at the airplane at my feet.

I opened it up and read his message:

YOU SUCK AT TRYING.

That hurt, not least of all because it was true.

I tried harder. I switched to organic cigarettes—those can't be that bad for you, right? They're organic!

Turns out organic tars and nicotine are still tars and nicotine. I quit for a day, then started again. I resolved not to go to the store so I couldn't be tempted . . . then found myself hunting through my jacket for an old packet, rifling around in my hiding places for a cigarette I'd forgotten.

Was that a half-smoked butt I saw on the ground?

Finally, I remembered one of the sayings SEALs live by: *Slow is smooth, smooth is fast.*

Not exactly the conventional advice one uses to stop smoking, but the conventional advice had failed me. For some reason I took the words and tried applying them to my heartbeat, slowing my pulse as it ramped up. It was a kind of mini-meditation, meant to take the place of a cigarette.

The mantra helped me take control. I focused on the thoughts that were making me panic, or at least getting my heart racing.

Slow is smooth. Slow down, heart. Slow down—and don't smoke.

I worked on my breathing. *Slow is smooth. Slow is smooth. And don't smoke.*

It worked, for a few days. Then I was right back into it, smoking more than ever.

One day I was out on the back patio—smoking—and a strange feeling came over me. I tried to pray, but couldn't.

You cannot smoke! You personally are going to pay!

It wasn't God talking to me in the literal sense—I wasn't hearing voices or anything—but the thought was so strong that it felt like a prayer, or more accurately an answer to one.

It was a moment of understanding, one of many. And it was a warning, also one of many:

If I could not pray, then I really was out of control.

My life was so crazed—and my cigarette addiction so deep—that my lifelong habit of talking directly to God was choked off. I felt so guilty about smoking that I had turned away not just from myself and my goals of being healthy, but from God. He was a friend I was ashamed to look at.

The only thing to do is quit. Quit!

A year before, I had heard a sermon about the walls we build, brick by brick, between ourselves and God. Everything we do that goes against His wishes puts another brick in that wall. Our shame makes it harder for us to reach Him.

I thought the sermon was silly at the time. I've never been the perfect person, but I've always been able to reach God. I could *always* pray.

But now I literally couldn't, because of the cigarettes.

Time to try again. And harder.

Gradually, over weeks and months, I was able to cut back. I still have a craving, and I still occasionally give in. But I know I've gotten a lot better at *trying;* if I'm not entirely prepared to say I've won—you always worry you'll slip back—I have definitely turned a corner.

Still, it's a battle I wish I didn't have to have.

Faith continued to prop me up, and in different ways than before. That fall, friends of mine invited me to a small church they attended not far from my home. It was comfortable and informal—there were actually couches and stuffed chairs instead of pews at the back of the nave. The pastor was amazing, down to earth and humble, yet inspirational at the same time. A family man with five kids, he had a knack for relating the Bible to everyday life. People mingled after services.

I was taken by the family atmosphere, and began attending as regularly as possible. Eventually I was moved to tithe, something I'd never done in my life. I'd always felt that helping individuals and giving to charity was enough. But tithing is specifically outlined in the Bible; as a friend put it, these financial commitments help build the church and its mission. This church's outreach to the poor as well as the congregation as a whole has had a continuing and lasting impact in the community. And just being a member has had a profound impact on me.

To be absolutely honest, I still don't go to services *every* Sunday. But I can also truthfully say that there hasn't been a time that the sermon I've heard hasn't directly related to something going on in my life.

FAMILIES IN GRIEF

It took the death of my close friends V and Jennifer's nephew to help me realize I was moving away from the deepest depths of my own grief. Being there for them was, in many ways, more therapeutic for me than it ever could be for them.

LT was the son of V's identical twin brother. The twins are so close that they share everything—including LT, who was in all but name V's son. A high school honor student who joined the Marines upon graduation, LT was a strong, polite young man with a huge future ahead of him when he died at age twenty-five during a workout. His heart failed; his time on earth was up.

As soon as I heard, I drove out to their house. I ended up going over every day for a week, helping any way I could. Small things, mostly—the dishes, cooking. Mainly, I just showed up, which often is what is most important.

Though I still wish there was more that I could do.

Seeing their grief put mine in perspective. My mourning was hard and deep. Yet it didn't rob me of everything. It didn't take away who I was, or who I could be.

Yes, I was pushing through what seemed like endless mud. But I was pushing, and that was something.

Grief is a simple emotion, but its complications can be endless. I've seen more than one family broken apart by the loss of a loved one.

One of the saddest things is to see the separation that can develop between in-laws and the remaining spouse or other surviving relatives. I haven't lost a child, so it's difficult for me to step out and see things from that side. Maybe parents feel that, when death has ended a marriage, the dead son or daughter "reverts" back to them—the spouse, after all, goes on with his or her life. They can remarry, they can build something new. And that's doubly true for a brother or cousin, aunt or uncle.

From my perspective, the widow or widower does have to move forward. But they do so without losing the love they had for their spouse. In my case, I'll always love Chris, no matter what. I don't move away from grief, but rather through it.

My relationship with Chris's family has not always been easy. We struggle to get beyond the difficulties and misunderstandings. Unfortunately, with Chris gone, things will never be the same. There will always be heartache at the center of our relationship.

I think in some cases, the heartache can be so deep that it becomes an obstacle. Maybe the strength of the relationship beforehand can ease not the pain, but at least the transition.

Then again, I don't know. Grief is still an open chapter in my life, and in the lives of everyone who knew and was close to Chris, his family most especially. The final story has yet to be written.

There was a day in autumn when every battle and every struggle came to a critical point at the same time: a decision on the Jesse appeal had to be finalized, a decision on the Craft disputes had to be made, important work for the foundation had to be squared away, and on and on. I spent the day driving from one attorney to another. I was constantly on my phone making child-care arrangements, arranging care for the dogs, finding help for household chores.

It was chaotic and crazy. And it was good. Everything was

moving forward. Things that had been started before Chris died were finally getting settled and I was moving on: not yet beyond them, but at least the possibility was there.

Somewhere on one of the drives, the tears started to come.

Nope, I told them. I'm moving forward.

They went away. I wish it were always that easy.

THE WEDDING RING

A few days later, I saw my psychiatrist to check on my progress.

"I notice that you're wearing your wedding ring," he said after I sat down. "Do you think you might be in denial?"

I guess it was a fair question, but it caught me off guard.

"I know Chris is gone," I said. "But I do feel as if I'm still married to him."

I looked at my ring. It didn't mean I was in denial; it meant I loved Chris. Yet the question bothered me.

My husband is dead, and of course I acknowledge it. But that's different than shouting about it.

The ring is a symbol of our love as well as our marriage. How should I treat that symbol?

Do I have a problem?

I left the office in a quandary.

The Bible says "until death do you part." I know that means that marriage lasts only until one death, and that it's okay for me to marry again. I know good friends who are widows, and I've encouraged them to marry, feeling it was right for them. One of my dearest friends decided to do just that this past summer. It hadn't been that long since her husband had died, but things had just come together, and her new love deserved to be acknowledged. It was another case, to me, of finding beauty through the ashes.

"I kept asking God, why now? Why so soon?" she confessed. "The answer that came back was, timing doesn't matter. Accept the gift."

She's right. People may judge her, but she had the courage and strength to admit that she had something beautiful, and that the right thing to do was act on it. I know with certainty that not only was the man right but the timing was as well. They have strengthened each other, and I'm sure will have a life together many can only dream of.

Not long after my session with the doctor, I met a married friend of Chris's who'd been a SEAL. We talked about some of the things he and Chris had done together. The memories were fun, and we laughed quite hard.

Suddenly his tone became very serious.

"You know what a Team guy's biggest fear is?" he asked.

"What?"

"That he'll die and his wife will never let herself be loved again."

I didn't know what to say.

"Yup," he continued. "I got a guy all picked out for my wife if I die. He's not quite as cool as me, but he'd make a good husband."

I've heard that general idea in different versions and permutations. Chris talked about the kids and me moving on if he died at war. Still, the idea of "moving on" breaks my heart. I still love him. I still feel married to him.

I don't want people to not see the ring and think, She's over it. She doesn't love him anymore.

But beyond the ring, does the pain have to be intense to prove that I loved him, and love him still?

I was finally reaching a point where I knew that was illogical.

More: I felt it was wrong. Pain proves nothing.

Both sides of my brain, logic and emotion, realized that continued suffering isn't the way to honor Chris. It's certainly not what the
marriage was about. The marriage, even in its imperfect moments,
was about support and love. It was a no-pain zone.

So what of its ultimate symbol? Keeping the ring on my finger
meant what? Denial? But taking it off meant what?

Acceptance?

I accept his death, but I don't accept that what we had is over.
The ring, and the love, remain important—even if the relationship
has changed.

I removed the ring from my left ring finger to recognize that
Chris was gone, and that, on earth, our relationship had changed.
Then I placed it on my right to symbolize the lasting nature of our
love.

It felt awkward and strange. And sad.

Not long afterward, I turned forty.

All grown up.

Bubba was born the day before I turned thirty. Ever since then,
I haven't really cared about celebrating my own birthday. I have a
lot of fun planning his parties; there's no need for something big to
mark mine. In fact, my biggest present each year is spending time
with the kids. Maybe that has made it easier for the years to slip by
without much fanfare.

But forty didn't slip past; it was too big a milestone. Two of
my best friends saw to that, taking me out to a nice restaurant for
dinner. It was splendid—I didn't want to do anything else.

On the one hand, the birthday itself was no big deal. The number,
though . . . Well, it does make me sound older, I have to admit.

Psychologically, there's a huge gap between "late thirties" and "oh no, forty!"

On the other hand, I think that instead of feeling *old*, I'm feeling surer of myself, and maybe more mature—*mature* being a good thing, not a synonym for *senile*.

Wiser.

Calmer, sometimes. Though that's still very much a struggle.

The decade that had passed had been an incredible one, both for good and bad. Who would ever have predicted all that happened in my thirties: I had children, moved to Texas, watched Chris become famous, endured his loss, struggled with court battles, worked to start a charity . . .

I flew around the country, made incredible friends, got a chance to inspire others . . .

What will my forties hold?

Less drama, I hope. No tragedies would be wonderful. But more of the other things that the thirtysomething me enjoyed: friends, family, helping others.

One thing did strike me, however, as I considered my thirties: *Maybe it's a blessing that we don't know what the future holds.*

CRAFT AND THE HOUSE

Jesse was only one of the legal combatants I had to endure in 2014. In some ways, the fight over Craft and the future of Chris's name and trademarks was even more difficult—it involved the future as well as the past.

Not to mention my home.

Kyle Bass had told many people—and me—that he was giving me the house Chris and I had lived in, meaning that he was forgiving the mortgage and renouncing any claims. He told me to stop paying the mortgage but to keep up with the taxes—an arrangement that was more than fair.

Somewhere he changed his mind. I have to wonder if the house became just another pawn in the battle over Craft and the rights to Chris's name and trademarks.

Or not "just another." It was an especially emotional one for me. And important: It was our family home.

Sometime after Chris died, one of his friends said something off-handed about us having to leave our house. I was shocked, and demanded to know why.

"Because a ghost lives there," he said.

He was speaking metaphorically about all of our memories. But that was exactly why I did *not* want to leave. I still felt Chris very strongly there, and I didn't want to lose that.

By the fall of 2014, I realized that I feel Chris strongly everywhere I go. He's so much a part of me that I can't lose him. Physical places may suggest memories, but that's all they do: suggest. The experiences are already deeply embedded in my brain and soul.

So by the time it became obvious that the best way to move past the ugliness was to offer to give up the house, I had already reconciled myself to the fact that I didn't need the physical structure to stay close to Chris. It still hurt to leave for many, many reasons, principle being one of them: *When is a promise not a promise?* But I've learned, painfully, that I can't control what other people do, much less what they think. I have to do what's best for myself and our children.

The negotiations stretched on for weeks. I wanted peace, but it was long in coming.

One of the most difficult things to accept for me—and maybe most women—is the fact that not everyone likes me. It's impossible to please everyone, whether in a lawsuit or in everyday life.

I've always had trouble with that. I want people to like me. I have since I was a little girl on the playground.

That just can't happen. And it was painfully obvious here, even though no one got into an actual fistfight with me.

Actually, I would have preferred a fistfight. It would have ended sooner.

But I'm evolving, I guess. I finally feel I've earned the right not to care what other people think.

Did I mention I turned forty?

By the terms of the settlement, I was allowed to live in the house rent free until October 2015, after which point I could either purchase or rent it. In return, I paid $50,000 for Chris's .338 Lapua sniper rifle, one of the guns he used in Iraq which he had originally pledged for the down payment on the house. All of the parties released each other from various liabilities and agreed to drop their suits. I gave up trying to figure out what had happened to Craft or CIRM. We agreed to cooperate in Craft's bankruptcy proceedings, to the extent possible.

Most importantly to me, I got full, undisputed rights to Chris's name, likeness, and logo.

A painful chapter of my life was closed. Chris's dream came to an end—but a new one that I shared fully was about to become a reality.

Even before we came to a final agreement, I accepted moving as inevitable, and began looking for a new house. I briefly flirted with the idea of relocating to Austin to be near Chris's grave. It's a beautiful, interesting city, with an art district and music festivals—a fun place to live. More important, many of our friends have homes in that area. But my heart really wasn't into it: I only looked at one house there. As lovely as it was, it convinced me the city wasn't for me. If I was going to stay in Texas, it was going to be someplace where we had a little room to roam.

Weeks of searching turned up a house with a barn and a good bit of property—enough land to have horses, and some peace of mind and privacy when you take a walk. It had a come-as-you-are air, the sort of place that says kids are welcome here. I made an offer and it was instantly accepted—and just like that, we had a new home.

The business side of my brain had taken over, instantly weighing the options and pushing ahead. I didn't second-guess myself, but the idea of moving was tough for the kids. There were a lot of tears as they struggled to understand why they had to leave their home. I think that was why so much of my focus was on finding a place where they could have fun. They're tough and very resilient, but at the same time very human. I can't take away all of their pain, but if I can mitigate it even slightly, I try.

When we first looked at the house, one of the owners took us to the barn.

"Do you have horses?" he asked.

I touched Angel. "No," I said. "But we want to have horses."

I could have stopped there, but I also felt obliged to move on.

"My husband knew horses," I said. "But he's gone now. We're going to have to learn on our own."

HAPPINESS

In my heart, we're four.

Day to day, there are only three of us. I feel so close to the kids, closer than ever; I know their rhythms and what they need.

But part of me realizes that if I do my job right, some day they'll grow up and leave. They'll marry and belong to someone else.

It's not easy to accept, but it's something all parents deal with.

A friend of mine who's a pediatrician says that she's been amazed by her kids at every stage of their lives. It hasn't always been easy to accept their independence, or stand by and watch them struggle, but they have grown into wonderful young adults.

"It is what you make of it," she says. "You either make the adjustments and grow with them. Or you'll be miserable, and so will they."

She has practical advice. The best: Be interested in what they're interested in. When her daughter was hitting the teen years, she started asking her to download the top ten songs on her playlist; my friend would listen to them as she worked out. It sounds like such a simple thing, but it gave them something to talk about and share.

More advice:

"Parents assume that when a kid—especially a boy—gets older and things get a little awkward, that they don't want to be hugged anymore," she says. "But they're the same people. And if you stop talking to them or hugging them—at night, when you're not embarrassing them in front of others—you will be disappointed. Your teenager is still the same kid they were when they were little. They're just going through different things. It's your job to stay strong and still believe in the relationship."

You have to tell them, "I love you no matter what. I will love you always. We're always going to be good. Even as you change and grow up. Even when you're independent."

In many ways, I have it easy now with the kids. They're still in elementary school; the teenage years will surely have their own challenges. I've tried to stay involved in their lives, though my participation in school events has declined because of my other commitments. I can't be the supermom who volunteers for every class trip anymore. But I do chaperone when I can, and one of my happiest days recently was watching Bubba give a class report.

It's been hard to realize and even harder to accept that that's enough.

The kids' emotional growth won't suffer if they don't have the most frightening zombie costume in their class? No? Really?

Can I get that in writing?

Things that are vital to their success in life as well as school—those things we still do. Chores, required reading, homework, of course—those are all still there.

And we still thank God every night for the things that mean a lot to us. We always say what we are grateful for that day—and from that, I've learned a lot about what's important to them, and I think they've learned the same from me.

One of the most remarkable things about children is their compassion. Mine continue to pray for others every night. Maybe it comes from the DNA. Maybe it comes from having been through adversity. But it's a wonderful quality, one that I hope stays with them as they grow.

Recently we went to a circus. It was fun to watch the kids enjoy the clowns and the animals and all the other acts. I used to lose myself like that. No more.

Why can't I find that pure joy, I wondered, watching them. I just don't have it in my heart.

Had Chris been there, I would have felt it was a perfect family moment, like that Christmas before he died. Now, of course, it's more complicated.

I'm not going to have that exact feeling ever again. But I sense that I can have a different joy—not better, but still joyful. I just have more mud to get through.

Some people tell me that I have to finally close the chapter that includes Chris. But I think, or at least I hope, that I can have it both ways—that he can join me in that new chapter, even if our relationship now has been changed.

The kids are not perfect. And while they are best friends in a brother-and-sister kind of way, they don't *always* get along. Every so often—rarely—they remind me they're just like other kids. But it makes them all the more precious to me.

Not all that long after Chris died, they were playing in another part of the house when I heard a commotion. I didn't think much of it until I called Bubba over for something a few minutes later. It took him a few minutes to answer.

"What were you doing?" I asked when he arrived.

"You're not going to like it."

Uh-oh.

"Tell me what you were doing," I insisted.

"I'd rather show you."

Oh-kay.

He led me to his sister's room. There on the painted door were the words ANGEL SUCKS!! written with a Sharpie pen. The exclamation marks ran all the way across the wood.

What was the appropriate punishment?

He scrubbed for twenty minutes, without getting the words off.

"So what are we going to do?" I asked finally, inspecting the not entirely blurred result.

"We could hang a sign over it," Bubba suggested.

"Okay. Make a sign. But it better be something nice."

I came back a little while later. He'd hung a very nice sign: ANGEL IS THE VERY BEST SISTER EVER.

"Aw," I said, truly impressed. "Do you think that?"

"Nope," he answered, truthful to a fault. "But you said it had to be nice."

They've both matured since then, and it's amazing to see not just how good friends they are but how protective they can be of each other. They almost never even raise their voices to each other. They have filled each other's void with laughter, kindness and compassion— their shared experience of pain bringing them even closer than they'd been before.

In late fall, I had a phone session with my Oregon therapist. For some reason, we started talking about happiness.

"Chris achieved happiness so easily," I said to him. "And I don't."

The counselor interrupted me. "Do you know how he did?"

I started to answer that I didn't. But then I realized that Chris had set out to do many things, and he'd achieved them. He'd wanted to be a rodeo competitor, work as a cowboy, join the SEALs. He'd done all of those. What's more, he excelled at them.

Those achievements made him happy, or at least confident enough that he could be happy.

As we talked, the counselor noted that I, too, had my own

achievements. But I told him—as he already knew—that I wanted to do so many more things. And I always do.

Was that a reason not to be happy?

The counselor pointed out that I tend to focus on what I haven't done, rather than what I've achieved. My thinking runs: If I do A, then B, then C, then I'll be happy. But when I achieve A, rather than saying "Yay!" I say, "I haven't done B and C, so I can't be happy."

Why focus on what I haven't done? Why not celebrate those things I have done, even as I look forward to doing other things on my list? Those achievements are accomplishments—I should feel good about them, confident I can do more.

And happy. Or at least happier.

Another lesson.

There are other components to happiness beyond achievement. "Smaller" things, like carving out time for workouts as well as the kids, are actually big things when they are added up. Yet I often feel those things are distractions from what I really want to achieve. Blockers, rather than stepping-stones.

Obviously, the wrong way to think about them.

On paper, it doesn't seem like a very profound realization. But put into practice, it means that I—we, all of us—have to keep things in the larger perspective. If you want to achieve a lot, then the reality is that you are *always* going to have something else you want to do. Keep trying to achieve, but don't beat yourself up for not getting everything done. The "smaller" things are just as essential to happiness.

So: the key to my happiness is appreciating what I have and what I've done, and realizing that I'll always have something else to do.

Profound?

No, but empowering.

I might never have realized it had I not been grieving so deeply. I would have felt silly, really, talking about achieving happiness when Chris was alive. Why wouldn't I be happy with a great husband and wonderful children?

I *was* happy. But not at the deepest level.

I'm not there yet, obviously. But it is possible now.

And yet I still wonder:

How can I possibly be happy with Chris gone?

It always seems to come back to some variation of that question. Can I miss Chris and still have a complete life? Can I grieve and not be swallowed up by depression? Can I love him, yet walk through the rest of this world without him?

Adversity—the court cases, loss, simple problems and life-altering ones—taught me I could survive. Feeling the pain every day taught me finally that I didn't need it to prove I loved Chris. I had too many other proofs of that: the kids, our memories, my own changes and perseverance.

There are still tears. But maybe they don't bar the way. A friend was over the other night and we watched an old video of Bubba's first few months. The beginning had many photos of Chris and the baby—so many photos that I was taken by surprise and felt like crying.

Ordinarily, I would have fought to hold the tears back. But somehow that night I felt it was right to just grieve. I reached my hand out to my friend; she took it and held it while the video played.

I was exhausted at the end of the video, and yet I felt as if I'd passed some sort of test. I haven't lost my grief or found true happiness, but maybe I understand both better.

THE MOVIE

In early November 2014, Warner Bros. called and told me that *American Sniper*, the movie, was ready for screening in L.A.

Even though I knew everyone had worked very hard to get the essence of Chris's life into it, I was still afraid that it wouldn't represent him properly.

But I had to see it.

They said I could bring anyone I wanted with me.

"Anyone?" I asked.

"Well . . ."

I thought of 180 people who I just had to have with me—relatives, friends, people who knew Chris, people who helped me in some way. They needed to be there. All of them.

The producers told me very gently that the first screening was really an experience I needed to go through with only a very small handful of friends, if not alone.

I invited the calmest people I knew—Melanie, my brother-in-law Stewart, and a SEAL friend and his wife who have been very close over the years. I steeled myself and went to the theater. It was the day before Veterans Day.

I cried as soon as the movie started. Soon, though, the tears dried as I watched the movie, absorbing everything.

It was beautiful, everything I'd hoped. Bradley did such a tremendous job—there were points when I thought it was Chris I was seeing on the screen, not an actor. Sienna was wonderful. Jason, the screenwriter, and Clint did a masterful job capturing the essence of his life.

If you're looking for a movie on the SEALs, or a guide to battlefield tactics—that's not what the film is about. Yes, there are parts that didn't happen the way they are portrayed in the book. But if you're looking for the deeper truth about what our veterans go through, what their families go through, it's all there. They definitely got Chris.

I felt a weight had been lifted from my shoulders. It's a great movie, true to its subject and true to Chris. I'm so grateful to everyone involved.

P.S.: Warner Bros. arranged for a special showing in Texas to thank those 180 people later on. *Thanks, WB!*

SIDE EFFECTS

As the year came to a close, I struggled with smoking. I worked to get my business sense back and take more control of my life. I learned that grieving didn't have to mean 24/7 pain and depression. The charity was nearing reality.

There was another lesson I had to learn: working isn't a substitute for breathing. Being a workaholic is ultimately destructive.

Since Chris's death, I'd worked nonstop at being a mom, organizing the charity, reviewing legal documents, preparing speeches, the books . . . I thought that was the way to do things: sprint to a finish, then rest. But life isn't a sprint; it's more a marathon. And once you finish one project, there's another. Some never finish—the kids will always be my kids. So I had to learn to trot rather than sprint. Working so hard and so late that you sleep through three alarms in the morning is not good.

There's a pun in there about it being a three-alarm disaster, but I can't seem to laugh about it yet.

I tried sleeping more. I tried slowing down. I got an assistant. And I leaned, heavily, on Stewart.

It was as I was learning a new pace that something odd began to happen: some people seemed to feel hurt if I didn't take all of their advice, or decided to do things in a different way than they wanted. As time went on, if I no longer needed quite as much help as I had a few months before, they somehow felt hurt.

I was surprised. Good friends thinking I was dissing them because I didn't need them as much?

Really?

Yes. Simple remarks to the effect of "I need a little space" became unintentional slights. If I wanted to have some time with the kids or just be alone, I took it for granted that people would realize it wasn't about them. But I was wrong.

I certainly didn't mean to insult people or turn my back on friends. I had to regroup and reach out, as I imagine they originally reached out to me, and make an effort to reassure them that I still needed them as friends, even if I couldn't talk to them every day or answer their emails or texts right away.

Someone said, "When is the old Taya coming back?"

The old Taya, unfortunately, is gone. But the friendships she made remain critical to me. I realize that I have to make more of an effort to keep my friends close, even as I struggle to balance my life.

It was another lesson: you can't take people for granted. But it was also a lesson that ran both ways: my friends, too, had to come to terms with a friendship that was still deeply emotional and important, but one that had less physical time to share.

I imagine many women have this problem. It doesn't have an easy solution—and won't until there are forty-eight hours in every day and ten days in every week. We talk, and somehow struggle to grow together.

I truly wish there were more time in the day. I guess everyone wishes that.

One thing I appreciate about living in a small community: people respect my privacy. From casual acquaintances to total strangers, I'm rarely bothered in town. Every so often someone will come up to me in Walmart or a store in town and mention that their husband went to high school with Chris, but that happens to everyone.

The thing that's different is their next line, which is always something like:

Bless you, and bless your heart.

It makes me doubly thankful to live here.

REMINDERS, EVERY DAY

Little things.

I drive by the funeral home where he was taken several times a week, if not a day. Ordinarily, these trips mean nothing. But one time not long ago I happened to glance at the building and my mind was filled with a vision of him laid out on the table, his body being prepared.

I started crying. I was still crying when I got on the freeway a short time later.

"You're gone," I whispered. "I can't believe you're gone."

I can't believe it. I can't believe he's gone.

I repeated the words over and over, until I started to hear something else above the rumble of the tires and the rush of the wind.

I'm still here. Always with you.

The other day I went to the pizza parlor with a friend and our kids. We ordered pizza and sat down.

Suddenly a song came on the sound system there.

There was a refrain about driving all night to get to his lover. It reminded me so much of Chris. He'd literally done that when we first met.

I crumbled.

"Just a song that got to me," I told the others through my tears. "I'm okay."

I ran through the streets the night of the murder, not knowing what else to do with myself. I metaphorically ran—overworking myself—for months and months after the murder, not knowing what else to do.

I'm still running, though I hope with more purpose. I try to pace myself more. I don't know sometimes if I'm just pushing to get things done, or if in some crazy way the feeling of being overworked has become a way of keeping Chris alive.

Images and memories hit me all the time. Before, I tried to ignore them. Now, I acknowledge them. A helicopter passes overhead and I remember being at the memorial. I see an actor with blondish hair on TV, and I remember touching Chris's hair in the casket.

The psychiatrist told me the other day I was nowhere near done grieving.

"Are you sure?" I asked.

"No. Nowhere near."

And yet, I realize how incredibly blessed I am. Truly. The kindness of others, the comfort of God—I appreciate those things more fully now. The beauty I have seen in the world buoys my faith. If it's not yet my motivation, I can at least think that perhaps someday it will be.

All of our stories are really tales of love, struggle, faith, and perseverance. They are all intermingled. Happiness comes with faith and compassion. Success means getting and giving a helping hand. Finding the strength within ourselves to overcome adversity can lead us to the point of recognizing that everyone has done or will try to do that.

I look at our wedding photo often. Many things strike me—how young we were, especially.

Am I still the same person?

Yes, and no. I'm much older, obviously. And if not wiser, at least more experienced.

The strength I had then? Some days I'm close, but not always.

Do I have the same optimism about the future? That one's hard to say.

I know my faith is stronger, and my blessings more plentiful—from our marriage I have two wonderful children, and my circle of friends has grown exponentially.

If there is any lesson to be drawn from that photo, it's this: You don't know what the future holds.

The other day, Angel found her old memory box toy and took it out to show me. It's a kind of recorder where you answer certain questions and then keep them as a keepsake.

"I want to share these with you," she said.

I listened to the questions and her answers, recorded some time before.

"Name your happiest memory," said the machine.

Angel talked about going on a roller coaster with her dad shortly before he died.

"What makes you sad?" asked the machine.

"I miss my dad," she replied.

I listened some more. Her most powerful memories were all about Chris. And yet her voice was always positive, and even when I asked about everything she remembers, she sounded genuinely happy. I know she misses Chris deeply, and grieves in her own way, but she is also unfailingly grateful for having known him. She is happy, and she is optimistic about the future. She has her dad in her heart, always.

And Bubba? He's always remembering the times when Chris made him laugh. Some of his happiest moments come when someone tells a funny story about his dad.

Their purity of spirit inspires me and gives me hope.

SEVEN

RENEWAL

Team Never Quit

I f you've read this far in hopes of finding an aha! moment where my grieving ended and the light of God shone down on me—sorry. Life doesn't work that way. At least mine doesn't.

I haven't found complete peace, nor have I stopped grieving.

I have gotten to the point where I am not paralyzed by depression. I have gotten to a place where I can recognize my blessings and thank God for them, where I can look toward the future as a bright place, not one filled with dark dread

My faith, as I have said, sustains me. The knowledge that one day I will be reunited with Chris gives me hope.

My children give me sustenance; my difficulties give me strength to persevere.

THE MURDER TRIAL

Months before Chris's alleged murderer was to go on trial, I sat in the prosecutor's office and listened to him talk about the case. He got off on a tangent at one point, speaking about the motives of most murders.

"They happen because someone wants something the other person has," he generalized.

This isn't always money or even material goods. Cain killed Abel because he was jealous of Abel's standing with God. He wanted it, but of course he couldn't have it.

Not long after Chris died, a national magazine published a story comparing his life with that of the man accused of killing him. There are some parallels; they both grew up in Texas. But the article skimped on the differences. Look at the decisions they made, look at what they did with their lives, look at the responsibilities they took on—or shirked.

Chris saw a great deal of combat. He never made excuses for his behavior. He didn't always do the right thing, but he tried to do the right thing by others. Chris got the good grace, as Abel did, not by his birthright but by his effort.

As I sat listening to the prosecutor, I thought his parallel extended through Chris's life—not solely to the man who shot him, but to the haters, to the people who ended up in legal disputes with him or his estate, for whatever reason. They all wanted something he had.

Not money, but authenticity. Real achievements. Soul.

Grace.

And of course that's the one thing you can't take from someone else, even if you steal his life.

Chris became famous without wanting to. Opportunities that others had to fight and claw for seemed to fall in his lap. But most of all, people just liked him for being who he was, with seemingly no effort on his part at all.

Of course, there was effort, and there was great struggle. He had to persevere—the Navy didn't want him at all when he first tried to enlist. But people don't see that part. They don't see the long days at BUD/S, or the pain of leaving your family. Nor do they logically analyze what toll the achievements take.

I don't want to sound like a Bible thumper, much less pretend that I have all the answers or am somehow an expert on faith. I have my own personal relationship with God, and I suspect everyone must find his or her own way to their faith.

I don't think I ever really believed that there was a devil in a literal sense. You know: the guy with horns and a pitchfork.

During a break in the Jesse trial, a friend argued that I was wrong—there is a lot of evil in the world, and while maybe the devil isn't exactly the way he's pictured in old books and B-grade movies, he is active and fighting on the side of evil.

"If you are a good person," she said, "you're going to get caught up in those battles. You have to fight."

"Maybe I should tell old Satan to back up his Evil Truck, load it up, and get the heck out of here," I joked.

"Tell him," she said, dead serious. "Live the good. Fight the battle."

Maybe my metaphor was silly, but I think she was right: those of us who believe in the good must battle evil. Those of us who believe in doing the right thing, who believe that God, not evil, should rule our lives, have to put those beliefs into practice.

It's not enough to simply avoid sin. We have to do good. And we have to go out of our way to do good.

Chris was a warrior on the battlefield, but he was also a fighter in everyday life—he fought to help veterans, and he fought to keep the kids and me safe and happy.

There's a strong amount of faith in that, a powerful brand. It's one I believe in.

When things are most difficult, I close my eyes and picture Jesus next to me. It calms me and restores my strength to fight on.

Someone asked me whether I thought grief was a kind of punishment for life.

"Of course not." I was adamant. "No."

But then I thought a little bit more as we talked. In some ways, I had seen it as a punishment. Or maybe I just punished myself if I started feeling too good: How can you feel good! Chris is dead! You have no right to feel good!

Now, my reaction is more complicated. I can't say that *all* of the guilt is gone. But there's a lot less. And I can reassure myself that Chris wouldn't have wanted me to feel pain.

CHRIS KYLE FROG FOUNDATION

After a great deal of hard work, on November 11, 2014, we were finally able to announce the foundation. Here is the press release we sent out:

HELLO FRIENDS,

I can't think of a better day than Veterans Day to be able to make this announcement!

In the past year and 9 months since Chris was taken from us, I have worked with a single goal in mind: to keep his legacy of service to God, family and country alive, I am passionate about serving the families who serve our country so heroically. Today, I am humbled, honored, and thrilled to announce the launch of the Chris Kyle Frog Foundation, a nonprofit dedicated to serving military and first responder families. Our goal is to provide experiences helping families reconnect after deployments, military involvement, and time spent serving those in crisis here at home. We will help couples create the new common ground they need to build a future together after the trauma of time apart. Our vision is to create a country of connected and thriving service members and first responder families.

My vision for CKF Foundation grew out of the common experiences all military and first responder families go through. Chris and I loved each other with all our hearts, and his deployments put a terrible strain on our marriage. Each time he came home, we each had to adjust to knowing another layer of our spouse. We had to adjust to the roles the other had taken on in our time apart and figure out how to manage them back into a working family structure until the next deployment. It was hard.

When Chris was home from deployments, he often had to go on training trips. On one rare occasion he had a couple of days off from work during a training trip. My mom offered to buy me a plane ticket to go spend two days with him while she watched our kids. It was something we couldn't afford at the time, and it was such a blessing. Escaping the stresses of everyday life— even for just a few days—let us reconnect and feel everything we loved about each other. It was stronger than anything that could ever tear us apart. It gave us new energy in our relationship, and strength to handle the challenges ahead.

Chris and I both believed in paying it forward, and we wanted to give this same opportunity to the other families in our community—first responder and military families. They serve bravely, but are struggling on the home front.

We know there is a real need that isn't being met. Right now, these American families are paying a huge price. Nearly three in four married veterans are likely to have had family problems after a deployment, and half say deployments have had a negative effect on their marriage. Divorce rates of over 80 percent in both groups affect not just the couple but the children too. These families don't need handouts; they need hand-ups— just an opportunity to find their feet, to reconnect with those roots of committed love and support that gave them the strength to serve so proudly in the first place. We want to treat them to experiences that will make finding the way home a little bit easier and help to build the resilience needed to continue in service to this country.

In the coming weeks, we'll be launching our website and sharing more details about opportunities to support the Chris Kyle Frog Foundation. We've filed for 501(c)(3) status, and will be announcing a series of events around the country to spread the word about our mission. With your help, the Chris Kyle Frog Foundation will be a one-of-a-kind force for good, celebrating core values of loyalty, empowerment, integrity and excellence, and honoring God and family for our country. We know we can make a real difference in the lives of so many families.

Chris and I, together, believed in this so strongly. There aren't words enough to say what it means to me to have the opportunity to bring our vision to life. His spirit, our marriage, and the challenges and triumphs of our friends are all guiding us.

We've been blessed by the support of so many. Thank you, to everyone who has generously blessed our family in your own unique way. Every one of you played a part in this foundation. You all allowed us the time and resources to make this day a reality. I can't thank you enough and I cannot wait to see what the future holds!

GOD BLESS,
TAYA KYLE

I want people to know that this isn't Taya Kyle's foundation, or even Chris Kyle's. It's been made possible by the book and everyone who's donated money to us, by all the friends and veterans who showered

Chris with love, and by everyone who has offered support in any way. I want people to know that I couldn't do it without them.

We're just starting as I write this, but already we're involved in some exciting projects. We're partnering with Boot Campaign to raise $500,000 to help musician Zac Brown add an Outward Bound–style leadership-building obstacle course and recreation area to his facility in Georgia. While the primary focus of the facility will be helping children using an already-built equestrian and aquatic center, we will be able to use it as a retreat area for spouses as well.

We're also planning marriage retreats, something a little more meaningful and hopefully longer lasting than simple vacations away from the kids—though those are important, too.

Years from now, if I can look back and say that what I went through ended up helping other people, then I'll feel as if I succeeded.

HOW TO GRIEVE

If I were to give a friend advice on how to grieve, the first thing I would say is: *There's no right way. There's no secret formula when grieving.*

I know how to stumble forward, crawling more than walking, moving through mud, climbing from the bottom of a pit, and struggling every day to keep moving.

I know the comfort of holding other people's hands. I know how to make my children a priority, not just for their sakes, but for mine. I know how to have fun, or at least do a dang good job of faking it. I know how to pray, which for me is probably the most important thing.

But if there's no right way to experience loss, there is no wrong way, either. As my friend Kelly said to me, "Time does have a way of stealing the pain from you." And as my brother-in-law Jeff said, "It doesn't really get better, but you do learn to live with it."

It can be difficult to remember, but God doesn't leave you in your pain. You're not being punished. Faith is not the only support, but it can be a powerful one.

For me, God, my family, and my friends have all been critical. But another thing that has helped has been the idea that, through the Chris Kyle Frog Foundation and through my speaking engagements, I may be able to help others. Focusing on the potential for good in a large way liberates me from the evil that I have experienced.

I don't know if that will work for everyone. But I do know it's important, whether you're grieving or not, to reach out beyond yourself and connect to a higher purpose.

I'm grateful for all the things I have that remind me of Chris— photos, videos, notes and emails he wrote, tangible pieces of him. We're blessed to have them, just as we are blessed to have his memory.

But I also know that sometimes those reminders can hurt, and not just me.

When we were preparing to move into the new house, Angel mentioned to me that she wouldn't mind having fewer pictures of Daddy in the hall.

"I love seeing him," she confessed, "but sometimes they hurt."

I know exactly what she meant. I love looking at them too, but sometimes I can't take the emotions they provoke. And I know, too, that there's a difference between building on the past and getting stuck in it.

I love that wedding photo of us because we're both looking off into the future. And that was Chris. That was the essential part of him: fearless and hopeful, always moving forward.

That's the part of him that I hold most dear, and that's the part of him that I struggle to bring with me every day: fearless and courageous, ready for anything, striding toward tomorrow, and tomorrow's tomorrow.

As we were wrapping up the book, I sat down and thought about all the lessons I'd learned over the past two years. I couldn't list them all, but here are a few:

> Never complain about the price of a gift from your spouse—accept it with love and gratitude. You can't put a price on romance.

> Take lots of videos, even of the mundane. You will forget the sound of your children's voices and you will miss your youth as much as theirs.

> Celebrate every wedding anniversary.

> Make time for dates. Hug your spouse every single morning. And always, ALWAYS, say "I love you."

> Believe in your partner.

> When you hit hard times as a couple, take a weekend away or at least a night out. The times that you least feel like doing it are likely the times that you need it the most.

Write love notes to your spouse, your children, and keep the ones they give you.

Don't expect a miniature pig to be an "easy" pet.

Live life looking forward with a goal of no regrets, so you can look back without them.

Be the friend you will need some day.

Often the most important thing you can do for another person is just showing up.

Question less and listen more.

Don't get too tied up in your plans for the future. No one really knows their future anyway.

Laugh at yourself, and with life.

People don't change their core character.

Be humble, genuine, and gracious.

Before you get into business with someone, look at their history. Expect them to be with you for the long haul, even if you don't think they will be. If they aren't someone you could take a road trip across the country with, don't do business with them in the first place.

Real families and real sacrifices live in the fabric of the Red, White, and Blue; stand for the national anthem.

Whatever your gift is, bring it to someone else in their time of need. No gift—singing, writing, painting—is too small to share.

Give without expecting to get back.

People's greed will shock you. Their generosity will shock you more.

Be unconcerned with what others think of you. If you are a good person, someone will always love you, and someone will likely hate you, too.

If you punch someone in a bar, get it on video.

Be unapologetic about your faith in God, Country and Family.

Everyone grieves differently. Don't judge. And don't be afraid to ask about a loved one who has passed.

Don't expect perfection from anyone, especially yourself.

Learn when to let go of people who bring only pain.

Time and distance don't change true friendship.

There is far more good in the world than bad.

Don't have the first cigarette.

PTS is not an excuse for murder.

This country has many, many patriots in it; you are not alone.

Look for divinity everywhere—I promise you will see it.

Desperate people do desperate things.

Stress will age you

Exercise relieves stress better than smoking.

When people lie about you, taking the high road can suck.

Pain does not have to consume you. When it's unavoidable, respect it and let it have its place in your life without letting it take over.

God promises beauty through ashes. Give it time and you will see it.

Fame doesn't bring happiness. Living a good life does.

All makeup artists are not created equal.

Accept that you are human, and eventually you need sleep.

When I die, this will happen:

Chris will be the first thing I see. He'll be youthful, full of energy and that spry sense of mischief that always took me off my guard. I'll hug him and kiss him, and feel his warm breath on my neck. We'll walk over to a park bench—I'm sure they have those in heaven, right?—and we'll sit down and talk. I'll ask him about everything he's seen. I imagine we'll talk a long time, but that's fine—we'll have all eternity.

Until then, I have another mission. Many missions, in fact: I have to raise our kids. I have to tend to Chris's memory. I have the foundation and the different causes he and I believe in. There will undoubtedly be many petty annoyances to get through, problems that will take an undue amount of time and a ridiculous amount of emotional energy.

From the moment I learned the horrible news of Chris's death, people have asked what they could do for me. I have always had one simple answer:

Pray.

Pray that I will always hear Chris's voice.

Pray that I will always understand his spirit and be able to share it with the world.

Pray that I will continue crawling forward, on my belly if I have to, until the day comes that God anoints me with those he has saved.

ACKNOWLEDGMENTS

Sometime in the spring of 2014, Jim and I began talking about doing this book. Peter Hubbard, who had been Chris's editor, was all for it, as were many other people at HarperCollins.

In fact, they may have been more enthusiastic than me. I was afraid of the stress working on it would cause. And I wasn't entirely sure anyone would want to read it.

I finally decided to write the book because I realized that if I did it, I wouldn't have to worry about forgetting. My memories would be there, in the book, in my notes, in the records of the conversations that helped shape the work.

I said before that *American Sniper* wasn't therapeutic for Chris; it meant reliving a lot of very nasty things, and getting back in touch with his dark side after having done so much to go beyond it. But this book has been a different experience for me. I feel it's the start of a new phase of my life, one where I can not only continue to remember Chris, but where I can carry on a mission that he would have wanted.

No one will ever know my story in its entirety, but I can at least preserve the essence.

I have learned over time that I cannot fight every battle; I can't keep every friend. Some days, the best I can achieve is to get out of bed.

Other days, I feel as if can accomplish *everything*.

I don't know what my life will look like after this book comes out. People say it will change. I don't know if that's true. I know that the core of who I am won't change, though of course we all change in big and small ways as we live our lives.

From the spring of 2014 until just before publication, Jim and I spent hours and hours on the phone talking, as well as conducting some interviews in person and simply "hanging out" as we gathered material for the book. Everything here is from memory. While dialogue has been used, it is approximate; too much time has passed to have the exact quotes.

With very few exceptions, we have avoided using the full names of people who helped me, out of a concern for their privacy. It should also be said that there were many, many more people along the way who helped me get to where I am now. There simply wasn't room to write about everything everyone did, to mention all of the contributions that family and friends made to my well-being, or to talk about all of the strangers who through their kindness helped keep me going.

I have many people I'd like to thank. Their names would fill a book several times this size. Here's a start:

Mom and Dad, thank you for raising me on a foundation of faith with the freedom to take it at my pace. Thank you for loving Chris and me both. Thank you for supporting us and loving us. You allowed us to be adults and put each other first, knowing our independence was no reflection of our love for you. You are extraordinary role models for parents of adult children. My humor, my ability to forgive, my commitment to marriage, and my belief in family comes from you. I remember the day you told me you both wanted to live in such a way that when you died, people would say they could count on you. You don't have to wait until then; you have consistently lived a life where others can count on you—none more than Ashley and me. I love you.

My precious children: your hearts, your humor, your patience with your mama, your insightfulness, faith and love—they all teach me, enlighten me, and make me believe it will always be worth putting one foot in front of the other. You are my most favorite of all time in the history of ever.

Ashley and Stewart (aka Uncle Poppy), you are two of the most generous people I know—I love you. There would be no book, no foundation, and certainly no sanity without you.

To Chris's parents, thank you for raising the love of my life. To Jeff and Amy, thank you for your love and support. I love you.

Any strength I have comes from the love and support of the following people who have never asked for anything in return. It is because of the following people that I have been able to climb out of the ditch every time I fall in (in absolutely positively no particular order):

Vanessa and Chet; Jennifer and V; Kim and Mike; Amy and Jay; Courtney and Craig; Melanie and Marcus; Sarah and Jarod; Jocelyn and Brian; Leanne, Deanne, and Amelia; Raegan and Debbie; Brad; Shannon and Cary; Kara and Bert; Laurie and Trapper; Rich and LeeAnne; David and Katie; David Drez; Ed Huddleston; Sherri; Dennis and Donna; Rick K; Connor, Maddie, Karen and Mark; Bryan and Angela; Janine and Trent; Teresa and Walt; Deryck and

Beth; Sean and Natalie; Danny; Jason and Elisha; Cheryl and John; Bill and Laura; Clint and Wendy; Kelly; René; Zane; Christine and Pepper; Gail and Marcus; Debra, Jim and Robert; Becky and Lee.

Lana Allen, Jason Kathman, Gerrit Pronske.

To all the people who have given their support and love, financially and in prayer, letters, and little gifts of encouragement. THANK YOU! I can't express enough how much you have blessed our family.

To the Stephenville jury, thank you for hanging through and paying attention to the details.

At William Morrow/HarperCollins, our editor, Peter Hubbard, was supportive and kind beyond measure. His assistant, Nick Amphlett, was always a great help. Copyeditor Greg Villepique watched our p's and q's and so much more. A special thanks goes to our publicist, Sharyn Rosenblum, who was an early and continued supporter of this project. I am blessed to call Sharyn and Peter good friends.

To Jim DeFelice: What a tremendous blessing to have had your skill, your humility, your compassion, and grit with *American Sniper, American Gun,* and now *American Wife.* With Chris and me both, you have been friend, writer, counselor who has laughed with us through the tears. You have taken on more work for less money and recognition than anyone probably should. With every New York snowfall, I think of you wielding a stogie, a beer, and a snow blower . . . life as a writer is good—except when your Yankees lose. I am honored to know you and to work with you. I look forward to our next literary adventures!

To everyone who read *American Sniper,* saw the movie, and had a dialogue about our veterans and first responders. Thank you.

To the veterans of all our wars—Vietnam and all others—as well as our first responders and their families: Thank you!!!